Skills for the Labor Market in Indonesia

Skills for the Labor Market in Indonesia

Trends in Demand, Gaps, and Supply

Emanuela di Gropello
with Aurelien Kruse and Prateek Tandon

THE WORLD BANK
Washington, D.C.

ISBN: 978-0-8213-8614-9
eISBN: 978-0-8213-8615-6
DOI: 10.1596/978-0-8213-8614-9

Library of Congress Cataloging-in-Publication Data
Di Gropello, Emanuela
  Skills for the labor market in Indonesia : trends in demand, gaps, and supply / Emanuela di Gropello, Aurelien Kruse, Prateek Tandon.
      p. cm.
  Includes bibliographical references and index.
  ISBN 978-0-8213-8614-9 — ISBN 978-0-8213-8615-6 (electronic)
  1. Labor market—Indonesia. 2. Skilled labor—Indonesia. 3. Occupational training—Indonesia. I. Kruse, Aurelien. II. Tandon, Prateek. III. Title.
  HD5824.A6D54 2011
  331.1209598—dc22

                                                                            2011005089

Cover photo: © BAGUS INDAHONO/epa/Corbis
Cover design: Quantum Think

Contents

Boxes

Figures

Tables

Foreword

Creating jobs and increasing productivity are key concerns for policy makers across the globe. For East Asian countries seeking to reduce poverty, expanding employment and productivity is at the top of the agenda.

If countries are to meet these challenges and grow in an inclusive way, improving the skills of the labor force is essential. Too many workers around the world are unprepared to meet the needs of firms, particularly in the more competitive and expanding sectors. And systems to provide training are often plagued by weak governance and poor incentives, which make them unreliable or ineffective. Moreover, in many countries, education systems are not providing young people with the basic cognitive and behavioral skills that make them effective in the work place.

This book is a comprehensive look at the demand and supply of skills in Indonesia—how skills have changed, how they will continue to evolve, and how the education and training sectors can be improved to be more responsive and relevant to the needs of the labor market and the economy as a whole. Using an innovative firm survey, the authors shed light on the functional skills that workers must possess to be employable and to support firms' competitiveness and productivity. They also assess the role of the education and training systems in providing those skills. Although this book focuses specifically on Indonesia, its methodologies, messages, and analysis will be instructive for researchers and policy makers who shape the delivery of education and training in other middle-income countries around the world.

Skills will continue to be a core issue for the World Bank and its client countries, and they will constitute a central pillar of the labor and educational agenda for years to come. But skills development is also an area where historically there has been a dearth of information. This book goes some way toward closing the gap. It will, I hope, lead to evidence-based policy making that will improve Indonesia's education and training systems and help align the demand and supply of skills. This book is an important tool in helping Indonesia to achieve the real promise of education for dynamic economies and robust growth.

Emmanuel Jimenez
Sector Director
East Asia Human Development Department
The World Bank

Acknowledgments

The preparation of this book was led by Emanuela di Gropello. The core task team also included Aurelien Kruse, Prateek Tandon, and Berly Martawardaya. Jill Armstrong provided excellent advice and support in the design and implementation of the employer and employee skill surveys.

This book was made possible thanks to the participation of a team from the Institute for Economic and Social Research, Faculty of Economics of the University of Indonesia. The team, which comprised Arie Damayanti, Desi Destriati, Ari Kuncoro, Uka Wikarya, and Lili Yunita, prepared, organized, and implemented the Indonesian employer and employee skill surveys.

The book also benefited from several newly commissioned background papers written (or co-written) by experts outside the core team, including papers on technological innovation, openness, and demand for skills in East Asia by Rita Almeida; skill demand and openness in Indonesia by Ana Fernandes and Ramya Sundaram; higher education and innovation in Indonesia by Hal Hill and Prateek Tandon; skill development strategy in Indonesia by Suahasil Nazara and Padang Wicaksono; and industry and skill wage premiums in East Asia by Chris Sakellariou and Emanuela di Gropello. Several other papers and reports were also used, including contributions from the recently published *Indonesia Jobs Report* for the section on secondary education.

Finally, the book incorporates the valuable comments received from policy makers, academics, and international donors during a dissemination event with Indonesia organized on March 3, 2010. The book also incorporates feedback from the Brown Bag Lunch on Skill Development Lessons in East Asia (held May 5, 2010) and the Human Development Network Workshop on Measuring Skills and Knowledge for Greater Competitiveness and Growth (held June 28, 2010). Peer reviewers of the book were Wendy Cunningham, John Giles, and Jee-Peng Tan.

Currency Equivalents

(Exchange rate effective December 30, 2009)

Currency unit = rupiah
US$1 = IDR9,435
IDR1 = US$0.00
Fiscal year: January 1 – December 31

Abbreviations

BAN-PNF	Badan Akreditasi Nasional Pendidikan Nonformal, or National Accreditation Agency for Informal Educational Units
BAN-PT	Badan Akreditasi Nasional Perguruan Tinggi, or National Accreditation Agency for Higher Education
BAN-S/M	Badan Akreditasi Nasional Sekolah dan Madrasah, or National Accreditation Agency for Schools and Madrasahs
BLK	*balai latihan kerja*, or vocational training center
EYE	Education for Youth Employment (program)
FDI	foreign direct investment
GCI	Global Competitiveness Index
GDP	gross domestic product
GER	gross enrollment rate
HEI	higher education institution
HELTS	Higher Education Long-Term Strategy
HRDF	Human Resource Development Fund (Malaysia)
ICS	Investment Climate Survey
ICT	information, communication, and technology
IMF	International Monetary Fund

ISO	International Organization for Standardization
KAM	Knowledge Assessment Methodology (World Bank)
KKNI	Kerangka Kualifikasi Nasional Indonesia, or National Qualification Framework
KPP	Kursus Para Profesi, or Professional Course (program)
MoMT	Ministry of Manpower and Transmigration
MoNE	Ministry of National Education
OECD	Organisation for Economic Co-operation and Development
OLS	ordinary least squares
PIAAC	Programme for International Assessment of Adult Competencies
PISA	Programme for International Student Assessment
PSG	Pendidikan Sistem Ganda, or Dual System of Education
R&D	research and development
SAKERNAS	Survei Angkatan Kerja Nasional, or National Labor Force Survey
SAR	Special Administrative Region (China)
SENAI	Serviço Nacional de Aprendizagem Industrial, or National Industrial Apprenticeship Service (Brazil)
SI	Survei Industri, or Manufacturing Survey of Large and Medium-Size Firms
SKKNI	Standar Kompetensi Kerja Nasional Indonesia, or National Competency Standard
SMAK	*sekolah menengah analisis kimia*, or chemical-analyst vocational secondary schools
SMK	*sekolah menengah kejuruan*, or vocational secondary schools
SMU	*sekolah menengah umum*, or general secondary schools
SUSENAS	Survei Sosial Ekonomi Nasional, or National Socioeconomic Survey
TIMSS	Trends in International Mathematics and Science Study
TVET	technical and vocational education and training

Overview

In Indonesia, the past two decades have been a time of great progress but also of massive transformations and abrupt setbacks. A period of fast economic progress between 1990 and 1997 was characterized by high GDP growth (averaging 7 percent) and profound changes in the structure of employment. At a pace not seen in other Asian countries, poor rural workers left their farms to find work in the industrial and service sectors. By 1997, almost half of working adults were employed in the formal sector, and in just a few years, the share of agriculture in total employment had shrunk by 14 percentage points, mostly to the benefit of the service sector, whose share grew by more than 9 percentage points. However, this trend came to an abrupt halt when the Asian financial crisis hit Indonesia, causing a massive contraction of economic activity (real GDP fell by 13 percent in one year); an escalation of poverty; and a movement of return to the farm, which reversed the previous evolution. Between 1997 and 1999, the share of agriculture in employment grew again at the rate of 1.3 percentage points yearly, and despite the rebound of the economy after the Asian crisis, agricultural employment has continued to grow as a share of the total and at the expense of formal employment, at least until 2003.

Labor regulations played a large part in explaining jobless growth, but workers' skills are also part of the equation. Although there are many reasons behind the Indonesian phenomenon of jobless growth, decomposition of the factors behind the slowdown in formal sector employment growth points to a sharp decline in employment elasticity of growth in the service sector. Whereas "high" wages have been blamed for undermining job creation, worker skills are an important part of the equation. Indications suggest that the skill profile of the Indonesian workforce has not evolved along with the demands of the labor market. The issue may thus be a lack of skills for employability in the country. High youth unemployment, though also related to other factors, may be another indication of this challenge.

Beyond employment issues, as the Indonesian economy returns to higher growth rates, identifying and addressing potential skill mismatches will be key not only to boosting job creation in the formal sector, but also to supporting higher productivity, competitiveness, and growth. Regaining momentum will obviously depend on many factors, but skills have a key role to play in supporting the further growth and competitiveness of the manufacturing sector (which has remained quite low in value added) and the service sector and, in general, in enhancing the long-term ability of the country to innovate and to adapt and assimilate new technologies. Unfortunately, and despite a significant increase in educational attainment, preliminary evidence, including global competitiveness rankings and educational quality indicators, suggests that this increase has not translated into higher productivity and competitiveness. Beyond the importance of other driving factors that need to be in place for competitiveness to grow—including the need for a comprehensive national innovation framework, which is still clearly underdeveloped in Indonesia—a lack of skills that would increase productivity and competitiveness is clearly evident in the country.

In this context, this book reviews the main characteristics of—and trends in—demand for skills in Indonesia. It seeks to document the existence of a possible skill mismatch between employer demands and available supply, as well as the ways in which the education and training sector may contribute to this mismatch. Finally, the book attempts to propose measures to improve the responsiveness of the education and training sector to the needs of the labor market and economy as a whole. To achieve this aim, the book proceeds in four main steps: (a) identifying the trends in the demand for skills, (b) examining its drivers, (c) identifying and understanding any skill gaps, and (d) identifying the main strengths and weaknesses of the education and training sector (figure O.1).

Figure O.1   Framework of the Book

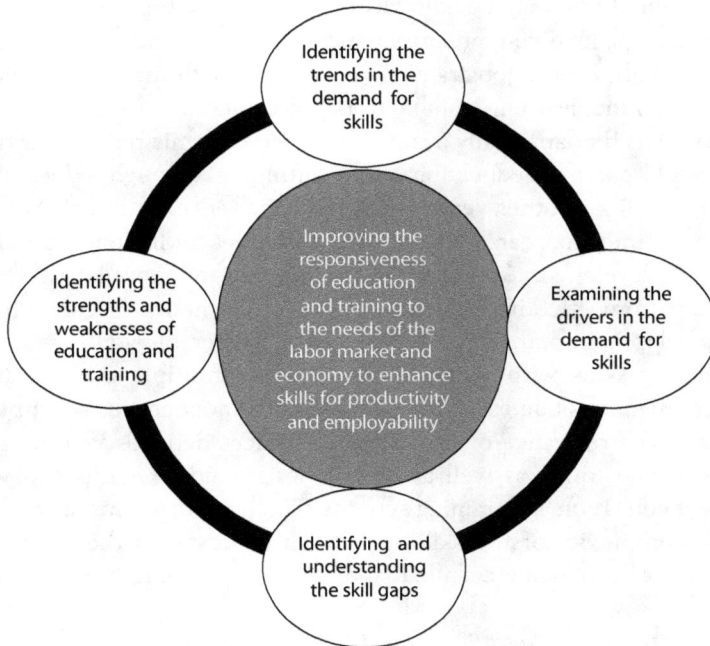

Identifying the trends in the demand for skills

Improving the responsiveness of education and training to the needs of the labor market and economy to enhance skills for productivity and employability

Identifying the strengths and weaknesses of education and training

Examining the drivers in the demand for skills

Identifying and understanding the skill gaps

Source: Authors' representation.

The book pays particular attention to (a) the functional skills that workers must possess to be employable and to support firms' competitiveness and productivity and (b) the role of the education and training system in providing them. Skills can be broadly disaggregated into three main categories:

- *Academic skills.* These skills are associated with subject areas (math, literacy, English) and are generally measured through standardized scores.
- *Generic (or life) skills.* This broader set of skills is transferable across jobs generally. It includes thinking skills (critical and creative thinking, problem solving, and so forth); behavioral skills (typically communication, organization, teamwork, and leadership skills); and computing skills.
- *Technical skills.* These skills are associated with a profession and are generally a mix of the specific knowledge and skills to perform a job.

Skill acquisition is a complex process. Although the book focuses on education and training, it acknowledges that skills are produced in many different ways, involving preemployment education and training (formal and informal), on-the-job training (formal and informal), work and life experience, and learning gained from peers at school and work. Skill acquisition is fundamentally a cumulative and dynamic process starting at birth with parental education and continuing through education at school, training in other venues, and life experience. Although skills can grow over time, they can also decay if possibilities for lifelong learning are not well developed. Additionally, a share of the population can be excluded from effective skill acquisition if alternative "second-chance" skill development pathways do not exist for vulnerable youth.

Mapping skills with skill providers or the multiple mechanisms to acquire them is not an easy task. A broad correspondence is attempted in box O.1. The relevance of the different sources depends very much on personal trajectories, as well as on the design and strengths and weaknesses of education and training systems, which are the focus of this book.

The complexity of the skill acquisition process and the interrelated objectives of producing a skilled labor force, continuing to update these

Box O.1   Where Are Skills Derived From?

Many mechanism help people gain skills:

- Academic skills are largely learned in formal (and informal) education institutions.
- Generic (or life) skills are gained from the following sources:
  ○ Early childhood parental education
  ○ Education and training institutions through curriculum and pedagogical approaches that enhance such learning
  ○ On-the-job training (including informal learning through co-workers and supervisors)
  ○ Work experience and learning by doing.
- Technical skills derive from the following:
  ○ Upper-secondary and tertiary education and training institutions through curriculum that enhances such learning
  ○ On-the-job training (including informal learning from co-workers and supervisors)
  ○ Work experience and learning by doing.

skills over time, and helping unskilled youth and adults gain skills necessarily lead one to consider skill development systems rather than focusing on isolated providers. What type of skill development system should be in place? Addressing this question is not easy because there is no magic bullet, and several options and arrangements are possible. But a benchmark can nonetheless be useful. Typically, a comprehensive skill development system would include the following:

- Sufficient high-quality and relevant school-based formal education and training opportunities at all levels to provide the following skills:
  - *Primary.* Basic academic and generic skills are included in this level.
  - *Secondary.* More advanced academic and generic skills, along with some technical skills, are considered secondary-level skills.
  - *Tertiary.* These skills include higher-order academic, generic, and technical skills.
- Quality informal education and training to accomplish the following:
  - Provide academic, generic, and technical skills to out-of-school groups.
  - Complement formal education with additional generic or technical skills.
  - Provide opportunities to update academic and technical skills over time.
- Sufficient firm training to do the following:
  - Complement formal and informal education and training with additional (job-relevant) technical and generic skills.
  - Provide opportunities to keep technical and generic skills up to date.

These different elements, in turn, need to be linked and integrated through a well-functioning national qualification framework that includes, among other aspects, effective skill certification.

Demand for Skills in Indonesia

What skills are most in demand? Today's job market in Indonesia appears to place a premium on theoretical and practical knowledge of the job. In terms of technical skills, the 2008 employer skill survey indicates that both theoretical knowledge and practical knowledge, acquired through primary schooling and on-the-job experience, are very important. And these skills are considered important for both (a) managers and professionals and (b) skilled production workers.

Skills based on core subjects, such as basic math and literacy (reflecting the finding that primary education remains the building block of worker quality), as well as generic skills such as thinking and behavioral ability, are also considered to be very important for the Indonesian workforce. Thinking and behavioral skills are particularly important for managers and professionals, whereas basic academic skills remain at a premium for skilled production workers (figure O.2). Among behavioral skills, communication skills and ability to work independently are particularly important for both managers and skilled workers. Employees' perceptions are generally aligned with those of employers. They stress the importance of communication and creative thinking skills (figure O.3).

Where are skills most in demand? Demand is higher in the service sector and export-oriented sector. Service firms appear to put greater emphasis on job-specific skills, irrespective of whether they are acquired in the classroom or on the job. The relative ranking is similar across sectors, although theoretical knowledge appears to be somewhat more important in the service sector. Behavioral skills are also given particular preeminence in the service sector, with special focus on communication and leadership skills (figure O.4). Finally, all generic and academic skills are in higher demand in the export sector (figure O.5).

Figure O.2   Importance of Core Subject-Based and Generic Skills

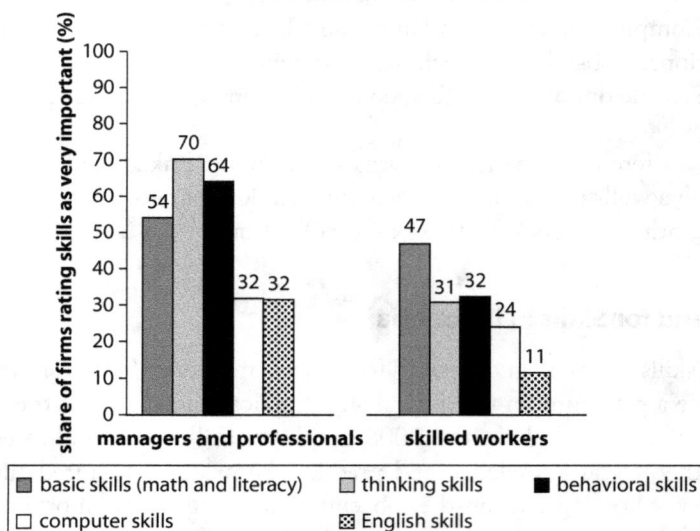

Source: Inconesia Employer/Employee Survey of Skills/Labor Demand and Job Vacancies 2008, Employer Module.

Figure O.3   Employees' Perceptions of the Importance of Skills

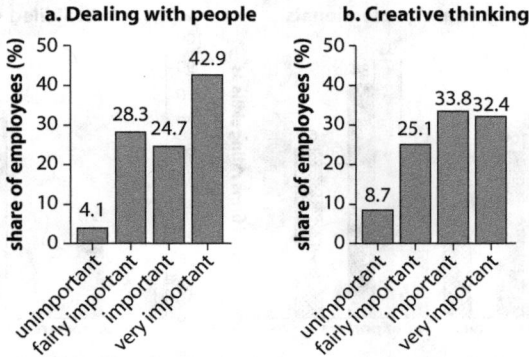

Source: Indonesia Employer/Employee Survey of Skills/Labor Demand and Job Vacancies 2008, Employee Module.

Figure O.4   Importance of Behavioral Skills, by Sector

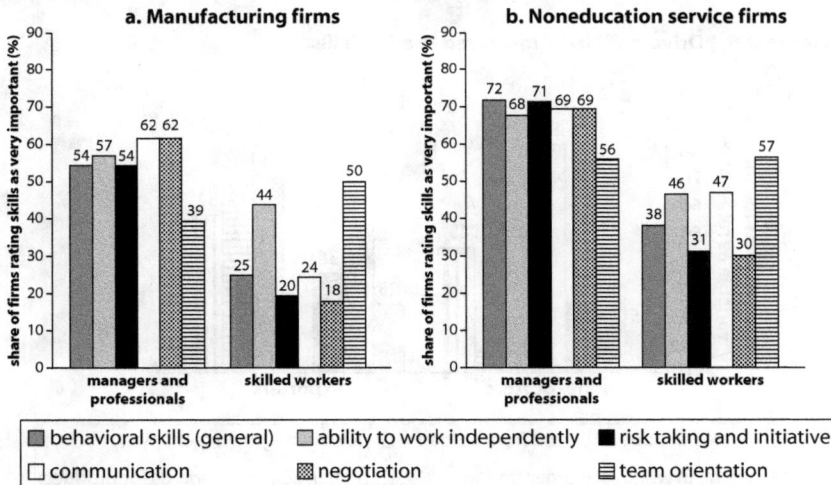

Source: Indonesia Employer/Employee Survey of Skills/Labor Demand and Job Vacancies 2008, Employer Module.

Other drivers of demand for skills are related to competitiveness, technology, and changes in workplace organization. Beyond differences across sectors and export orientation, employers also point to other drivers of demand for skills, underlining the role of higher product-quality standards (as a proxy of product innovation) and a more competitive business environment (figure O.6). Virtually all drivers take heightened significance for firms engaged in exporting, including higher relative relevance

Figure O.5   Importance of Skills in the Export and Nonexport Sectors

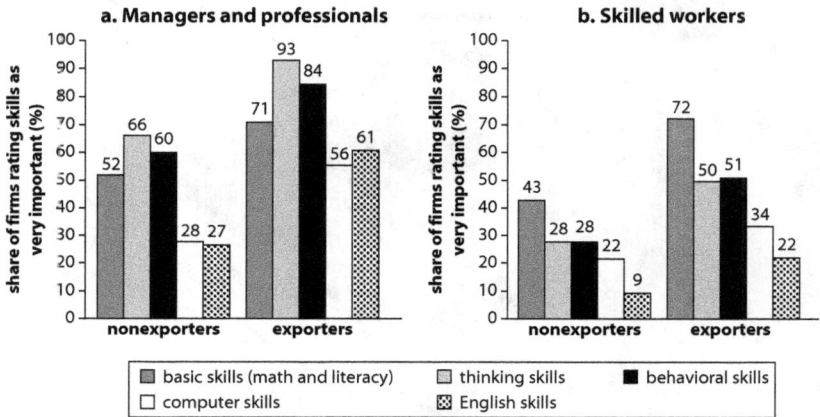

a. Managers and professionals

b. Skilled workers

- ■ basic skills (math and literacy)
- □ computer skills
- ▨ thinking skills
- ▨ English skills
- ■ behavioral skills

Source: Indonesia Employer/Employee Survey of Skills/Labor Demand and Job Vacancies 2008, Employer Module.

Figure O.6   Drivers of Firms' Increased Use for Skills

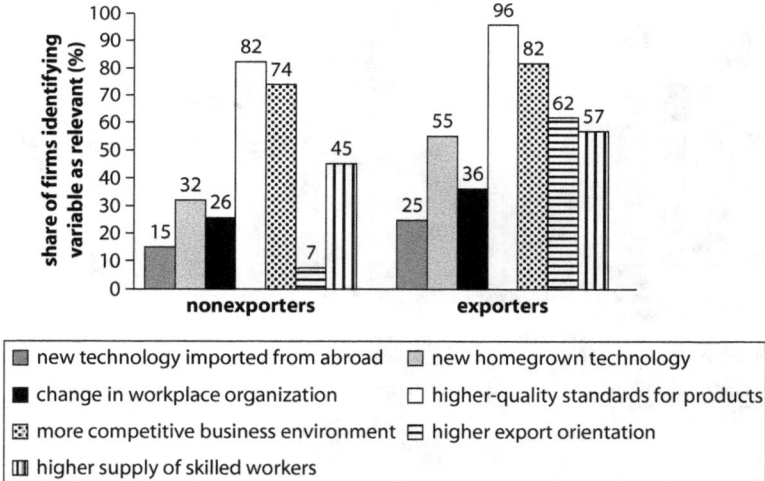

- ■ new technology imported from abroad
- ■ change in workplace organization
- ▨ more competitive business environment
- ▥ higher supply of skilled workers
- ▨ new homegrown technology
- □ higher-quality standards for products
- ▤ higher export orientation

Source: Indonesia Employer/Employee Survey of Skills/Labor Demand and Job Vacancies 2008, Employer Module.

of homegrown technology. Changes in workplace organization are also important drivers of demand for skills and include greater client orientation and teamwork, more innovative processes, more managing duties, and use of computers (figure O.7). An obvious correspondence exists between the greater client orientation and the need for communication

Figure O.7   Changes in Work Organization Driving Demand for Skills

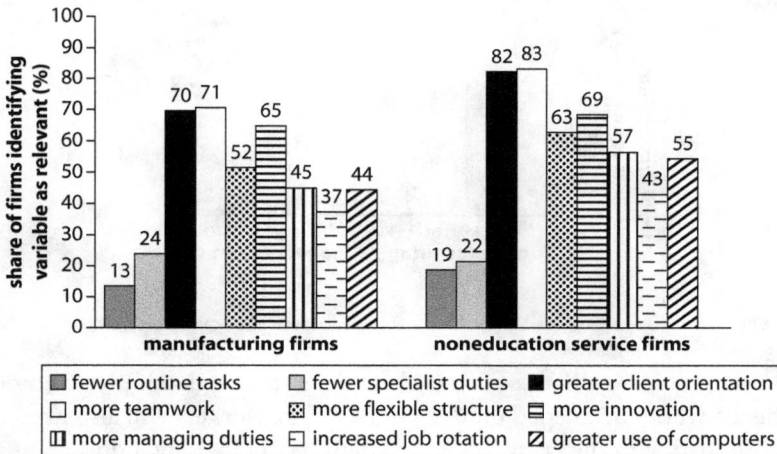

Source: Indonesia Employer/Employee Survey of Skills/Labor Demand and Job Vacancies 2008, Employer Module.

skills, and in general, there is higher correlation between changes in work-place organization and demand for skills in the service sector.

Will demand for skills continue to grow? In all likelihood it will. All employers point to the fact that skill requirements will continue to increase over the next 10 years (figure O.8). Other data pointing in the same direction are the changing employment shares across sectors over the long run—which have seen a gradual but steady increase of the share of the service sector—and import-export projections. The increasing importance of the service sector will demand continued emphasis on behavioral skills. As far as exports are concerned, the export orientation of Indonesian firms, which had reached a peak of 60 percent of GDP in 2000, decreased to about 20 percent of GDP in 2009, making it less of a driver. However, the most recent International Monetary Fund (IMF) projections indicate an upward trend, at least until 2014, returning the ratio to at least 30 percent of GDP.[1] This figure is quite significant (comparable to China). It implies that exports will remain a significant driver of demand for skills and stresses the need for an adequate mass of workers with the adequate skills who can be absorbed into this sector and make a real difference. Critical skills for the export sector include thinking, negotiation, computer, language, and practical knowledge skills. Finally, according to the latest IMF projections, imports over GDP have picked up again from 2009, which implies that the role of imported technology may increase and that technology may therefore remain or even increase

Figure O.8   Employers' Perceptions of Skill Requirements in the Next 10 Years

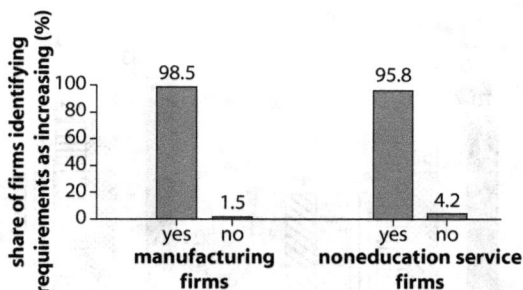

Source: Indonesia Employer/Employee Survey of Skills/Labor Demand and Job Vacancies 2008, Employer Module.

its importance as a driver of demand for skills (although admittedly more evidence would be needed on this point).[2] If so, workers will also need to be equipped with the critical skills to adapt technology, including creativity, critical thinking, command of information and communication technology, as well as proactivity, curiosity, and broad-based understanding of company operations and the industry. Overall, combined with the need to foster higher value added in manufacturing, this evidence suggests that Indonesia should very actively invest in building a stronger skill base.

Skill Gaps

Are skill gaps emerging in Indonesia? Gaps can be assessed in various ways. This book uses two main definitions. One is based on gaps in relation to employers' (and employees') expectations. The other, when available, is based on gaps in relation to an international average or an average in higher-income countries. The first definition is based on a demand-side approach and is often the only way to measure gaps in higher-level skills. The second definition is based on a supply-side approach (standardized international testing) and is still available only up to lower-secondary education and, therefore, only for more basic skills (mostly, though not solely, academic skills).

Although skills do not yet appear to be among the most important constraints for the economy, the situation is different for larger, more export-oriented manufacturing firms, and subjective assessments of difficulties of matching needs with available skills provide evidence that skills are becoming an issue overall in Indonesia. Although unskilled positions are logically—almost by definition—easy to staff, finding the right profile for director and professional jobs is perceived to be difficult by more than

80 percent and 60 percent, respectively, of respondents. Respondents in the manufacturing and export sectors tend to report greater difficulty in finding employees with the required skills, but services also face serious difficulties (figures O.9 and O.10).

The widest gaps across professional profiles are for English and computer skills, followed by thinking and behavioral skills (figure O.11). The gaps in thinking and behavioral skills are particularly critical given their overall level of importance for employers. Gaps in computer and English skills are likely to be more important in the export- and technology-oriented sectors and subsectors. Within behavioral skills, leadership, team orientation, and ability to work independently are considered particularly weak. The strongest gaps in job-specific skills are confirmed to be theoretical and practical knowledge of the job, in accordance with what

Figure O.9   Difficulties in Filling Vacancies, by Sector

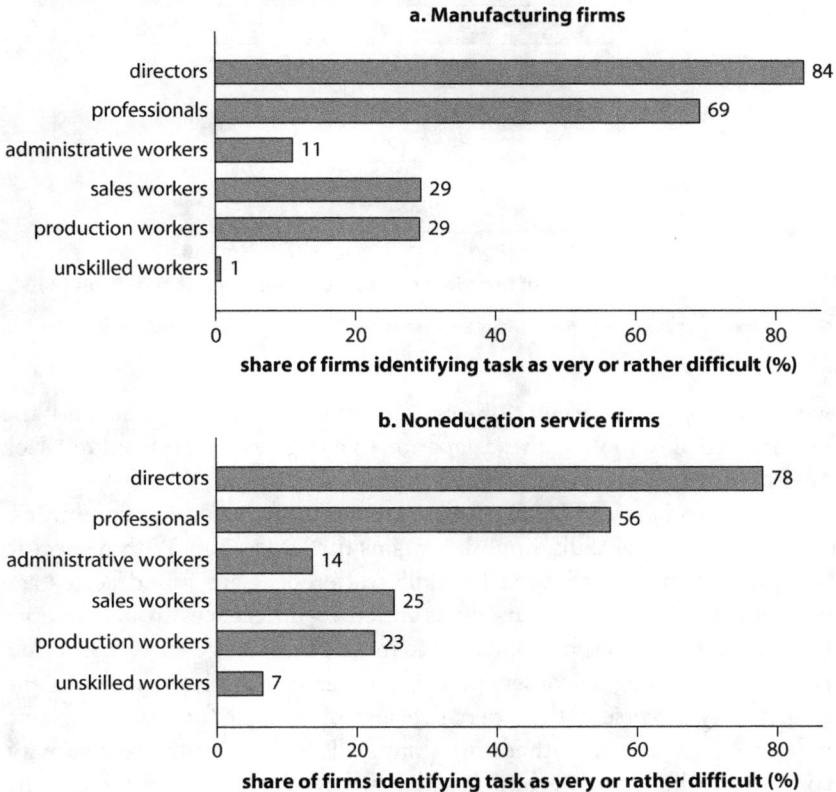

a. Manufacturing firms

directors	84
professionals	69
administrative workers	11
sales workers	29
production workers	29
unskilled workers	1

share of firms identifying task as very or rather difficult (%)

b. Noneducation service firms

directors	78
professionals	56
administrative workers	14
sales workers	25
production workers	23
unskilled workers	7

share of firms identifying task as very or rather difficult (%)

Source: Indonesia Employer/Employee Survey of Skills/Labor Demand and Job Vacancies 2008, Employer Module.

Figure O.10   Difficulties in Filling Vacancies, by Export Orientation

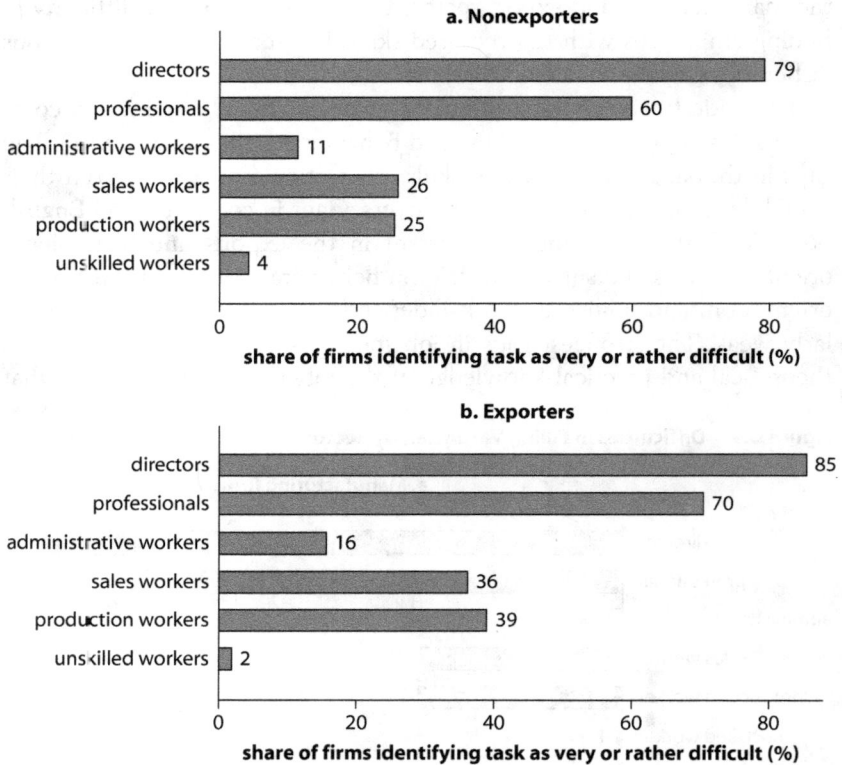

a. Nonexporters

directors	79
professionals	60
administrative workers	11
sales workers	26
production workers	25
unskilled workers	4

share of firms identifying task as very or rather difficult (%)

b. Exporters

directors	85
professionals	70
administrative workers	16
sales workers	36
production workers	39
unskilled workers	2

share of firms identifying task as very or rather difficult (%)

Source: Indonesia Employer/Employee Survey of Skills/Labor Demand and Job Vacancies 2008, Employer Module.

were the most important job-specific skills. Interestingly, beyond the importance of schooling, these gaps are, to a large extent, related to a lack of experience in the same field.

Young workers experience important gaps in creativity, computing, and some technical skills. English remains the largest gap. With respect to the workers' perceived need for skills, differences are found across age groups that may be attributable as much to differences in occupations (including level of responsibility) as to more profound generational shifts.[3] For instance, younger workers perceive a greater need for team skills and adaptability. Inversely, they perceive less of a need for leadership and independent thinking. Other important skills for the youth are creativity, computing skills, and technical skills (figure O.12, panel a). Gaps are even more difficult to compare across generations, so it is interesting to

Figure O.11   Gaps in Core Generic and Subject-Based Skills

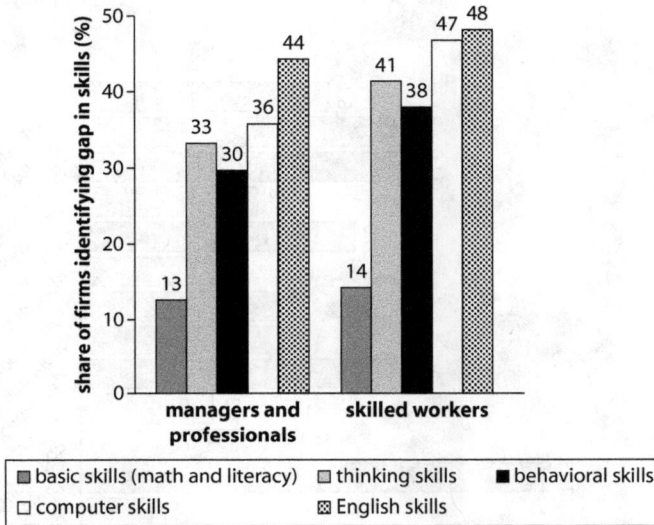

Source: Indonesia Employer/Employee Survey of Skills/Labor Demand and Job Vacancies 2008, Employer Module.

compare skills most lacked with skills most needed within the young generation. Although English may not be considered that relevant, it is, however, perceived as the most serious gap (and by younger and older workers alike), matching employers' perceptions. The other most important gaps reckoned by young workers are in leadership, problem solving, creativity, computing, and some technical skills (figure O.12, panel b). Of those skills, creativity, computing skills, and technical skills are currently the most needed.

Youth unemployment is almost 25 percent in Indonesia versus 5 percent for the overall population and is particularly high for secondary school graduates (approaching 40 percent). Beyond slow employment growth, these results, which come from regression analysis that controls for family wealth, are likely due, to a large extent, to insufficient skills because of lack of previous experience (which, as discussed earlier, is a very important source of skills) and because of poor quality and relevance of schooling. Along the same line, for the lucky ones who are employed, the survey shows that, despite their higher relative educational attainment, they mainly have jobs that do not require their educational qualifications. Slow overall employment growth and a misalignment between occupations and educational attainment are likely to explain, to

Figure O.12 Skills Most Needed and Most Lacked, according to Younger Workers

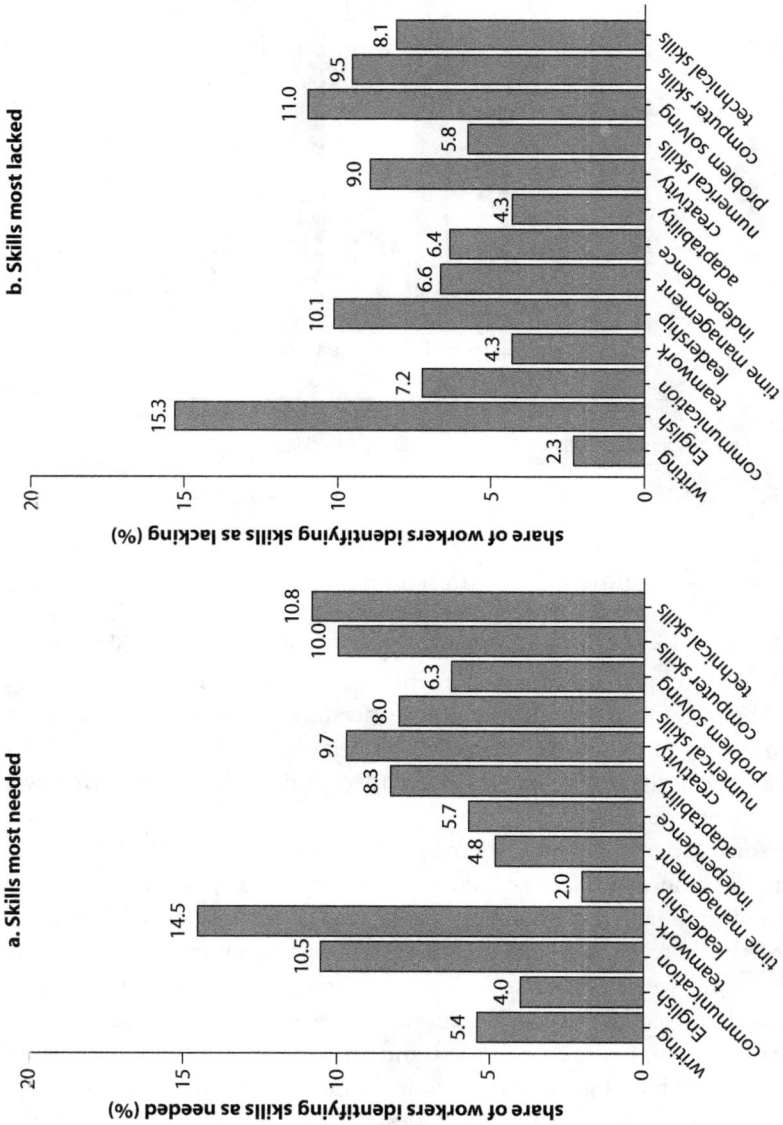

a. Skills most needed

b. Skills most lacked

Source: Indonesia Employer/Employee Survey of Skills/Labor Demand and Job Vacancies 2008, Employee Module.

Figure O.13 Workers' Perceptions of Educational Preparedness for Their Jobs

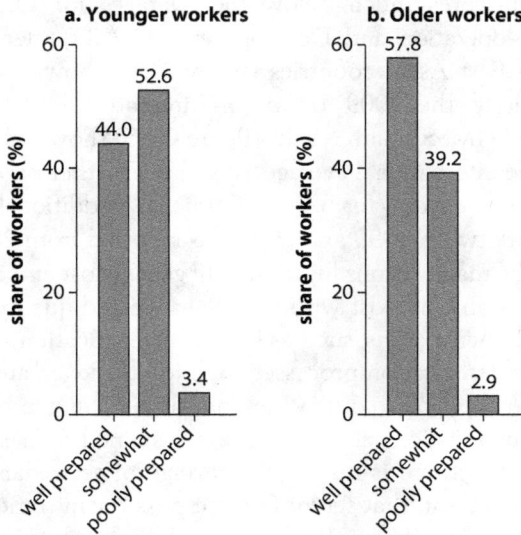

Source: Indonesia Employer/Employee Survey of Skills/Labor Demand and Job Vacancies 2008, Employee Module.

a major extent, this poor employment situation, but insufficient skills and the skill requirements of the labor market are other reasons. The majority of young workers experience a somewhat low sense of preparedness or qualification for their jobs or for professional life in general (figure O.13), and along this line about 40 percent very much agree that additional skills would improve their performance. At the same time, though it is not surprising that older workers feel overall more prepared owing to their much longer job exposure, the fact that 40 percent consider themselves to be only somewhat prepared points indeed to an element of skill decay that may not be sufficiently addressed in the Indonesian context.

Finally, standardized testing also shows significant room for improvement in basic academic skills. Although employers and employees alike do not highlight significant gaps in subject-based skills such as literacy and numeracy, international standardized assessments do. The difference may in part be because testing is capturing these academic skills only at the lower-secondary level, and such skills may improve with further education. The difference may also arise in part because testing provides a more accurate picture of academic strengths and weaknesses, which are typically difficult to measure at the workplace. Although significant improvements have been achieved between 2000 and 2006 in Programme for International Student Assessment (PISA) scores in all disciplines, Indonesia still scores much below the averages for Organisation for Economic Co-operation and Development (OECD) members and for upper-income East Asian countries (figure O.14 shows the 2006 math results). Similarly, the 2009 Trends in International Mathematics and Science Study (TIMSS) math results (figure O.15) show Indonesian pupils still lagging the international average as well as all other participating East Asian countries (except for the Philippines). Additionally, the slight improvement between 1999 and 2003 was reversed from 2003 to 2007.

What are the main reasons for these skill gaps? Most empirical evidence confirms that problems exist with the relevance and quality of education and training. Other reasons, such as lack of diversification in recruitment practices, poor certification processes, high job turnover, and low starting wages, can also explain the difficulties in skill matching in both manufacturing and noneducation services. Despite sustained demand for skills in the service sector, there is no major shortage of secondary and higher-education graduates in that sector (except possibly in some specific subsectors); moreover, there is only limited evidence of possible shortages in the manufacturing sector overall (figure O.16).

Figure O.14   Programme for International Student Assessment: Math Results, 2006

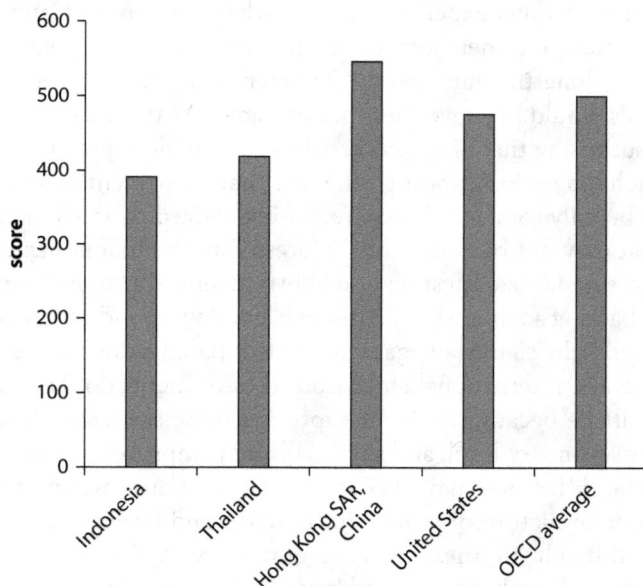

Source: OECD 2009a.

Figure O.15   TIMSS Math Results, 1999–2007

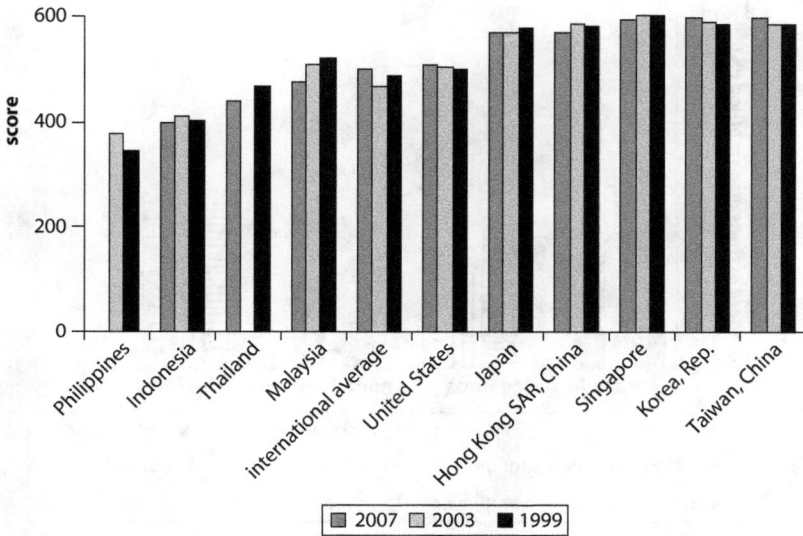

Source: IEA 2008.

Figure O.16   Causes of Skill Shortage

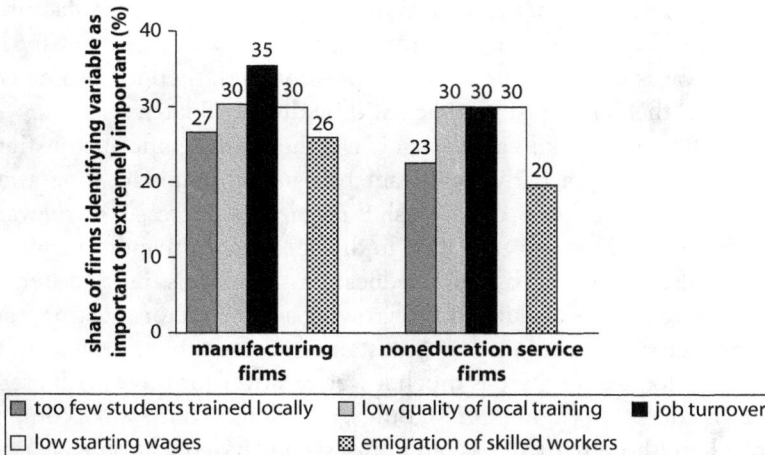

Source: Indonesia Employer/Employee Survey of Skills/Labor Demand and Job Vacancies 2008, Employer Module.

The way in which firm executives assess applicants' skills reveals a less than perfect alignment between schooling and actual job-relevant skills (figure O.17). Interviews and probation periods are the most popular methods, ahead of educational level as attested by diplomas. This finding

Figure O.17   Methods of Assessing Applicants' Skills

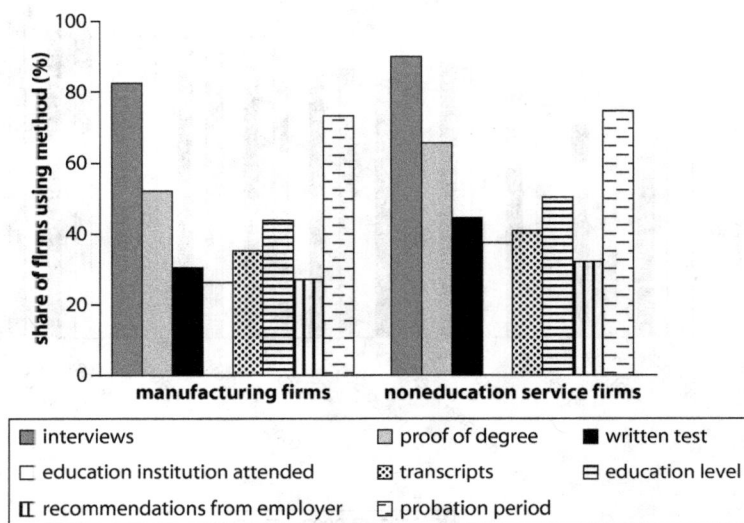

Source: Indonesia Employer/Employee Survey of Skills/Labor Demand and Job Vacancies 2008, Employer Module.

points to a possibly important constraint in job matching: lack of adequate skill certification. High job turnover, particularly in manufacturing, can also be a proxy for lack of experience in the same field. Finally, low starting wages can indicate wage compression and, therefore, some constraints on the demand side, which will be discussed later.

Quantity gaps in skills are certainly not the most significant constraint, but they still play a fairly significant role in the manufacturing sector. Such gaps suggest that a supply push is required to increase the relevance of secondary and tertiary education to the needs of the manufacturing sector (as also indicated by high education premiums in that sector). However, relevance of skills to the growing service sector must be maintained. Demand for education is sustained in Indonesia, driven by the service sector, where there is much lower turnover for those with greater levels of education (figure O.18). But signs of longer-term wage compression, where those with at least an upper-secondary education have experienced declining skill premiums in recent years (figure O.19), educational "overqualification," and high unemployment rates point to some constraints in the ability of the economy to absorb educated workers. These constraints could hamper the generation of secondary and tertiary graduates. In other words, while the demand for skills is growing and

Figure O.18   Education of Net Hires, by Sector

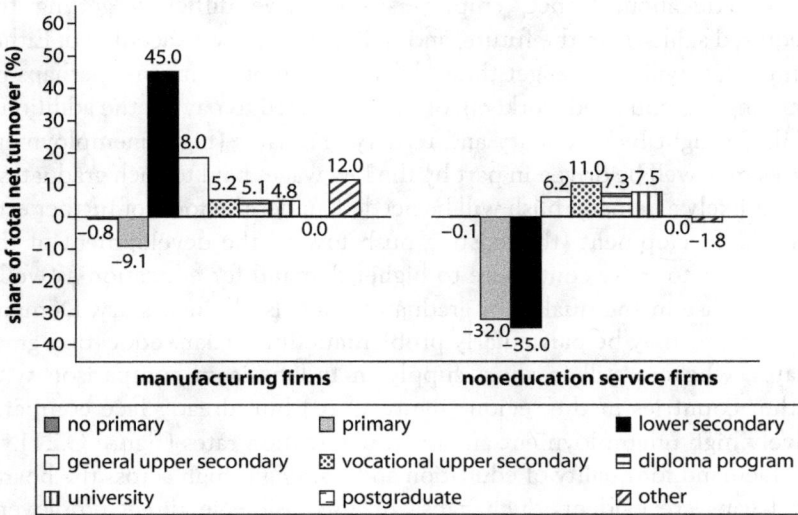

Source: Indonesia Employer/Employee Survey of Skills/Labor Demand and Job Vacancies 2008, Employer Module.

Figure O.19   Trends in Education Premiums and Educated Workforce

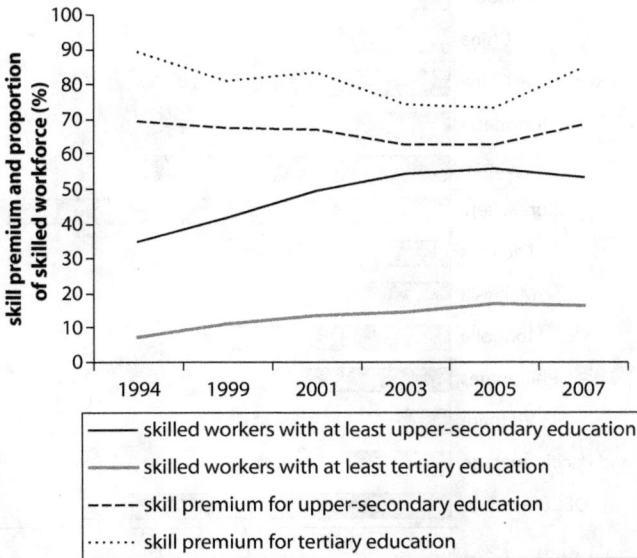

Source: Indonesia Employer/Employee Survey of Skills/Labor Demand and Job Vacancies 2008, Employer Module.

will continue to grow, it will not necessarily translate into workers with more education. Hence, employers may have difficulty getting the required skill sets in the future, and skill gaps may be exacerbated. Either employers will have to get these skills through other means (perhaps by training less educated workers), or they will need to pay for the additional skills brought by secondary and tertiary graduates (high unemployment rates may well be driven in part by the low wages paid to such graduates). Most likely a demand push will be needed, under the form of further economic development (the existing push toward the development of the service sector may contribute to higher demand for education as well); an increase in the quality of graduates may also be necessary. Demand constraints may be particularly problematic for tertiary education graduates, who are still in short supply in Indonesia in comparison with other countries in the region (figure O.20) but already face comparatively high unemployment and overqualification rates (figure O.21).

Demand for quality of education and training is high across the board, and gaps are evident. Such gaps are also visible in direct employers'

Figure O.20   Tertiary Gross Enrollment Rates in Selected Countries, 2007 or Latest Year Available

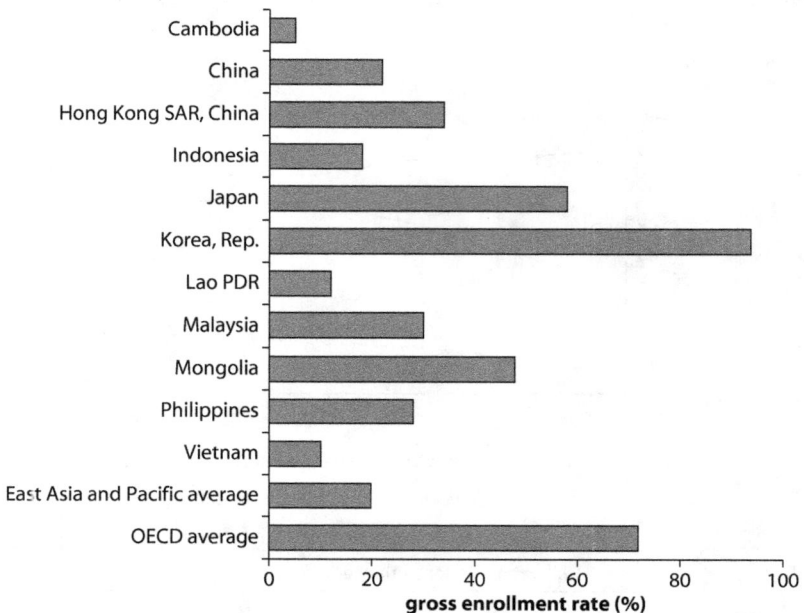

Source: UIS 2008.

Figure O.21   Labor-Market Outcomes of Tertiary Graduates in Selected Countries, 2008

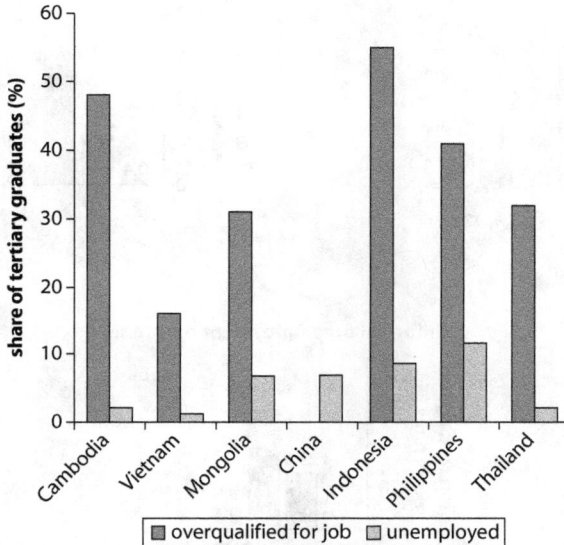

Source: World Bank 2010.

assessments of the quality of graduates. Almost one-third of secondary education graduates are considered to be below average or very poor, and most of the rest are just fair (figure O.22). Although tertiary education graduates have a somewhat better reputation, the majority are considered only fair, and just a very small proportion are rated very good (figure O.23).

Gaps in the Quality and Relevance of Education and Training

To go more in depth into quality and relevance issues, the book provides an overview of the characteristics, outcomes, and challenges facing the education and training sector in Indonesia, with particular focus on the secondary and tertiary subsectors. The book takes a comprehensive approach by also touching on the sector's capacity to provide skill development opportunities for unskilled workers ("second-chance" programs) and on on-the-job training. Emphasis is put on three core aspects of skill production: the general ability of a system to produce a skilled labor force, the ability to continue updating these skills over time, and the ability to help unskilled younger and older workers gain skills. These three interrelated dimensions characterize a skill development system.

Figure O.22   Quality of Secondary Education Graduates

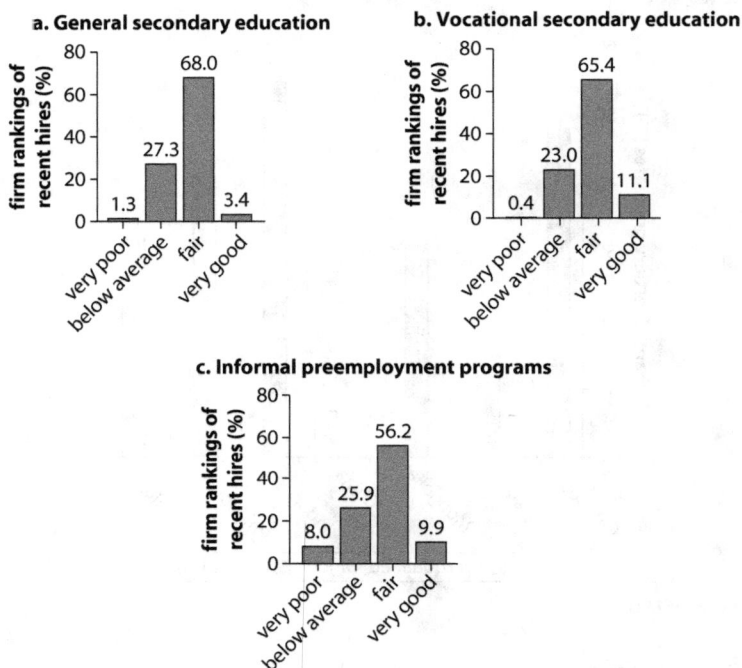

a. General secondary education

b. Vocational secondary education

c. Informal preemployment programs

Source: Indonesia Employer/Employee Survey of Skills/Labor Demand and Job Vacancies 2008, Employer Module.

Ability to Produce a Skilled Labor Force: Formal Secondary and Tertiary Education

A separate analysis of secondary education suggests a situation in which formal vocational and general secondary schools both have specific advantages and shortcomings and urgently need to be improved. Gaps in quality and relevance are particularly strong in secondary education. According to both employers and employees, vocational secondary schools have an advantage in terms of curriculum relevance to specific labor-market needs and in terms of links with the productive world that may somewhat increase employability, particularly for youth (figure O.24 [vocational secondary school]). However, they also have disadvantages in terms of general curriculum and related skills and quality of the teaching-learning process, which hamper earnings (particularly in the medium to longer term and possibly the service sector) and employment in jobs that match their qualifications (figure O.25, panel a). At the same time, the curriculum of

Figure O.23   Quality of Tertiary Education Graduates

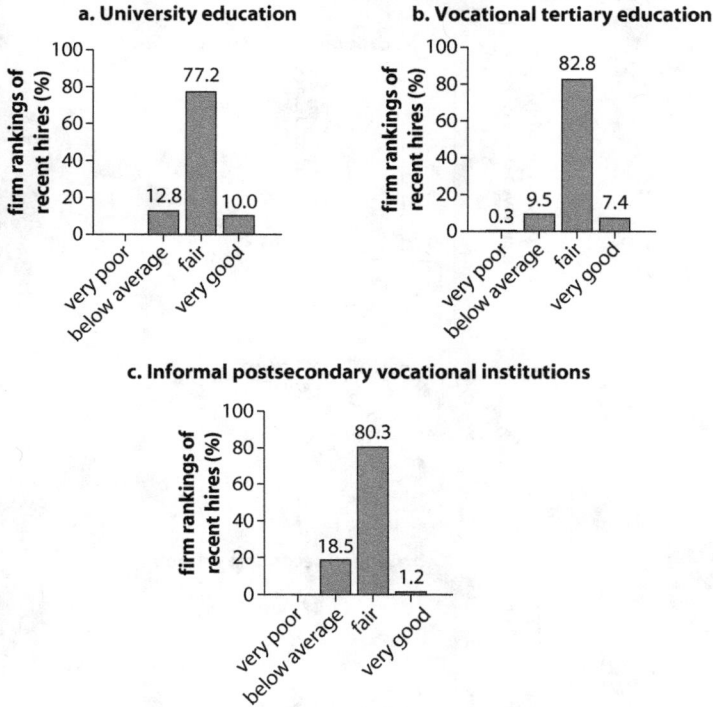

a. University education

b. Vocational tertiary education

c. Informal postsecondary vocational institutions

Source: Indonesia Employer/Employee Survey of Skills/Labor Demand and Job Vacancies 2008, Employer Module.

Figure O.24   Major Strengths of Vocational and General Secondary Schools as Perceived by Employers

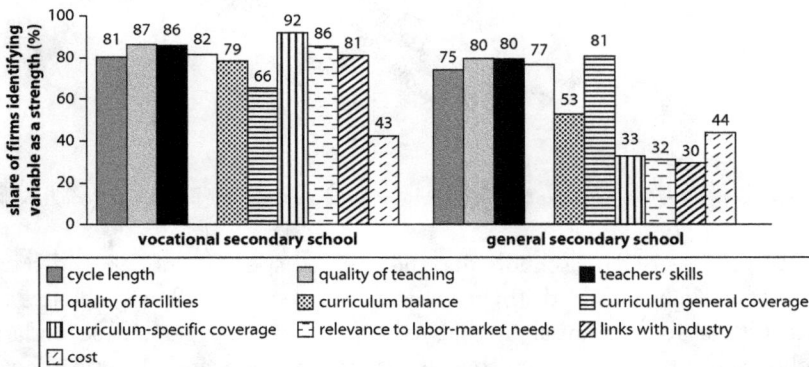

Source: Indonesia Employer/Employee Survey of Skills/Labor Demand and Job Vacancies 2008, Employer Module.

Figure O.25   Major Weaknesses of Vocational and General Secondary Schools as Perceived by Employees

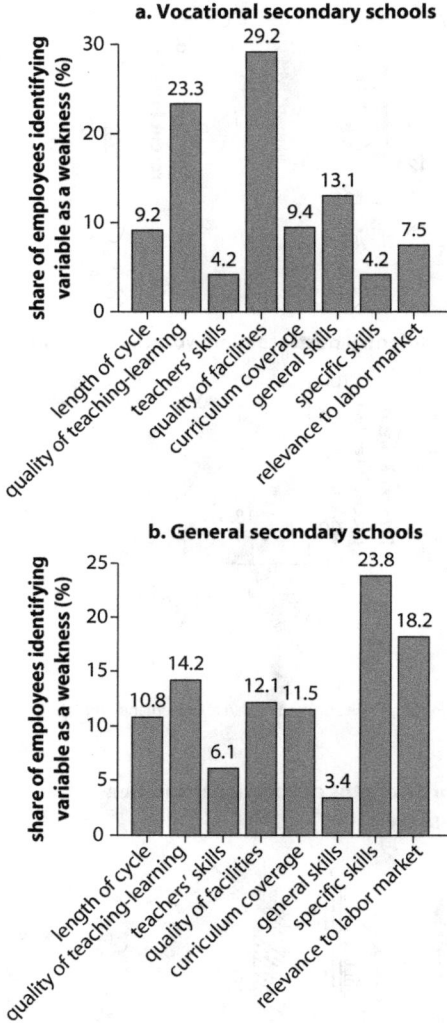

a. Vocational secondary schools

b. General secondary schools

Source: Indonesia Employer/Employee Survey of Skills/Labor Demand and Job Vacancies 2008, Employee Module.

vocational secondary schools may not yet be specific enough and have strong enough links with the manufacturing sector to allow graduates to meet their full potential in that sector. In contrast, general secondary schools produce graduates that are more rounded and flexible. These graduates clearly satisfy an important fraction of the labor market (and have more options of mobility across jobs), but they significantly lack in specificity of education and in contacts with the productive world (figure O.24 [general secondary education] and figure O.25, panel b), which complicates job placement, particularly for youth.

Costs also differ for general and vocational secondary education. A public general high school education costs Rp 5.3 million per year, whereas a public vocational high school education costs Rp 6.8 million per year. The cost-effectiveness of vocational secondary schools is particularly doubtful given their mixed labor outcome results, as exemplified by declining returns and increasing unemployment rates (figure O.26).

An analysis of tertiary education shows that although universities are generally considered to be of better quality than secondary education institutions, they still have a way to go to produce high-quality graduates who can meet the needs of both the manufacturing and the service sectors. Issues exist at both the lower end and the upper end of tertiary education. Practical knowledge is still weak across the board, and universities remain quite unconnected to the needs of the labor market, judging from the rather negative opinions employers and employees hold about universities' capacity to link with industries and adapt to changing labor-market needs (figures O.27 [universities] and figure O.28, panel a). Lack of links to industry is likely to be particularly serious in manufacturing given the difficulty that the sector encounters filling its professional positions. Universities have an even longer way in being able to support innovation through applied research and technology transfer, and given that Indonesia lags in all innovation indicators, their provision of innovative skills also needs improvement. At the same time, while more connected to labor markets according to employers (figure O.27 [diploma programs]), diploma programs are considered weaker across the board by employees (figure O.28, panel b). In general, standard employment indicators suggest that graduates of diploma programs perform more poorly than university graduates in the labor market; thus, curriculum balance, variety, and flexibility remain at a premium in higher education in Indonesia, and the role and design of diploma programs urgently need to be reexamined. Finally, weaknesses are greater for private tertiary institutions across the board.

Skilling the Unskilled and Updating the Skills of the Labor Force: Informal Education and Training and On-the-Job Training

Few hard facts allow us to make an overall judgment on the coverage, quality, and relevance of informal education programs in Indonesia. Overall, they are below par with formal education, but some trends are

Figure O.26   Returns and Unemployment Rates Related to General and Vocational Secondary Education

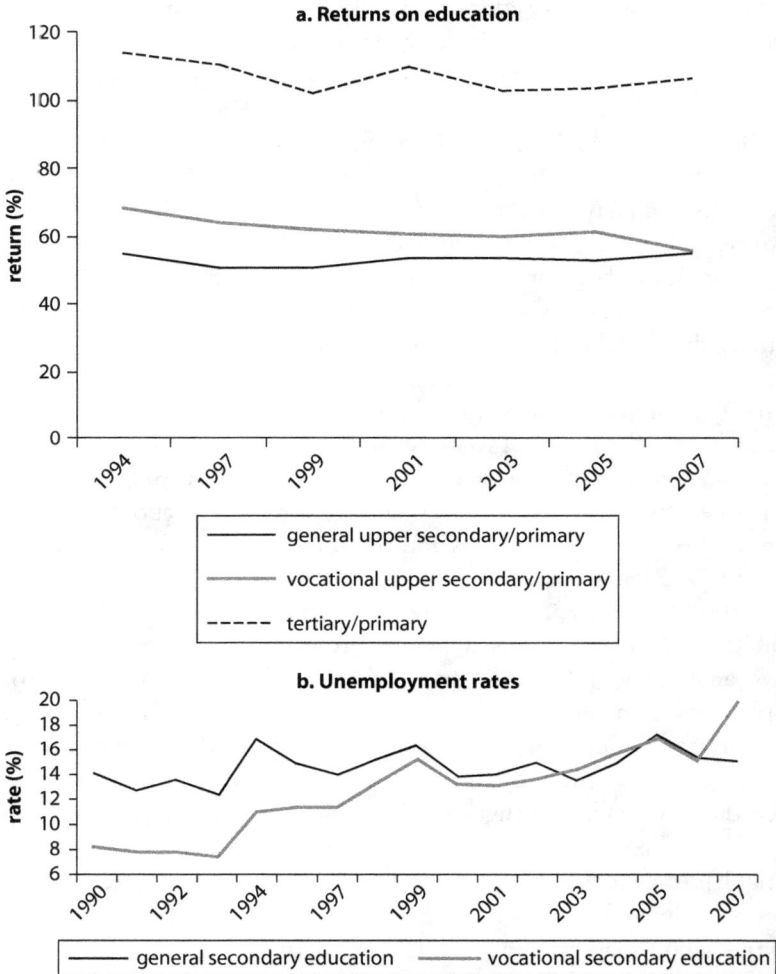

a. Returns on education

b. Unemployment rates

Source: di Gropello 2009; World Bank 2010.

promising. The employer and employee skill surveys suggest that informal education programs are of lower quality than formal programs, but that they tend to be reasonably responsive to labor-market needs, like the line of vocational formal options (figures O.29 and O.30). The initial results of programs such as the Kursus Para Profesi and Education for Youth

Employment (EYE) programs appear to support these findings; however, those outcomes need to be more thoroughly evaluated. The EYE program, in particular, which supplements the education equivalency package with life skills training, improved education management, and teacher training modules while placing youth in jobs through networking in the industrial or business world, has had some initial promising success: 82 percent of EYE participants were employed after three to four months of training, and employee retention rates remained above 80 percent after three years.[4] An achievement is the recent development of a skill-based competency and qualification framework that creates bridges between the informal and formal sectors and lays the groundwork for a lifelong learning approach. Along this line, it would be useful to reexamine the role of the vocational training center (*balai latihan kerja*, or BLK) in light of an increasing focus on lifelong learning, because BLKs are the main public providers of informal education.

Firms tend to provide short-term remedial skill development rather than longer-term development. Manufacturing and exporting firms do not train to the level that would allow their professional and managerial employees to become generally more competitive and innovative. Formal training programs that firms offer to their employees constitute an important source of practical on-the-job skills. Training areas tend to reflect the ascertained skill gaps and relative firms' strengths by focusing on job-specific skills across all sectors and more thinking, behavioral, and computing skills

Figure O.27   Major Strengths of University and Diploma Programs as Perceived by Employers

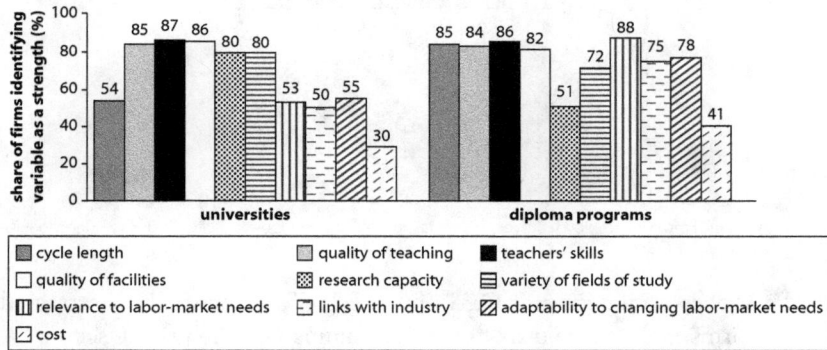

Source: Indonesia Employer/Employee Survey of Skills/Labor Demand and Job Vacancies 2008, Employer Module.

Figure O.28   Major Weaknesses of University and Diploma Programs as Perceived by Employees

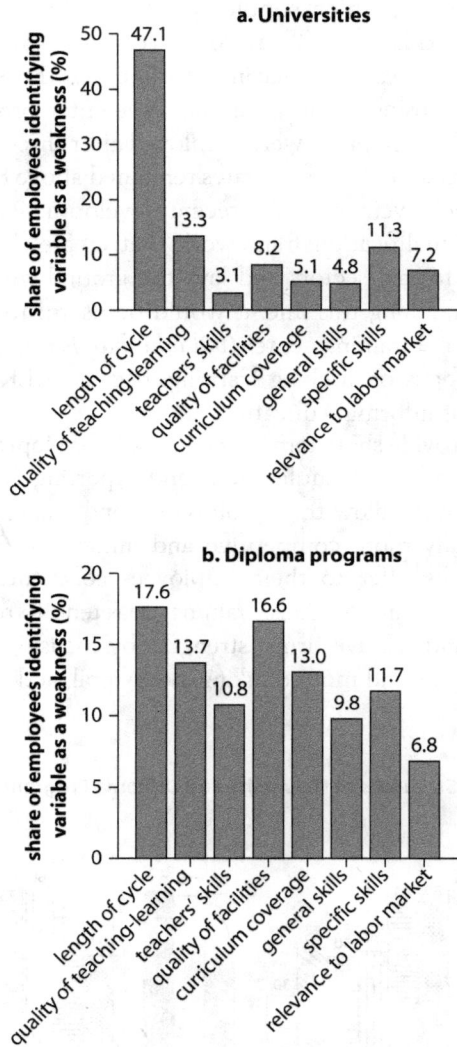

a. Universities

b. Diploma programs

Source: Indonesia Employer/Employee Survey of Skills/Labor Demand and Job Vacancies 2008, Employee Module.

in the service sector (figures O.31 and O.32). Less financially constrained service firms make more use of external training and the private sector.

These findings confirm rationality in firms' decisions, but they also indicate a short-term approach to training. In the absence of significant financial incentives to train and gaps in the preparedness of youth and

Figure O.29   Main Strengths of Informal Education as Perceived by Employers

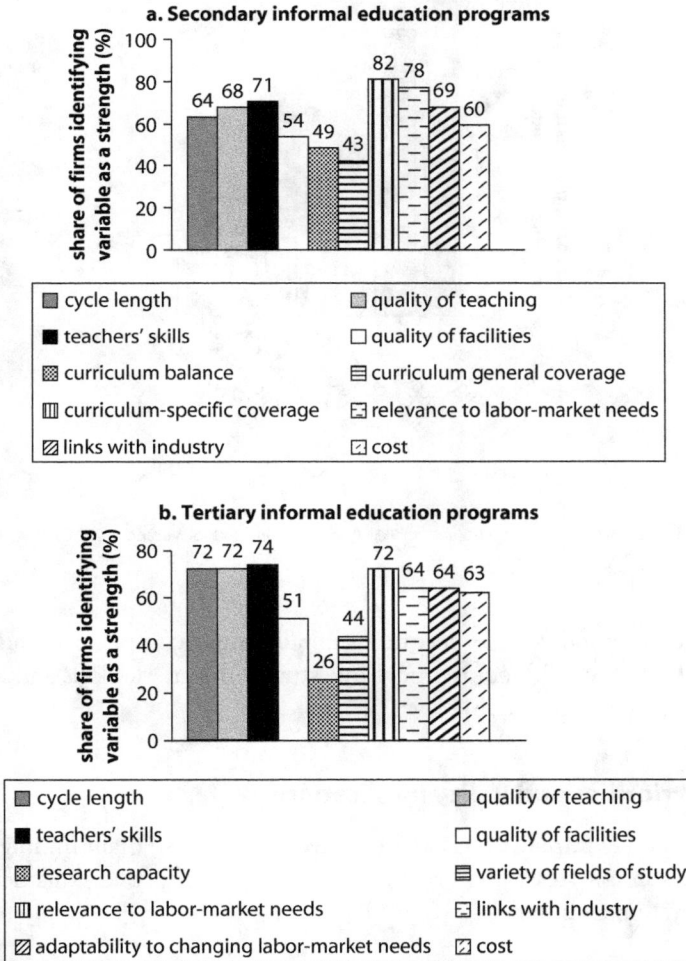

a. Secondary informal education programs

cycle length ☐ quality of teaching
teachers' skills ☐ quality of facilities
curriculum balance ☐ curriculum general coverage
curriculum-specific coverage ☐ relevance to labor-market needs
links with industry ☐ cost

b. Tertiary informal education programs

cycle length ☐ quality of teaching
teachers' skills ☐ quality of facilities
research capacity ☐ variety of fields of study
relevance to labor-market needs ☐ links with industry
adaptability to changing labor-market needs ☐ cost

Source: Indonesia Employer/Employee Survey of Skills/Labor Demand and Job Vacancies 2008, Employer Module.

secondary education, firms focus most of their efforts on upgrading the skills of young workers and skilled production workers (figure O.33), while relying, to a large extent, on informal training and learning by doing for professionals and managers. This approach is not conducive to addressing the needs of lifelong learning. There is also a sense that manufacturing and exporting firms, in particular, may not train enough, and certainly not to the level that would allow their professional and

Figure O.30   Main Weaknesses of Informal Education as Perceived by Employees

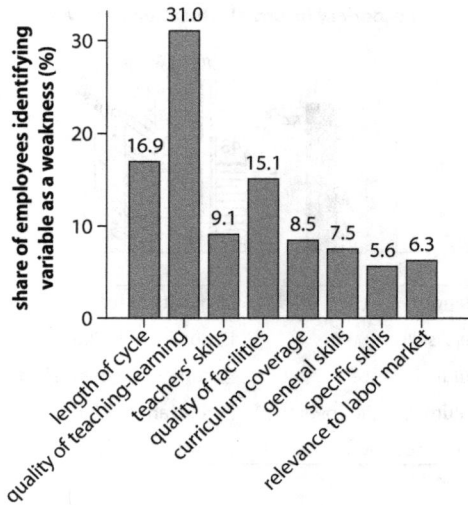

Source: Indonesia Employer/Employee Survey of Skills/Labor Demand and Job Vacancies 2008, Employee Module.

managerial employees to become generally more competitive and innovative (which would require more investment in generic skills and higher-level industry knowledge).

Main Priorities and Policy Implications

Several policy implications can be derived from these main findings. This section summarizes those critical to building an effective skills development system in Indonesia.

Overall Priorities
Five general skill-related priorities can be highlighted for Indonesia:

1. *Improve skill measurement to get a fuller understanding of skill needs and gaps.* Following the example of this book, Indonesia needs to get better understanding of what skills are needed and what skills are lacking. Both demand- and supply-side sources could be used to undertake this diagnostic, ranging from employer and employee skill surveys (which can simply be integrated with existing firm surveys) and better and increased use of firm and tracer surveys, to participation in

Figure O.31   Training Provided by Manufacturing Firms, by Type of Skills

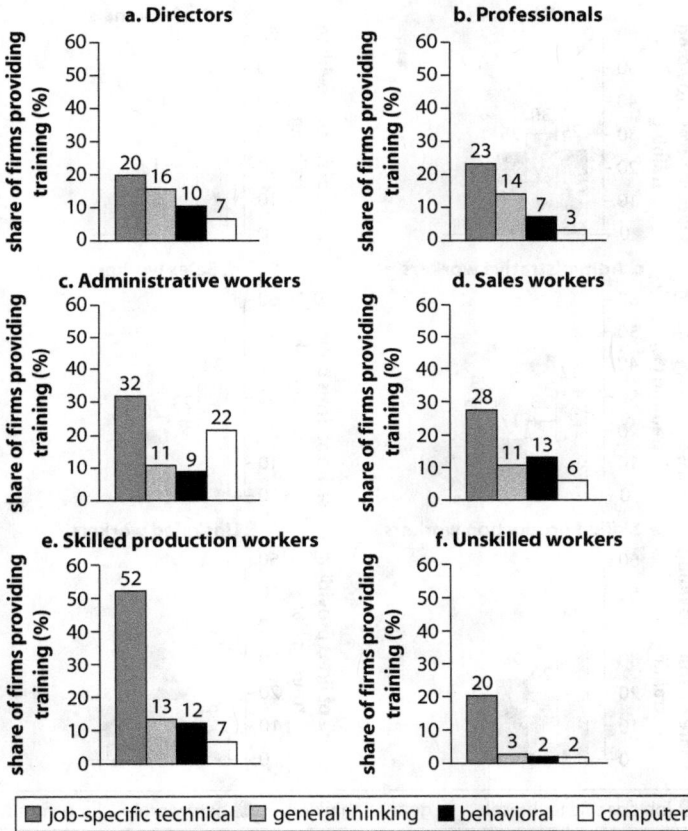

a. Directors

Category	Value
job-specific technical	20
general thinking	16
behavioral	10
computer	7

b. Professionals

Category	Value
job-specific technical	23
general thinking	14
behavioral	7
computer	3

c. Administrative workers

Category	Value
job-specific technical	32
general thinking	11
behavioral	9
computer	22

d. Sales workers

Category	Value
job-specific technical	28
general thinking	11
behavioral	13
computer	6

e. Skilled production workers

Category	Value
job-specific technical	52
general thinking	13
behavioral	12
computer	7

f. Unskilled workers

Category	Value
job-specific technical	20
general thinking	3
behavioral	2
computer	2

(y-axis for all panels: share of firms providing training (%))

Legend: ■ job-specific technical ▨ general thinking ■ behavioral □ computer

Source: Indonesia Employer/Employee Survey of Skills/Labor Demand and Job Vacancies 2008, Employer Module.

adult competency tests, such as the upcoming Programme for International Assessment of Adult Competencies (PIAAC).[5]

2. *Address the unsatisfactory quality and relevance of formal education.* More than quantity, quality and relevance are the critical issues for the formal education and training sector of Indonesia. Changes are needed at all levels to improve the quality of the teaching-learning process and to strengthen links with firms. It is particularly imperative for secondary education to improve so that Indonesian youth learn the skills they need in the labor market, thereby improving their labor-market outcomes.

Figure 0.32   Training Provided by Service Firms, by Type of Skills

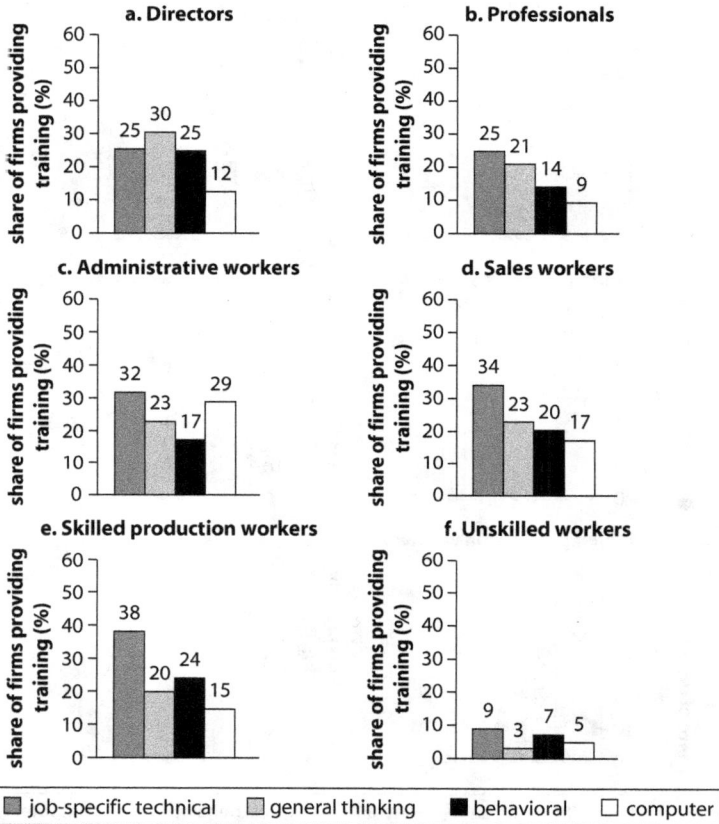

Source: Indonesia Employer/Employee Survey of Skills/Labor Demand and Job Vacancies 2008, Employer Module.

3. *Set up multiple pathways for skill development.* Beyond addressing the quality and relevance of its formal education, Indonesia needs to continue building a skill development system that creates opportunities for use of existing skills, updates skills over time, and provides skills to out-of-school and vulnerable youth and adults. Although development of a national qualification framework that will articulate the country's goals is a promising step, the framework needs further strengthening (including institutional accreditation, skill standardization and certification, and regulating bodies). The constraints to building a multipurpose system need to be fully understood, and appropriate actions must

Figure O.33   Incidence of Training, by Sector and Occupation

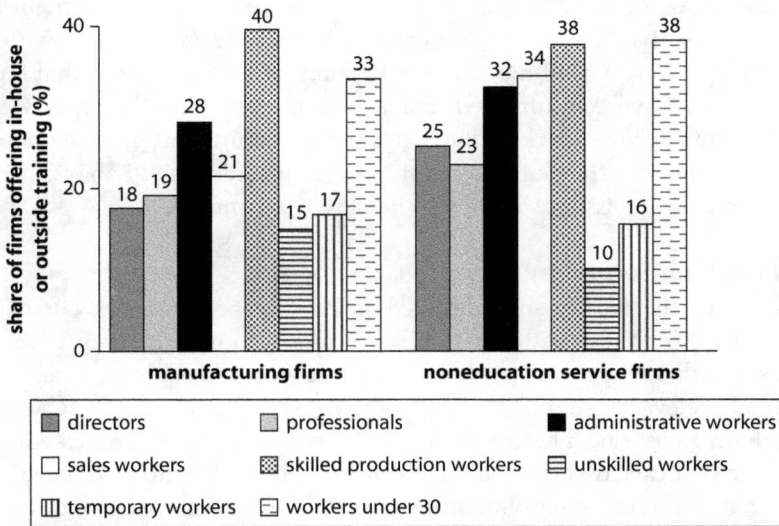

Source: Indonesia Employer/Employee Survey of Skills/Labor Demand and Job Vacancies 2008, Employer Module.

be identified to address those constraints. For instance, better institutional and funding incentives for lifelong learning, including incentives to firms for fulfilling a longer-term training role, are needed. At the same time, fuller and more rigorous assessment is required of the outcomes of existing informal education and training institutions and programs and of their potential as providers of relevant skills for vulnerable youth and adults, complementary skills, and skill development over time.

4. *Develop an integrated approach to tackle skill development for youth.* Despite youth's increased educational attainment, the skills of youth are insufficient in Indonesia and contribute to poor labor-market outcomes. An integrated approach is needed, including improving formal education (particularly secondary education); further developing and improving informal "second-chance" programs; building more bridges between education and the labor market through school-to-work transition programs that provide labor-market information, placement, and complementary life and technical skills; and focusing firms' training role for youth on complementary job-specific skills.

5. *Tackle labor-market constraints that affect the skill-matching process.* A diagnostic of labor-market constraints is necessary to complement an analysis of skill supply and demand. Such a study would provide a broader view of skill-matching constraints and would ensure that inefficiencies were minimized. For instance, even if skill supply were greatly improved, lack of diversification of recruitment practices could still constrain the skill-matching process in Indonesia. Labor-market segmentation issues should also be closely examined.

Priorities for Secondary Education

Improving the quality and relevance of secondary education is currently Indonesia's first imperative. This effort is all the more important because most youth stop attending school at the secondary level. Improving educational relevance should start by improving relevance within each track (including ensuring a better allocation of technical and vocational education graduates across the manufacturing and service sectors) rather than by changing relative enrollment across tracks. Evidence presented in the book does not support the Ministry of National Education's target of shifting the ratio of students enrolled in general secondary schools to vocational secondary schools to 30:70 by 2015.

This book suggests five specific priorities:

1. *Maintain a balanced curriculum.* The most important policy implication is to maintain a balanced curriculum irrespective of the general or vocational track, which, in a nutshell, implies the need for more specific and practical knowledge to be included in the general secondary track but also, conversely, for vocational education to retain a solid transversal set of core academic skills. The current situation is quite imbalanced and will therefore need to change.
2. *Improve academic and generic (thinking and behavioral) skills.* Another overall lesson is the need for better academic and generic skills across all tracks in secondary education. This need derives from the gaps that have been ascertained in math, literacy, and English on the one hand and thinking and behavioral skills on the other. Although employers generally tend to be less preoccupied with core subject skills than with more specific skills and, therefore, see fewer weaknesses from this perspective, it is nonetheless clear that the general coverage of the curriculum is an issue in vocational schools, and the quality of teaching and learning could be further improved in both tracks (at least according to employees' perceptions). The curriculum will need to

enhance proficiency in core subjects while introducing generic skills. Such changes imply pedagogical modifications. Vocational schools will need to ensure a good balance between teachers with academic backgrounds and those with practitioner backgrounds.

3. *Better design and implement the specific components of the curriculum in secondary vocational schools.* The example of Sekolah Menengah Analis Kemia and German experience with vocational education suggest that there is scope for designing a more demand-driven curriculum for vocational schools. Such designs require more systematic industry input (including financial input), sufficient practitioners on staff, and stronger consultation mechanisms with the industry and relevant ministries and government bodies. Meanwhile, support for the dual education system methodology (including the dual skill certification) should continue through internships in firms. This approach, which is now being more widely applied, would particularly help improve the demand-driven focus of the technology and industry curriculum, which, by nature, is more difficult to design and implement well than the business and management curriculum (perhaps explaining why there are relatively fewer technology and vocational education graduates in manufacturing). In Indonesia, where firms and vocational secondary schools tend to be small, the government may need to step up its role to make the model work, which will necessarily imply more selective support that imposes consequences and sets school and enrollment targets. Consolidating private vocational schools would help ease the financial burden.

4. *Increase emphasis on specific skills and improve links with industry for the general stream.* This approach would not imply adding very specific technical subjects to the curriculum, but rather more applied subjects, such as business, economics, computing, and English courses. It would also imply making the pedagogy itself more varied by supporting ways to communicate more effectively and planning short internships in relevant economic sectors. These changes would make general secondary graduates more appealing to the service sector, which is currently "overusing" vocational graduates in relative terms. Conversely, strengthening the emphasis in the general curriculum on science, math, and information and communication technologies, as well as on development of analytical and creative thinking, could better serve the needs of the manufacturing sector.

5. *Undertake a thorough set of tracer studies to follow graduates and learn lessons about the relevance of their education.* Such studies could interview both graduates and employers on a regular basis, ascertain

what the most desirable skills for particular industries are, determine which fields of education are in increased (or decreased) demand, and identify how secondary education institutions can benefit from this information and incorporate it into their curriculum.

Priorities for Tertiary Education

There is also strong ground for improving tertiary education, focusing on six main priorities and policies:

1. *Maintain a balanced curriculum.* Like secondary institutions, tertiary institutions need to maintain a more balanced curriculum. Doing so will require universities to increase their capacity to provide practical knowledge and to generally adapt to labor-market needs. Diploma programs should ensure that they provide a solid transversal set of core academic skills.
2. *Build incentives to improve university-industry links.* Universities need to be further encouraged to link with industries for purposes of curriculum (particularly in the manufacturing sector), training, and research. Although more management flexibility will help, the government may also need to play a role by improving the legal framework and incentives for collaboration. More incentives for technology transfer are needed, including setting up universities' internal technology licensing organizations to help promote collaboration with industry and industrial technology transfer. Legislation protecting intellectual property rights should also be strengthened.
3. *Undertake a thorough set of tracer studies to follow graduates and learn lessons about the relevance of their education.* Such studies could interview both graduates and employers on a regular basis, ascertain what the most desirable skills for particular industries are, determine which fields of education are in increased (or decreased) demand, and identify how higher education institutions can benefit from this information and incorporate it into their curriculum.
4. *Rethink the role of diploma programs.* Diploma programs do not fulfill their function of providing valuable higher-level vocational skills. It is imperative to reexamine their role and focus. What should they provide? How? A separate diagnostic and policy analysis of this educational level would be worth doing.
5. *Step up provision of skills for innovation.* Additional emphasis is needed on the provision of skills for innovation. In that respect, universities are particularly well positioned to address the general lack of international

exposure and knowledge on the part of firm employees, which is presumably linked to language barriers. They can also enhance creative thinking by exposing students to different learning-teaching methodologies.

6. *Review the quality of private institutions and publish accreditation results.* Although they are part of the accreditation process, private tertiary education institutions continue to have quality issues and should be more closely monitored. Remedial actions should be taken to decrease the number of underperforming institutions, including, if needed, closing failing and nonperforming institutions. This effort—together with regular publication and dissemination of outcomes and accreditation results—would signal a commitment to quality, guide and influence the behavior of tertiary education institutions, and provide clearer information to students about which institutions provide better education.

Priorities for Informal Education and Training

Informal institutions and programs have a huge potential in Indonesia given the situation of young and unskilled workers. Moreover, they could help fulfill the growing need for lifelong learning. Main priorities and policies should include the following:

1. *Collect better data and undertake systematic monitoring and evaluation.* Information systems should be set up that include collecting data on individual programs and participants and conducting tracer studies. More comprehensive and rigorous monitoring and evaluation of ongoing programs should be undertaken (particularly when the incentives for providers and users of training services are changed).

2. *Learn from international experience in setting up successful school-to-work transition programs.* Indonesia has started putting in place programs that have good potential, but policy makers need to look at successful examples elsewhere.

3. *Improve input quality in school-based vocational training.* More emphasis needs to be put on ensuring that all programs are more demand driven. Also, to improve the core weaknesses in their teaching-learning processes, these programs need to address the quality of facilities, instructors' qualifications, and curriculum coverage. Revitalizing BLKs should clearly continue to be a priority. Reexamining their role in light of an increasing focus on lifelong learning may also be useful.

4. *Pursue efforts to develop the skill competency and qualification framework.* The effort to develop a well-functioning competency and qualification

framework should be pursued to help support better quality of the informal system (and improved skill certification) and to build a life-long learning approach to education and training. This effort should include focus on (a) developing a competency-based curriculum; (b) providing skill certification, including dual certification by the school and a professional association; (c) gaining industry participation; (d) ensuring consistent quality of vocational training; and (e) building the framework for lifelong learning.

Priorities for Firm Training

Firms need to play a stronger role both in the short term by upgrading job skills and in the longer term by maintaining skills and strengthening them to increase competitiveness and productivity. Two policies are discussed in the book:

1. *Consider innovative ways of financing firm-based training.* It is urgent to consider new ways of financing firm training in Indonesia to allow firms to focus on updating skills and to help exporting and manufacturing firms build the skills they need for higher competitiveness and innovation. In this respect, the experience of successful training funds may be particularly helpful to look at.
2. *Provide more incentives for employees to pursue outside training on their own.* Firms, the government, or both should provide more incentives for employees to pursue training on their own. According to survey results, such training should focus mostly on improving career opportunities offered by firms, reinserting employees into the firm, and certifying the new skills they acquire. Training vouchers and education savings accounts may also give employees a further motivation to seek training.

Notes

1. These data are 2009 projections from the Global Financial Statistics Database. They are based on IMF Article IV Medium-Term Expenditure Framework data.
2. These data are 2009 projections from the Global Financial Statistics Database. They are based on IMF Article IV Medium-Term Expenditure Framework data.
3. Comparisons among generations are made difficult by the possibility of selection bias ("survival of the fittest") and skill decay for older cohorts—two somewhat counteracting effects—and thus need to be made with care.

4. These results need to be taken with care because they do not control for the possibility of selection biases.

5. The PIAAC is promoted by the OECD.

References

di Gropello, Emanuela, ed. 2009. "Demand for Skills and Skill Gaps in Indonesia." Background report for *Indonesia Jobs Report: Towards Better Jobs and Security for All*. World Bank, Jakarta.

IEA (International Association for the Evaluation of Educational Achievement). 2008. *TIMSS 2007 International Mathematics Report*. Boston: TIMSS & PIRLS International Study Center, Lynch School of Education, Boston College.

OECD (Organisation for Economic Co-operation and Development). 2009a. *PISA 2006 Technical Report*. Paris: OECD. http://www.oecd.org/document/41/0,3343,en_32252351_32236191_42025897_1_1_1_1,00.html

————. 2009b. *PISA 2009 Assessment Framework: Key Competencies in Reading, Mathematics and Science*. Paris: OECD.

UIS (United Nations Educational, Scientific, and Cultural Organization Institute for Statistics). 2008. Database. Key Statistical Tables on Education. http://stats.uis.unesco.org/unesco/ReportFolders/ReportFolders.aspx?IF_ActivePath=P,50&IF_Language=eng

World Bank. 2010. *Indonesia Jobs Report: Towards Better Jobs and Security for All*. 2 vols. Jakarta: World Bank.

CHAPTER 1

Introduction

In Indonesia, the past two decades have been a time of great progress but also of massive transformations and abrupt setbacks. A period of fast economic progress between 1990 and 1997 was characterized by high GDP growth (averaging 7 percent) and profound changes in the structure of employment. At a pace not seen even in other Asian countries, poor rural workers left their farms to find work in the industrial and service sectors. By 1997, almost half of working adults were employed in the formal sector, and in just a few years, the share of agriculture in total employment had shrunk by 14 percentage points, mostly to the benefit of the service sector, whose share grew by more than 9 percentage points. However, this trend came to an abrupt halt when the Asian financial crisis hit Indonesia, causing a massive contraction of economic activity (real GDP fell by 13 percent in one year); an escalation of poverty; and a movement of return to the farm, which reversed the previous evolution. Between 1997 and 1999, the share of agriculture in employment grew again at the rate of 1.3 percentage points yearly (see table 1.1).

Despite the rebound of the economy after the Asian crisis, agricultural employment has continued to grow as a share of the total and at the expense of formal employment, at least until 2003. Although foreign direct investment as a percentage of GDP plunged in the late 1990s in

Table 1.1   Labor Trend Indicators, Growth by Period

Indicators	1990–97	1997–99	1999–2003	2003–07
Employment				
Employment ratio growth	–0.2	–0.1	–0.4	–0.1
Unemployment growth	0.1	0.8	–0.2	0.5
Labor structure				
Nonagricultural employment share growth	2.1	–1.3	–0.8	1.3
Formal employment share growth	1.5	–0.9	–0.3	1.2
Wages				
Median wage growth	7.1	–11.0	8.9	–3.8

Sources: SAKERNAS (Survei Angkatan Kerja Nasional, or National Labor Force Survey); SUSENAS (Survei Sosial Ekonomi Nasional, or National Socioeconomic Survey) for 1992–97 unemployment rates; World Bank 2010.

the immediate aftermath of the Asian economic crisis, reaching a low of –2.76 percent of GDP in 2001, it has gradually recovered, reaching 2.92 percent of GDP in 2005. Similarly, GDP growth picked up again, at about 5.6 percent from 2003 to 2007.[1] However, despite the rebound of the economy, the growth in nonagricultural employment and formal employment continued to be negative up to 2003. This pattern of jobless growth has begun to recede since 2005, but employment creation in Indonesia's industrial and service sectors remains modest—especially by regional standards and in comparison with fast-growing economies such as China and Vietnam.

Labor regulations played a large part in explaining jobless growth, but workers' skills are also part of the equation. Although many reasons underlie the Indonesian phenomenon of jobless growth, decomposition of the factors behind the slowdown in formal sector employment growth points to a sharp decline in employment elasticity of growth in the service sector. In other words, Indonesia's services, which still make up the highest employment share (figure 1.1), have failed to translate growing activity into an equivalent increase in employment. Although "high" wages have been blamed for undermining job creation, workers' skills are also an important part of the equation. Indications suggest that the skill profile of the Indonesian workforce has not evolved along with the demands of the labor market, which may have contributed to slow employment growth in the service sector.[2] Therefore, lack of skills for employability may be an issue in Indonesia. High youth unemployment is another clear indication of this challenge. An adequately skilled workforce would bring increases in productivity that, beyond possible employment losses in the short term, would lead to more employment creation

Figure 1.1   Sectors as a Share of Total Employment in Indonesia, 1990–2007

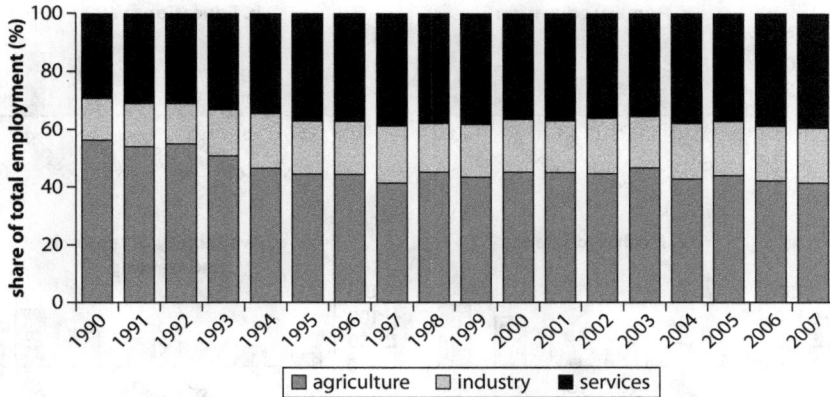

Source: World Bank's World Development Indicators database.

in the longer run through output and competitiveness gains. This insight leads to the next point.

Beyond employment issues, as the Indonesian economy returns to higher growth rates, identifying and addressing potential skill mismatches will be key not only to boosting job creation in the formal sector, but also to supporting higher productivity, competitiveness, and growth. Regaining momentum will obviously depend on many factors, but skills have a key role to play in supporting the further growth and competitiveness of the manufacturing sector (which has remained quite low in value added) and the service sector and, more generally, in enhancing the long-term ability of the country to innovate as well as adapt and assimilate new technologies. Unfortunately, and despite a significant increase in educational attainment, preliminary evidence suggests that this increase has not translated into higher productivity and competitiveness. Indonesia was in 44th place on the 2010–11 Global Competitiveness Index (GCI), ahead of only the Philippines and Vietnam among the East Asian countries assessed (see table A.1 of appendix A). Within the GCI, Indonesia ranks particularly poorly in primary and higher education (see table A.1). Along the same lines, a simple snapshot of some education quality indicators provides preliminary evidence of quality-related gaps, although Indonesia is better positioned than the Philippines and Thailand, two other middle-income countries (figure 1.2). Therefore, a lack of skills for productivity and competitiveness in the country also exists.

Figure 1.2   Quality of Education in a Sample of East Asian Countries

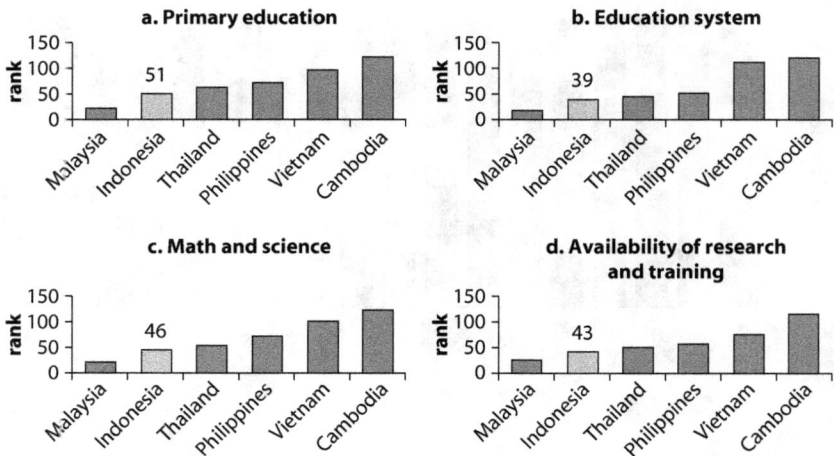

a. Primary education

b. Education system

c. Math and science

d. Availability of research and training

Source: Schwab 2009.
Note: A total of 134 economies were ranked.

Purpose and Conceptual Framework

In this context, this book reviews the main characteristics of and trends in demand for skills in Indonesia, seeking to document the existence of a possible mismatch between employer demands for and available supply of skills. In addition, the book seeks to ascertain the contribution of the education and training sector to this mismatch. Finally, the book proposes measures to improve the education and training sector's responsiveness to what the labor market and the economy need. Improving skills for employability and productivity requires, first of all, a better understanding of the evolving demand for skills and of the critical skills most needed to support the changing demand and drive economic development, followed by identification and understanding of any emerging skill gaps. Beyond other causes that can lead to skill mismatches, assessing to what extent the education and training sector is providing the skills relevant to the labor market and the economy is imperative. Critical policy and market failures must be identified, as well as possible remedies to address them. A very simplified depiction of this conceptual framework is provided in figure 1.3. Understanding how the Indonesian education and training system is able—or unable—to produce the types of skills demanded by employers is also of immediate interest to the government of Indonesia, which has recently adopted an ambitious plan to drastically

Figure 1.3   Framework of the Book

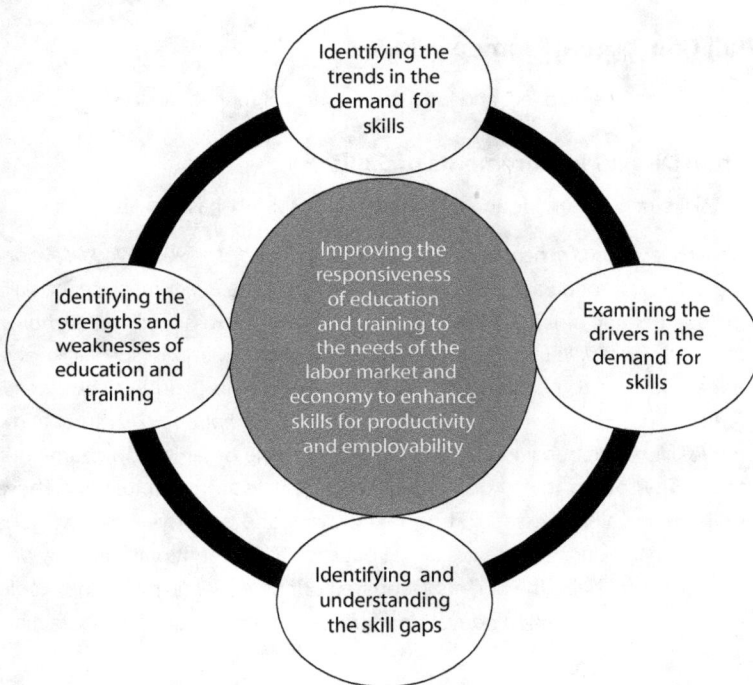

Identifying the trends in the demand for skills

Identifying the strengths and weaknesses of education and training

Improving the responsiveness of education and training to the needs of the labor market and economy to enhance skills for productivity and employability

Examining the drivers in the demand for skills

Identifying and understanding the skill gaps

Source: Authors' representation.

expand enrollment in vocational education and to put renewed emphasis on the development of higher education.

This book pays particular attention to the functional skills that workers need to be employable and to support firms' competitiveness and productivity and to the role of the education and training system in providing those skills.

Functional skills include three main categories (further described in box 1.1): (a) generic (or life) skills, (b) technical skills, and (c) subject-based (or academic) skills. These skills are central to performing well in the workplace and are the cumulative result of all education received, including formal schooling, in-service training, and on-the-job and life experience.[3] From that perspective, education levels such as secondary and tertiary education, which refer to formal education received, can be useful proxies of academic and nonacademic skills at basic, intermediate, and advanced levels. These data are also widely available. Nonetheless,

Box 1.1

Skill Conceptual Framework

This book focuses on direct and indirect measures of functional skills.

Actual Direct Measurements of Skills

Such skills include generic and technical skills or subject-based skills:

- *Non-subject-based generic and technical skills.* Following the 2007 *World Development Report* (World Bank 2006) and Stasz (2001), these direct measures of skills include generic or life skills, which are transferable across jobs, and *technical* and *vocational skills* (associated with one's profession: a mix of specific knowledge and skills to perform jobs). In turn, generic skills include *thinking skills* (critical and creative thinking, problem solving); *computing skills* and *behavioral skills* (basic behavioral skills,[a] leadership, time organization, teamwork, the ability to negotiate conflict and manage risks, communication). These skills are usually assessed through employers' and employees' perceptions (although specific tests are available), but such assessments capture only one side of overall skills (the non-subject-based or nonacademic skills). These skills can be acquired through education (formal or informal),[b] on-the-job training, experience, and so on.
- *Subject-based skills.* Academic skills are generally associated with subject areas (math, literacy, English). They are typically taught in schools and measured through standardized tests. Employers' surveys allow only some (imperfect) measure of these skills. The available international standardized tests at the secondary level allow measurement of some of these skills for Indonesian students in a comparative way.

Education and Training Levels

This measure includes education levels attained or completed, such as secondary and tertiary education, and, when available, training programs completed (pre- or postemployment). Education and training levels are a widely available measure that can potentially indicate a broad range of skills—from academic to generic and technical skills at the basic,[c] intermediate, and advanced[d] levels, depending on the education and training level completed. However, although attaining a certain education and training level can "signal" skills, it is not necessarily synonymous with "possessing" those skills (because it is only an indirect measure) if education and training are of poor quality and poorly relevant to labor-market

Box 1.1 *(continued)*

needs—especially considering that skills are acquired in several different ways. Hence, measures of education attainment and completion are often also complemented by measures of quality and relevance of that education or training to labor-market needs of education and training graduates. The quality and relevance of individual institutions and programs can also be measured to provide a fuller picture of skills, and analyses of different skill providers are similarly important.

Workers' Occupations

Skilled and unskilled occupations covered in this book include those of unskilled workers, skilled production workers, sales workers, administrative workers, professionals, and managers or directors. This indirect measure of skills is quite widely available in firm surveys and potentially captures both generic skills and technical or vocational skills (both of which are important to enter and keep occupations). To a lesser extent, it also captures more academic skills. Workers' occupations can be more or less aligned with education and training levels.

a. Basic behavioral skills are often related to personal traits and are generally defined as noncognitive skills because of their limited capacity to be shaped by outside factors.
b. Literature has highlighted the ways in which the education and training system can support the development of these skills in the labor force (see Heckman and Lochner 2000).
c. At a basic level, these skills can include the set of minimal abilities needed for further learning, work, and life, including numeracy and literacy and basic levels of behavioral skills, such as perseverance, self-discipline, and self-confidence.
d. At a postbasic level, these skills can include thinking skills; higher-order behavioral skills (decision-making skills, teamwork, the ability to negotiate conflict and manage risks); advanced academic skills; and technical or vocational skills.

they are only indirect measures, because "signaling" skills is not necessarily synonymous with "possessing" those skills if education is of poor quality or, conversely, if skills have been acquired through any other source. Finally, workers' occupations, from unskilled laborers to professionals and managers or directors—which can be more or less aligned with education and training levels—can potentially capture, although again only in an indirect way, nonacademic technical and generic skills. The labor force survey, existing firm surveys, the employer skill survey, and standardized testing jointly provide a detailed overview of labor force occupational composition and education as well as information about the most sought-after workers' actual skills, thereby allowing these different skill-related dimensions to be studied.

Outline and Sources

Part I of this book investigates trends in demand for skills in the country, both overall and by sectors. It explores the possible determinants of this demand and attempts to identify emerging skill gaps. Chapter 2 provides baseline data and general trends in the demand for skills, whereas chapters 3 and 4, respectively, go deeper in identifying the various drivers of demand for skills and in investigating the possible existence of a skill gap caused by a mismatch between skills supplied by the education system and those most demanded by firms. With this perspective, part II looks at the skills supplied by the education and training sectors in Indonesia through both formal and informal skill acquisition pathways.

The analysis undertaken in the book is based on data from the National Labor Force Survey (Survei Angkatan Kerja Nasional, or SAKERNAS); the Indonesia industry census and investment climate surveys; and new employer and employee skill surveys, which were fielded in 2008 (see box 1.2 for a brief description of the survey sample and characteristics), as well as from secondary institutional data gathered through specific case studies.

Box 1.2

The Employer and Employee Skill Surveys, 2008

Employer and employee skill surveys were undertaken on 473 medium-size and large firms and 200 employees in the manufacturing and service sectors to ascertain the magnitude and nature of the demand for skills at the employer and employee levels and the drivers of that demand, to explain any possibly developing skill mismatch and its drivers (such as lack of quality of educational institutions), and to assess firm strategies to develop workers' skills. The surveys focused on the five provinces where most of the economic development is concentrated and, within these five provinces, on representative samples of manufacturing and service firms. The focus on services is new because all other existing surveys focus only on manufacturing. Thus, the surveys represent a significant contribution to the data, because they aim at getting a better understanding of the skills demanded (and provided) in a sector that has traditionally been skill intensive and has had a consistent upward trend in its demand for skills.

Box 1.2 *(continued)*

The accompanying table provides the main characteristics of the employer survey sample, which has been stratified according to some key variables to ensure proportional representation of some key firms' characteristics. All the results in the chapter are derived from the weighted sample.

Main Characteristics of the Employer Survey

Sample size and coverage	Stratification variables	Distribution by economic activity
473 medium-size and large firms:[a]	Manufacturing:	Manufacturing (57%)
• 273 manufacturing	• Employment size	Construction (3%)
• 200 services	• Propensity to export	Wholesale and retail
Five provinces:	• Propensity to import	trade (10%)
• Kepulauan Riaou (15%)	• Foreign or domestic	Hotels and
• Daerah Khusus Ibukota	ownership	restaurants (7%)
Jakarta (18%)	• Skill intensity	Transportation,
• West Java (35%)	Services:	warehouse, and
• East Java (24%)	• Employment size	communication (4%)
• Banten (8%)	• Propensity to import	Financial services (4%)
	• Propensity to export	Real estate, rental,
	• Skill intensity	and services (5%)
		Health and social
		assistance (4%)
		Other services (6%)

Source: Authors' compilation.
a. Defined as firms with more than 20 employees.

The employee portion of the survey was less comprehensive, but the 200 interviewed employees were randomly sampled across firms. The quality of both surveys was judged to be satisfactory. In the employer survey, responses were obtained from 473 firms of an initial sample of 500 firms, which maintained representativeness. The refusal rate was low, and nonrespondents were systematically replaced by equivalent firms taken from the larger firm pool. Interviews were conducted in person after the questionnaires were sent in advance. Most questions were well answered, generally by both the human resource manager and the firm manager, with relatively few missing data. In any event, for both surveys, the book presents the most robust findings only, leaving aside questions that either were not well answered or had too much missing data. Significant time was also taken to double-check all figures.

Notes

1. Data are from the World Bank's Knowledge Assessment Methodology (KAM). For more information, see the KAM Web site at http://www.worldbank .org/kam.
2. Possible mechanisms for such slow growth could include a substitution of labor by capital, an increase in the wage of skilled workers, or a push of the inadequately skilled workforce toward the informal sector.
3. Skill acquisition is fundamentally a cumulative and dynamic process starting at birth with parental education and continuing through school education, training, and experience. Although skills can grow over time, they can also decay if possibilities for lifelong learning are not well developed. Additionally, a share of the population can be excluded from effective skill acquisition if alternative "second-chance" skill development pathways do not exist for vulnerable youth.

References

Heckman, James J., and Lance Lochner. 2000. "Rethinking Education and Training Policy: Understanding the Sources of Skill Formation in a Modern Economy." In *Securing the Future: Investing in Children from Birth to College*, ed. Sheldon Danziger and Jane Waldfogel, 47–83. New York: Russell Sage.

Schwab, Klaus, ed. 2009. *The Global Competitiveness Report 2009–2010*. Geneva: World Economic Forum.

Stasz, Cathleen. 2001. "Assessing Skills for Work: Two Perspectives." *Oxford Economic Papers* 53 (3): 385–405.

World Bank. 2006. *World Development Report 2007: Development and the Next Generation*. Washington, DC: World Bank.

———. 2010. *Indonesia Jobs Report: Towards Better Jobs and Security for All*. 2 vols. Jakarta: World Bank.

PART I

Demand for Skills and Skill Gaps in Indonesia

This first part of the book describes trends in demand for skills in Indonesia, both overall and by sectors; it explores the possible determinants of demand and attempts to identify emerging skill gaps. The following key questions are addressed:

- How is the demand for skills changing, and what are its key drivers?
- What are the critical skills most in need for supporting the changing demand and driving economic development?
- Are any skill gaps emerging? What are they, and where are they?

Chapter 2 provides baseline data and general trends in the demand for skills, whereas chapter 3 goes deeper into identifying the various drivers of demand for skills and investigating the possible existence of a skill gap. Chapter 4 attempts to determine to what extent a skill gap is caused by a mismatch between skills supplied by the education and training system and those most demanded by firms.

Conceptually, this part relies on a set of comprehensive indicators based on direct and indirect skill definitions to measure demand for skills, drivers of this demand, and any emerging skill gaps, as identified in table I.1. The main sources used for the analysis are the National Labor Force Survey (Survei Angkatan Kerja Nasional, or SAKERNAS), the industry census and surveys, and the employer and employee skill surveys.

Table I.1 Indicators and Data Sources for the Analysis of Demand for Skills and Skill Gaps

Topic	Indicators	Data source
Demand for skills	1. Trends in wage skill premiums and shares of educated workforce, overall and by sector	Labor force survey
	2. Trends in unemployment and creation of skilled occupations	Labor force survey
	3. Total and net employment by education level, overall and by sector	Employer skill survey
	4. Actual skills demanded by employers and employees	Employer and employee skill surveys
Drivers of demand for skills	1. Regression analysis of skilled occupations and educational attainment ratios over measures of openness and technology	Industry census and investment climate survey
	2. Drivers of demand for skills according to employers	Employer skill survey
	3. Education level and actual skills by firm characteristics	Employer skill survey

Table I.1 *(continued)*

Topic	Indicators	Data source
Skill mismatches	1. Measures of skill bottlenecks	Investment climate survey and employer skill survey
	2. Difficulties in finding the right skills for skilled and unskilled occupations according to employers, by firm characteristics	Employer skill survey
	3. Main causes of skill mismatches according to employers, by firm characteristics	Employer skill survey
	4. Vacancy analysis by occupation level (filled versus unfilled; time to be filled), by firm characteristics	Employer skill survey
	5. Employers' perspectives on the quality of newly hired graduates, by firm characteristics and education level	Employer skill survey
	6. Gaps in actual skills, according to employers	Employer skill survey
	7. Gaps in actual skills and employment outcomes for youth	Employee skill survey and labor force survey

Source: Authors' compilation.

CHAPTER 2

Trends in the Demand for Skills in Indonesia

What are the trends in the demand for skills? This chapter investigates those trends in Indonesia (see figure 2.1), using largely microeconomic evidence from labor force and firm surveys and looking at measures of educational attainment, occupation type, and functional skills. Using the labor force survey, one can outline long-term trends in labor force composition by education level as well as rates of return (the wage premium) to educational attainment, overall and by sector. Additionally, the employer skill survey gives detailed information on labor force composition and education, as well as the worker skills and qualifications most sought after by employers, thereby providing a snapshot of the latest trends in demand for skills.

In terms of education levels and actual skills, the overall picture is one of generally sustained demand for skills across sectors. In today's Indonesian job market, a clear premium is put on upper-secondary and tertiary education, with stronger demand in the service sector. Nevertheless, confirming the importance of looking at direct measures of functional skills, concrete knowledge—particularly theoretical and practical knowledge of the job and core generic and subject-based skills—appears to be more important than nominal educational level.

Figure 2.1   Skill Trends

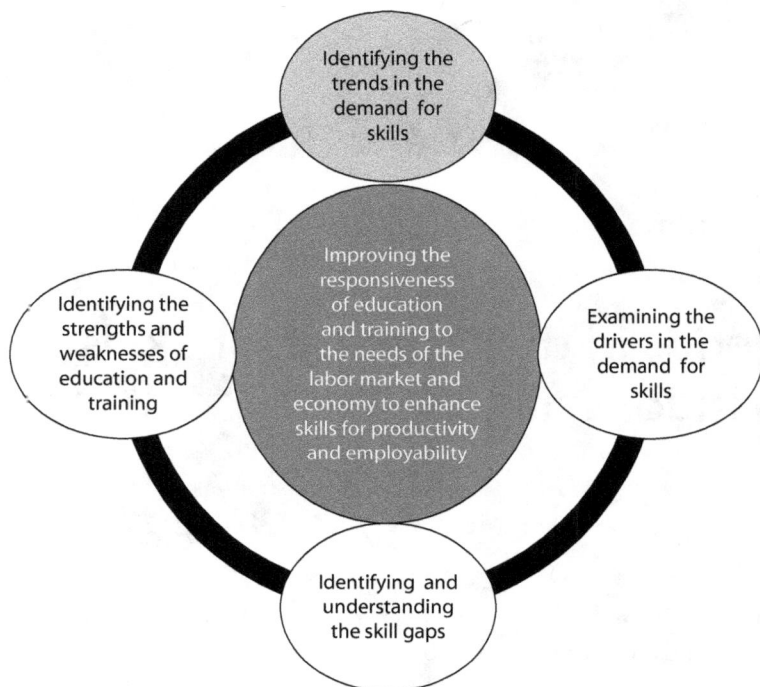

Identifying the trends in the demand for skills

Improving the responsiveness of education and training to the needs of the labor market and economy to enhance skills for productivity and employability

Identifying the strengths and weaknesses of education and training

Examining the drivers in the demand for skills

Identifying and understanding the skill gaps

Source: Authors' representation.

Educational Attainment and Private Returns to Schooling

In recent years, educational attainment has increased significantly in Indonesia, yet this improvement has not translated into a significant decline of returns to education. Together, these trends point to the existence of sustained demand for educational skills and to the continuing ability of the Indonesian job market to absorb new graduates.

From 1994 to 2007, overall schooling has increased materially, thereby improving the skill profile of the labor force. Between those years, the proportion of workers who at least completed the secondary education cycle rose from about 35 percent to 53 percent. Additionally, the share of workers with tertiary-level education more than doubled. The trends in schooling levels can be seen in figure 2.2 (see also table A.2 of appendix A).

Persistently high education premiums—albeit declining slightly[1]—suggest that the increase in educational supply is matched by sustained

Figure 2.2   Trends in Educational Attainment, 1994–2007

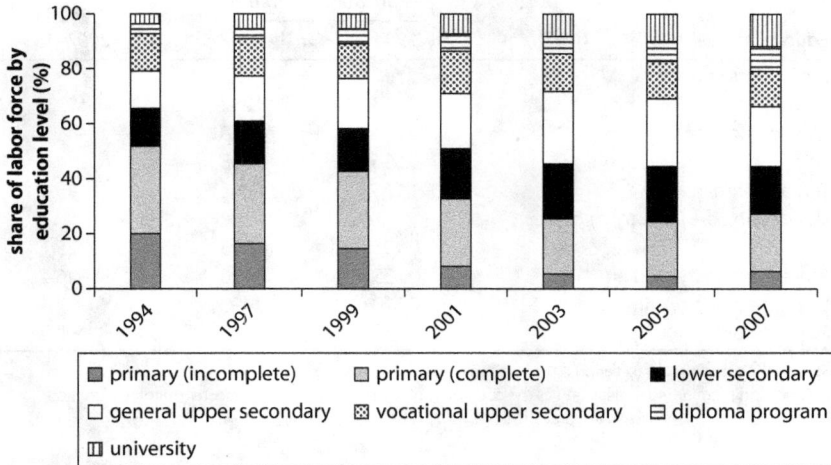

Source: Table A.2 in appendix A.

demand for education. Indeed, premiums to primary education continued to grow, while premiums to senior secondary and tertiary education remain high, even if they are declining slightly. Upper-secondary education graduates earn about 50 percent more than primary graduates, all other things being equal, and tertiary education graduates earn about 100 percent more, which remains a substantial benefit (table 2.1). A simple equivalence exists between education premiums as calculated in this book and the more traditional annualized rates of return. The estimate of 1.084 for tertiary over primary is the difference in coefficients for tertiary and primary in the estimated earnings equation. Dividing 1.084 by the difference in years of education between tertiary and primary education (10 years) implies an annualized return of about 10.8 percent. Similarly, if one wants to derive an estimate of the return to tertiary over upper secondary, the calculation would be the difference between 1.084 and 0.508, or 0.576; annualized, this figure implies an average return of 14.4 percent for each year of tertiary education over upper secondary. These annual rates of return are significant. They are comparable with those of upper-income Asia and most countries of the Organisation for Economic Co-operation and Development (see figure 2.3), although lower than those of Latin America.[2] Within the group of workers educated through at least

Table 2.1   Education Premiums of People Employed for Wages

Education level	Education premium[a]		Change (%), 2007–1994
	1994	2007	
Basic controls only			
Primary	0.213	0.242	13.6
Lower secondary/primary	0.234	0.128	−45.3
Upper secondary/primary	0.596	0.508	−14.8
Tertiary/primary	1.125	1.084	−3.6
Basic controls + Industry dummies			
Primary	0.195	0.243	25.1
Lower secondary/primary	0.235	0.126	−46.4
Upper secondary/primary	0.610	0.498	−18.4
Tertiary/primary	1.137	1.070	−5.9

Source: di Gropello and Sakellariou 2010.
a. Education premiums are measured as the coefficient of the skill variable in a Mincerian earnings function, controlling for workers' personal characteristics.

Figure 2.3   Private Rates of Return for an Individual Obtaining a University-Level Degree (International Standard Classification of Education 5/6)

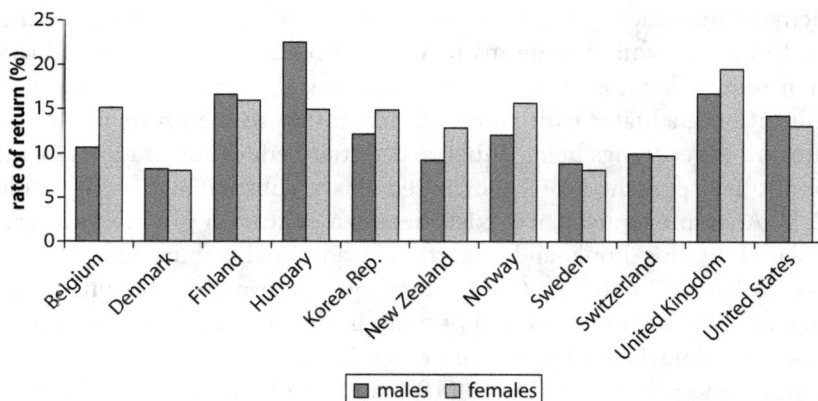

Source: OECD 2007.
Note: The figure shows the rate of return when the individual immediately obtains the next-higher level of education.

secondary levels, the decline in education premiums has been inversely related with the level of education. For instance, whereas the premium to tertiary education fell by less than 4 percent between 1994 and 2007, premiums to upper-secondary and lower-secondary education fell by 14.8 percent and 45.3 percent, respectively, over the same period.

In line with the previous comparison, when a single dummy for education is used with two alternative specifications—(a) upper secondary and above compared with lower secondary and below and (b) tertiary compared with upper secondary and below—one sees that education premiums in Indonesia are comparable with those of other middle-income East Asian countries (lower than Thailand and, recently, Cambodia,[3] but higher than China, the Philippines, and Vietnam; figure 2.4). At the same time, the observed slight decline of these premiums over time (in contrast with regional trends showing increases in both premiums and workforce skill ratios) suggests that the quality and relevance of the skills acquired in school will increasingly be driving returns (rather than educational attainment per se) and differentiating students with similar levels of schooling. This trend also indicates longer-term wage compression, which, together with education "overqualification" and high unemployment rates (discussed later), may be pointing to some emerging constraints in the ability of the economy to absorb educated workers.

Although the proportion of educated workers has increased in all sectors, the service sector—because of its relative dynamism and skills intensity—has absorbed most of these workers. Together with stable or slightly rising education premiums in the service sector, this trend indicates increasing demand for education (in particular, tertiary education) in the service sector, reflecting an East Asian trend. Some evidence exists of education imbalance across sectors. Over the past decade, the proportion of skilled workers (at least as measured by education levels) increased substantially, on average, but particularly in the service sector,[4] where a substitution of highly educated workers for less educated ones has occurred. This change probably reflects more capital- and technology-intensive processes but also lower overall quality of the skill supply. Mirroring this trend, the evolution of education premiums across sectors in Indonesia has been rather sector specific, with generally decreasing returns in agriculture, a mixed performance in manufacturing, and stable or even slightly increasing returns in the service sector (figure 2.5). A comparison across countries in the evolution of education premiums is shown in table A.3 of appendix A, confirming that returns have been stable or increasing in most East Asian countries in the service sector. Although this finding would justify a sustained focus on skills for the service sector, it also suggests a somewhat imbalanced distribution of education levels across sectors. (For example, does manufacturing[5] have too few highly educated workers or

Figure 2.4 Education Premiums and Educated Workforce in a Sample of East Asian Countries

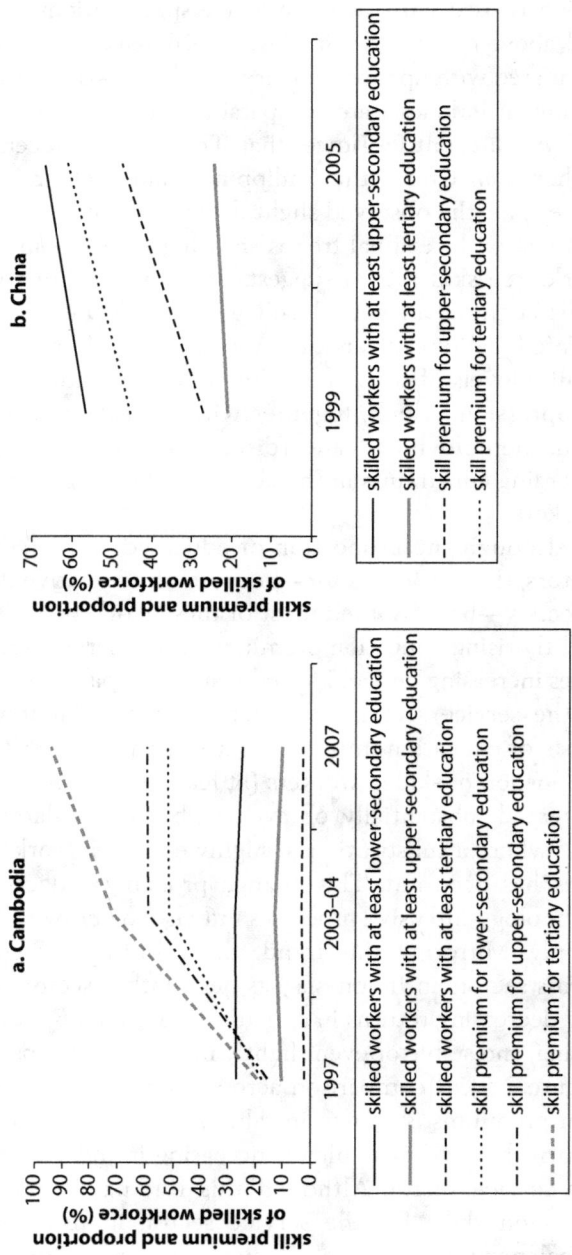

a. Cambodia

skill premium and proportion of skilled workforce (%)

100
90
80
70
60
50
40
30
20
10
0

1997   2003–04   2007

— skilled workers with at least lower-secondary education
— skilled workers with at least upper-secondary education
- - - skilled workers with at least tertiary education
······· skill premium for lower-secondary education
–·–· skill premium for upper-secondary education
– – – skill premium for tertiary education

b. China

skill premium and proportion of skilled workforce (%)

70
60
50
40
30
20
10
0

1999   2005

— skilled workers with at least upper-secondary education
— skilled workers with at least tertiary education
- - - skill premium for upper-secondary education
······· skill premium for tertiary education

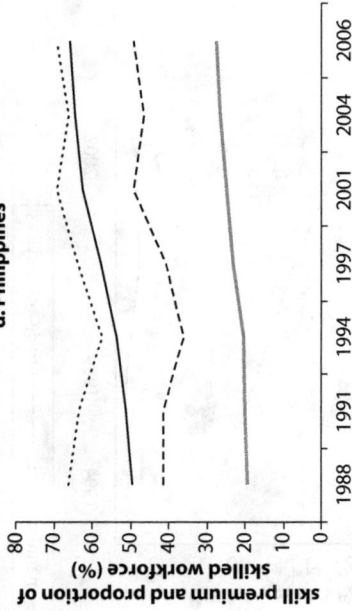

c. Indonesia

skill premium and proportion of skilled workforce (%)

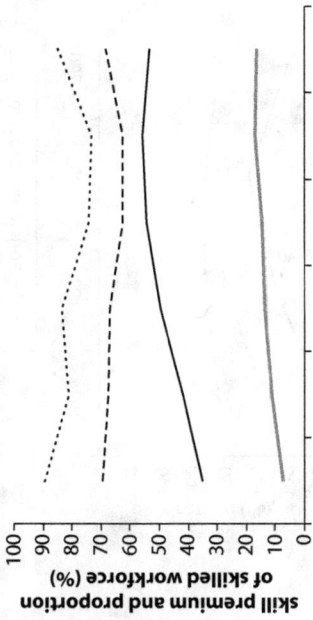

e. Thailand

skill premium and proportion of skilled workforce (%)

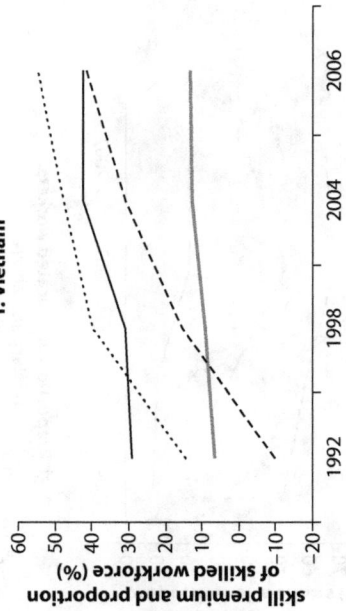

d. Philippines

skill premium and proportion of skilled workforce (%)

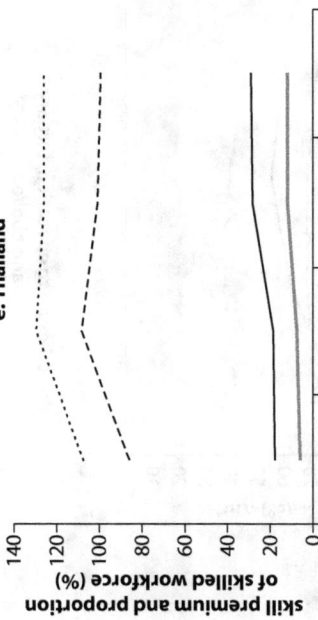

f. Vietnam

skill premium and proportion of skilled workforce (%)

— skilled workers with at least upper-secondary education

----- skill premium for upper-secondary education

— skilled workers with at least tertiary education

.... skill premium for tertiary education

Source: di Gropello and Sakellariou 2010.

Figure 2.5 Education Premiums and Educated Workforce in Indonesia, by Sector

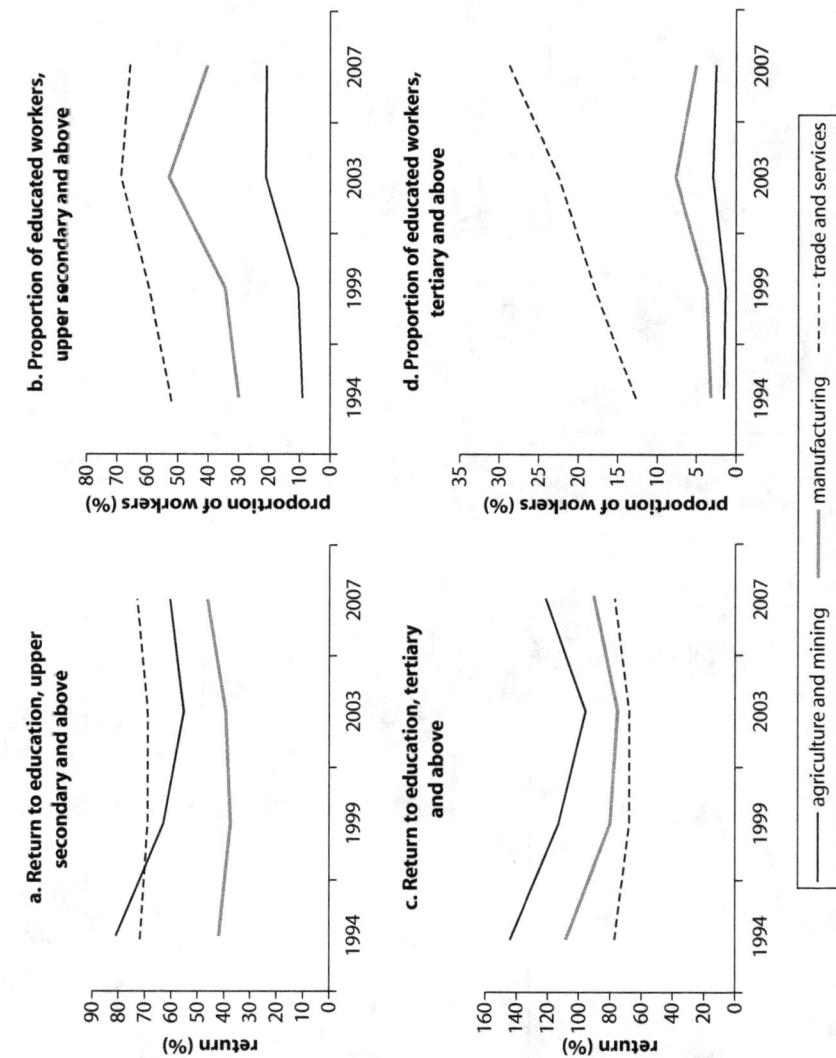

a. Return to education, upper secondary and above

b. Proportion of educated workers, upper secondary and above

c. Return to education, tertiary and above

d. Proportion of educated workers, tertiary and above

agriculture and mining — manufacturing — - - - trade and services

Source: di Gropello and Sakellariou 2010.

services too few moderately educated workers?) Such imbalances may have consequences on the productivity growth of the manufacturing sector and the employment growth of the service sector and may therefore also need to be addressed. Labor-market segmentation issues may be preventing higher mobility of workers across sectors (which is difficult to assess), or broader issues may affect the relevance of different skilled workers to the needs of each sector. Chapter 4 and part II examine this issue further.

Confirming this trend, a subsector analysis of demand for workers with at least secondary education shows increased demand for education in the service sector and some manufacturing subsectors (figure 2.6). The analysis shows a decline in demand for education (that is, declining premiums) in the primary sector (agriculture and mining) but increased demand—manifested by an increasing skilled employment share and education premiums—in timber and furniture; nonmetallic mineral production; electricity, gas, and water; retail; transport and communication; and finance and real estate (which has the highest skill premium of all sectors). The education premium has tended to increase homogeneously across service subsectors but more unpredictably for manufacturing, confirming higher demand in the service sector.

The focus on the service sector is mirrored in the employer skill survey, which shows that over 60 percent of service sector firms have seen an increase in skill requirements over the two years preceding the survey. The increase is also real, albeit more modest, for manufacturing firms. Interestingly, looking ahead, virtually all firms expect their skill requirements to increase over the next 10 years (figure 2.7).

Other Employment Outcomes

Not only do education premiums remain significant, but also employment outcomes of educated workers in finding a job have generally improved in time. Whereas the overall unemployment rate has remained practically stable from 1998 to 2006, unemployment of educated workers, although generally higher than the average because of higher reservation wages, has decreased in this same period, confirming a sustained demand for educated workers (figure 2.8). This decrease has been particularly sharp for university graduates. Unemployment has, however, been increasing for secondary vocational graduates and has stayed practically stable for lower-secondary graduates.[6]

Figure 2.6   Education Premium and Proportion of Skilled Labor, by Sector (at Least Secondary Education), 1996 and 1997

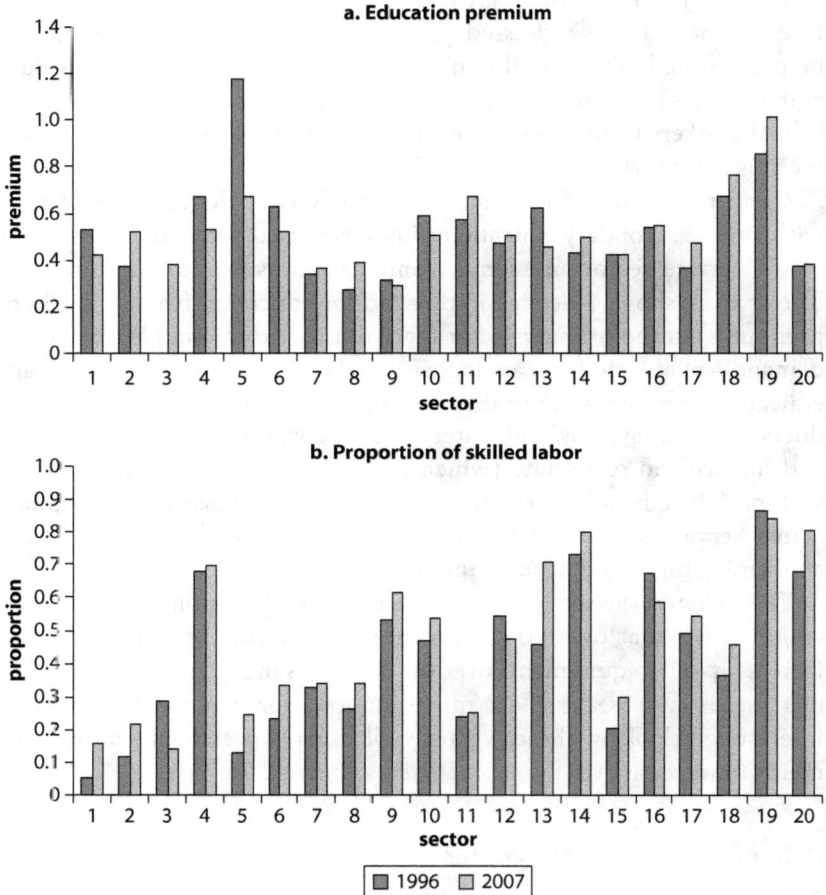

a. Education premium

b. Proportion of skilled labor

■ 1996   □ 2007

Source. SAKERNAS (Survei Angkatan Kerja Nasional, or National Labor Force Survey).
Note: 1 = agriculture; 2 = forestry; 3 = fishery; 4 = coal mining and oil; 5 = other mining; 6 = food, drinks, and tobacco; 7 = textiles; 8 = timber and furniture; 9 = paper, printing, and publishing; 10 = chemical; 11 = nonmetallic mining production; 12 = native metal industry and metal-made production, machinery, and equipment; 13 = other industries (other machinery, computing, radio and television broadcasting, medical instruments, vehicles, and so forth); 14 = electricity, gas, and water; 15 = building construction; 16 = wholesale and accommodation; 17 = retail; 18 = transport and communication; 19 = finance and real estate; 20 = public, social, and personal services.

At the same time, Indonesia's unemployment rates remain the highest in East Asia.[7] Higher relative unemployment rates for Indonesia at the regional level (figure 2.9) point to slow employment creation as well as to issues with the quality and relevance of secondary and higher education[8]—particularly secondary education, given that unemployment rates are now

Figure 2.7   Employers' Perceptions of Skill Requirements

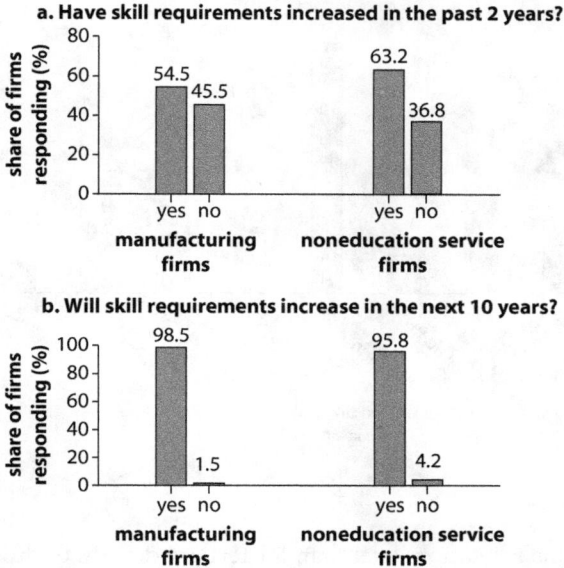

a. Have skill requirements increased in the past 2 years?

b. Will skill requirements increase in the next 10 years?

Source: Indonesia Employer/Employee Survey of Skills/Labor Demand and Job Vacancies 2008, Employer Module.

Figure 2.8   Predicted Probabilities of Being Unemployed, by Education Level, 1996–2008

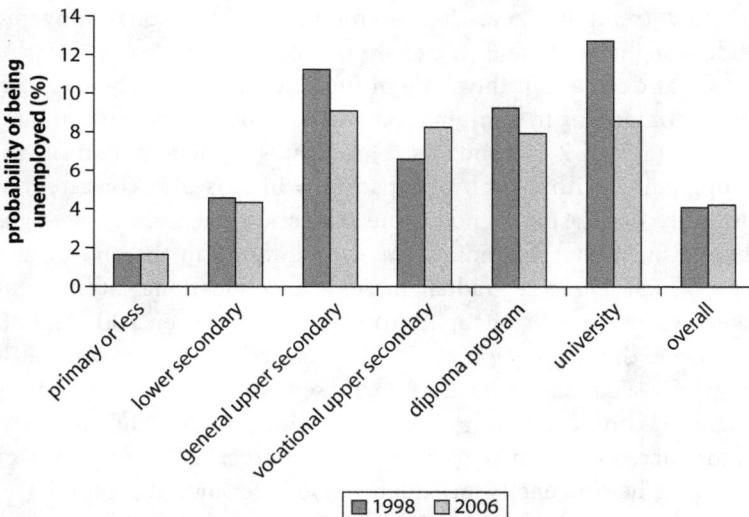

Sources: SUSENAS (Survei Sosial Ekonomi Nasional, or National Socioeconomic Survey) 1996, 2008.
Note: Data are for the population 22 to 65 years of age.

Figure 2.9   Unemployment Rates in East Asian Countries

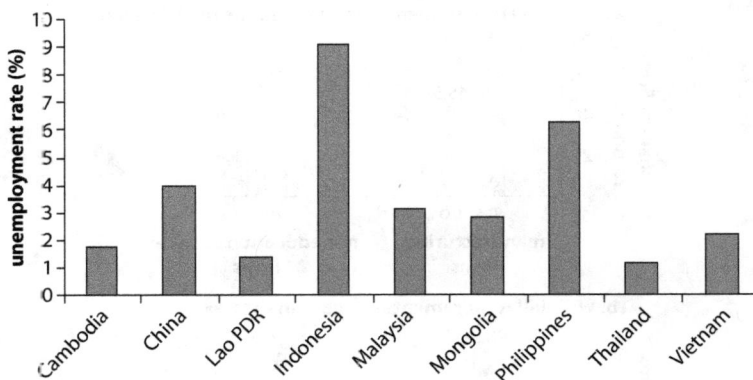

Source: World Bank's World Development Indicators database.
Note: Data are for the population 15 to 60 years of age.

higher for this education level than for tertiary despite traditionally lower reservation wages.

Additionally, the decrease in unemployment may have come at a price: the overall occupational structure of the economy does not seem to have fully kept pace with the increase in educational attainment. Signs of job overqualification are evident, helping to explain the slightly decreasing trend in education premiums. Occupational movements include a slight increase in the share of sales workers and professionals and a slight decrease in the share of unskilled workers. The rise in educational attainment in combination with a broadly stable occupational structure (table A.2 of appendix A) indicates a phenomenon of education upgrading within each occupation, which is also consistent with the slightly decreasing trend in the education premium. The signs of such an educational upgrading can also be found in the employer skill survey, which shows a gradual increase in educational attainment of workers within specific occupation categories. Between 2005 and 2007, for instance, the proportion of skilled production workers with at least some upper-secondary education increased from 59 percent to 61 percent, and the proportion of professionals with at least a higher-education diploma increased from 65 percent to 68 percent. The relative lack of (or at least heterogeneity in) quality and relevance of secondary and higher education could in part explain this phenomenon whereby higher educational attainment often fails to translate into occupational mobility. Other reasons may include labor regulations, wage levels, and slow employment creation. Nevertheless, even if the broad allocation of labor across employment categories has not changed markedly, some specific professional categories have expanded at the expense of others. In particular, reflecting the increasing relative importance of services over industrial activity, the number of sales workers and professionals has risen since the mid-1990s, whereas the share of unskilled workers in the labor force has dropped by roughly 5 percentage points over the past decade (table A.2).

A more in-depth look at the results of the employer and employee skill surveys allows a better understanding of the demand for skills and its patterns.

Demand for Skills according to Employers

The survey data give a closer look at the demand for skills in terms of education levels, occupations, and direct measures of skills. At the same time, one can examine how such demand varies systematically across sectors and according to firms' integration in world markets (this analysis is presented in chapter 3).[9]

Evidence from the employer skill survey confirms sustained demand for skilled workers, proxied by education levels. Overall, educational attainment increases the probability of employment and continues to determine the type and quality of jobs that graduates can aim for. In today's Indonesia, most jobs in the formal sector require a minimum education level. Although the bulk of job creation remains in occupations that are relatively simple (such as crafts and machine operation), employers tend to expect a minimum level of education even for such jobs. For machine operators, completion of lower-secondary level is the minimum required, and most employers expect craft, sales, and clerical workers to be educated at or above upper-secondary level. Managers, professionals, and even technicians are expected in a majority of cases to have a diploma or university education (figure 2.10).

As a result of the occupation structure and minimum education requirements, the educational profile of new recruits is biased toward the secondary level, and there are relatively larger increases of workers with at least a diploma level. The employer skill survey confirms the continued relevance (for finding employment) of the secondary and university tracks; firms recruiting in the 12 months preceding the survey

Figure 2.10   Minimum Education Level Required of New Hires in Past 12 Months

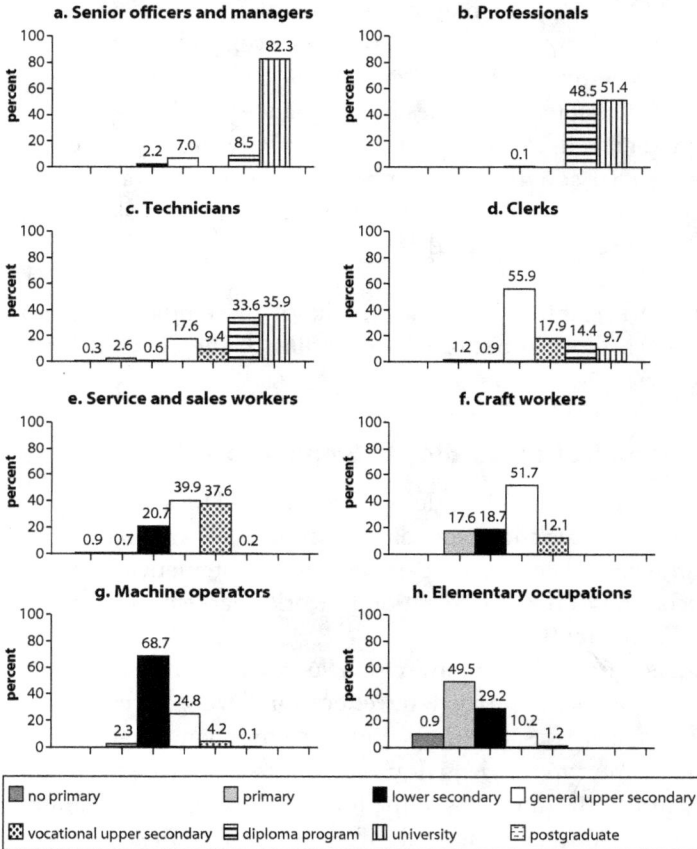

a. Senior officers and managers

b. Professionals

c. Technicians

d. Clerks

e. Service and sales workers

f. Craft workers

g. Machine operators

h. Elementary occupations

Legend: no primary | primary | lower secondary | general upper secondary | vocational upper secondary | diploma program | university | postgraduate

Source: Indonesia Employer/Employee Survey of Skills/Labor Demand and Job Vacancies 2008, Employer Module.

did so predominantly at the secondary level or higher, with a very significant reduction of hires at the primary level. Because of the occupation and education-level structure, a clear relative bias exists toward secondary as opposed to higher education (see figure 2.11, panel a). In fact, during the 12 months preceding the survey, jobs filled at the secondary-only level (73.7 percent of the total) outnumbered those staffed by higher-education graduates (17 percent) by a factor of 4.3. However, when the education of new hires is compared with the education of discharges (figure 2.11, panels a and b), the stronger relative

Figure 2.11   Education of New Hires and Discharges

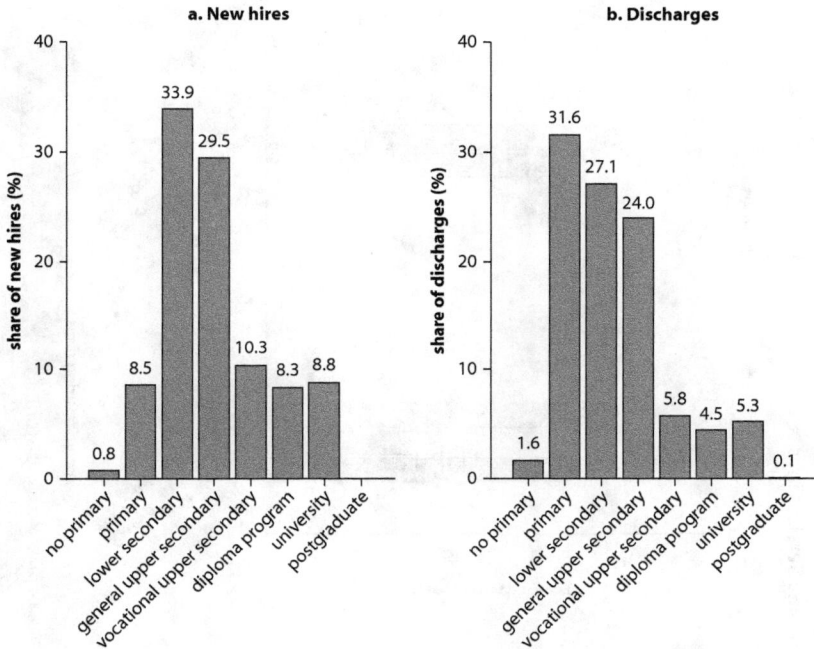

Source: Indonesia Employer/Employee Survey of Skills/Labor Demand and Job Vacancies 2008, Employer Module.

upgrade occurs in vocational and higher education (which almost double their share in the new recruits).[10] Although these trends partly reflect an increase in the *supply* of secondary and tertiary graduates, together with the trends in education premiums, they also confirm the hypothesis made previously of sustained *demand* for upper-secondary and higher education.

The bias toward upper-secondary graduates is particularly pronounced in the service sector, which also accounts for a significantly higher proportion of higher-education graduates. Although almost 40 percent of those entering the workforce do so with only lower-secondary education or below, this share is largely driven by manufacturing. Disaggregating the data by sector (figure 2.12) shows a rather sharp contrast between the manufacturing sector, on one hand (where more than 50 percent of new recruits have no upper-secondary schooling), and the service sector, on the other hand (where this proportion is

Figure 2.12 Education of New Hires and Discharges, Manufacturing and Service Firms

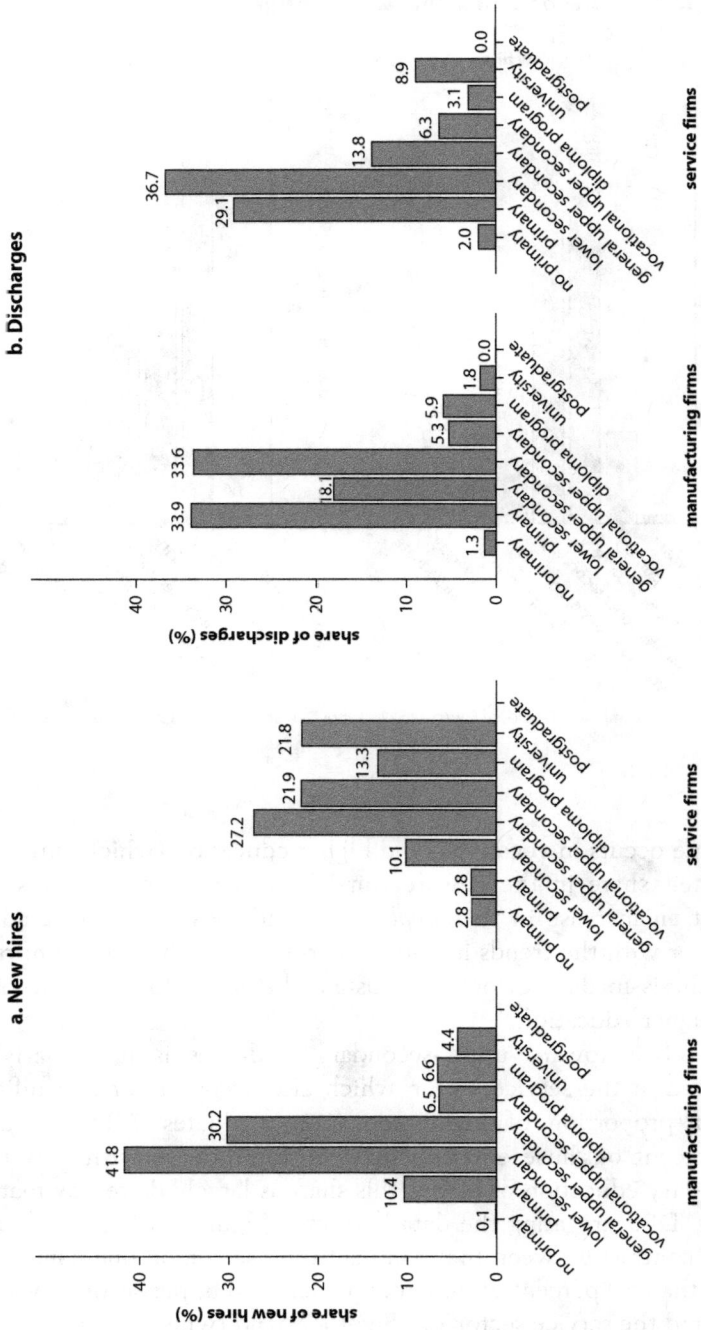

a. New hires

manufacturing firms

education	share of new hires (%)
no primary	0.1
primary	10.4
lower secondary	41.8
general upper secondary	30.2
vocational upper secondary	6.5
diploma program	6.6
university	4.4
postgraduate	

service firms

education	share of new hires (%)
no primary	2.8
primary	2.8
lower secondary	10.1
general upper secondary	27.2
vocational upper secondary	21.9
diploma program	13.3
university	21.8
postgraduate	

b. Discharges

manufacturing firms

education	share of discharges (%)
no primary	1.3
primary	33.9
lower secondary	33.6
general upper secondary	18.1
vocational upper secondary	5.3
diploma program	5.9
university	1.8
postgraduate	0.0

service firms

education	share of discharges (%)
no primary	2.0
primary	29.1
lower secondary	36.7
general upper secondary	13.8
vocational upper secondary	6.3
diploma program	3.1
university	8.9
postgraduate	0.0

Source: Indonesia Employer/Employee Survey of Skills/Labor Demand and Job Vacancies 2008, Employer Module.

barely 15 percent). Likewise, a much higher proportion of new hires in services received tertiary-level schooling (over 35 percent in services compared with barely over 12 percent in manufacturing), which also confirms the trends in the higher-education share shown in figure 2.5. The service sector also has a significantly higher share of workers with vocational secondary education. Overall, the increase in education levels appears much stronger in the service sector than in the manufacturing sector.

This trend is confirmed by data on outstanding vacancies, which show a sharp contrast between education levels expected of candidates in manufacturing and services. In the manufacturing sector, over 50 percent of vacancies require no more than lower-secondary schooling. In the service sector, this share is barely 3.5 percent. Meanwhile, over 70 percent of vacancies in the service sector are expected to be filled at the tertiary level, against 12.3 percent in the manufacturing sector (figure 2.13). Pulling together the data on new hires and vacancies, one gets an initial indication that service firms may actually be facing some skill shortages as higher-education vacancies outstrip recruitment of higher-education graduates. (However, the fact that this situation does not yet translate into a drastic increase in the higher-education skill premium in services tends to indicate that the issue is more about gaps in terms of quality and relevance than mere quantity.) If it exists at all, shortage of skills may be more of an issue for technical and vocational education and training (TVET) and higher-education workers in manufacturing according to data on

Figure 2.13   Expected Education Level for Vacant Positions

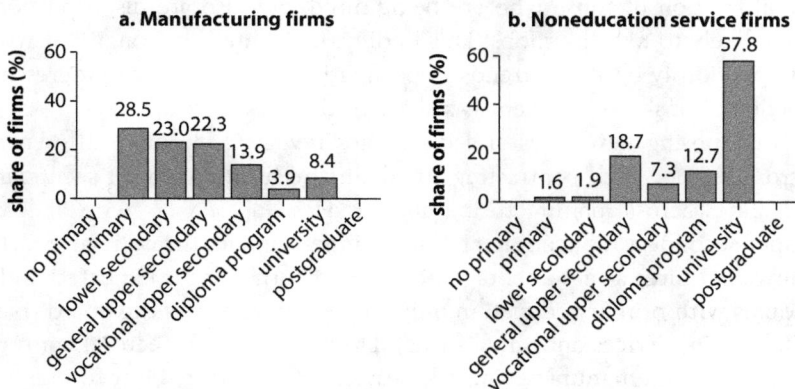

Source: Indonesia Employer/Employee Survey of Skills/Labor Demand and Job Vacancies 2008, Employer Module.

hires, vacancies, and rates of return (at least with respect to secondary and tertiary education).

Within the group of new hires educated at the upper-secondary level, most are accounted for by the general education track rather than the vocational stream. The service sector hires more vocational graduates than the manufacturing sector. The share of the former is approximately three times that of the latter, which corresponds roughly to the share of enrollment in each track (and therefore hints at the fact that hiring ratios may reflect supply of upper-secondary graduates more than a strong preference for either track). There again the sectoral divide is striking: service sector firms appear more eager to hire graduates of the vocational track than do manufacturing employers. Although the ratio of new hires from general to vocational stream is roughly 5.0 to 1.0 for manufacturing, it is barely 1.2 to 1.0 in services. This difference might indicate that vocational institutions have closer links with service than with industrial activities, but it is also an indication of the higher availability of service tracks than manufacturing specialized tracks within secondary TVET.[11] This situation is in sharp contrast to that in the Philippines, where most workers with vocational education are employed in the manufacturing sector (see di Gropello, Tan, and Tandon 2010) and deserves further analysis. The low proportional hiring of general secondary graduates in the service sector compared to TVET graduates is also a curious trend deserving further analysis. Relative demand for general versus vocational secondary graduates and other employment outcomes of these different tracks are further investigated in chapter 4 of this book.

Another clear-cut trend is the precarious situation of those laborers with no schooling or only primary education. They not only represent a small fraction of those who are being hired, but also are disproportionately likely to lose their jobs. This finding, incidentally, is congruent with the previously observed trends in occupation shares and the progressive decline of unskilled workers as a share of the labor force.

Juxtaposing new hires and discharges reveals additional differences across sectors, with contrasting trends in the hiring of lower-secondary graduates across manufacturing and services. Job seekers with at least upper-secondary education are net winners in all firms. Figure 2.14 shows net hires as a percentage of total net turnover. As expected, individuals with primary education only are net losers across the board (particularly in services and small firms). However, a sharp sectoral contrast exists between manufacturing and service firms with respect to individuals with lower-secondary education only (they are strong net winners in

Figure 2.14   Education of Net Hires, Manufacturing and Noneducation Service Sectors

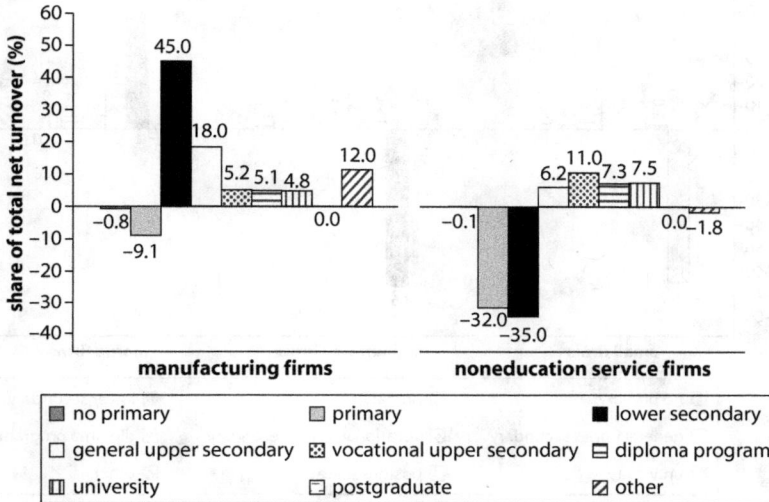

Source: Indonesia Employer/Employee Survey of Skills/Labor Demand and Job Vacancies 2008, Employer Module.

manufacturing and sharp losers in services). To a lesser extent, the contrast also exists for this category between medium-size firms and large firms, where they are, respectively, net losers and winners (figure 2.15). The net hires analysis shows that job seekers with upper-secondary education are net winners in all firms, as well as those holding a diploma or university degree, and that service firms appear more eager to create positions for students of vocational institutions.

Notwithstanding the evidence of some educational upgrading within occupations and a resulting imperfect alignment between education and occupation, education levels not only are related to the likelihood of finding employment but also continue to determine the level at which new hires enter the workforce and the types of occupations to which they may aspire (with related higher relative earnings). This finding is illustrated by a review of the typical education profiles by type of occupation.

The survey data show that top managers are typically educated at the tertiary level, particularly in the service sector, where more than 90 percent of managers have completed at least secondary schooling and 67 percent are educated at the tertiary level. Predictably, the average education

Figure 2.15   Education of Net Hires, by Size of Firm

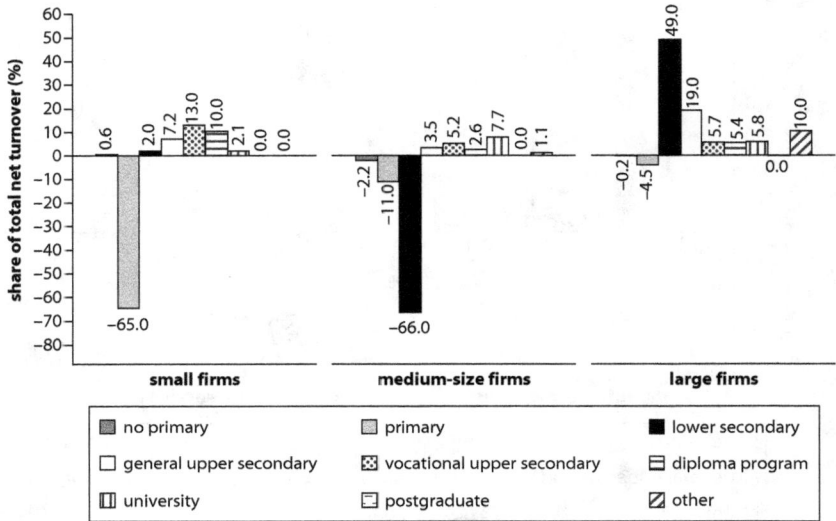

Source: Indonesia Employer/Employee Survey of Skills/Labor Demand and Job Vacancies 2008, Employer Module.

of top managers tends to rise with firm size as well as firm formality (as proxied by International Organization for Standardization, or ISO, certification). Among firms that received ISO certification, over 90 percent had top managers educated at the tertiary level (compared with 57 percent otherwise).

The educational profile of those hired as managers and professionals is strikingly similar. The tertiary-track graduates are by far the largest group, and within it, university students dwarf diploma holders by a factor of six (figure 2.16). But within the group of secondary graduates, the situation is much more even between general and vocational students.

Administrative and sales staff members are educated predominantly at the secondary level and in the general stream (figure 2.17). Interestingly, those who did follow a tertiary cycle did so largely in vocational diploma institutions. Taken together, the profile of managers and professionals, on the one hand, and that of administrative and sales staff, on the other hand, appear to suggest that the diploma stream may be operating mainly as an extension of the secondary education level, perhaps commanding higher positions relative to secondary only, but not really opening the door to those occupations dominated by university graduates. A nonetheless still

Figure 2.16   Average Education Levels of Managers and Professionals Recruited in 2007

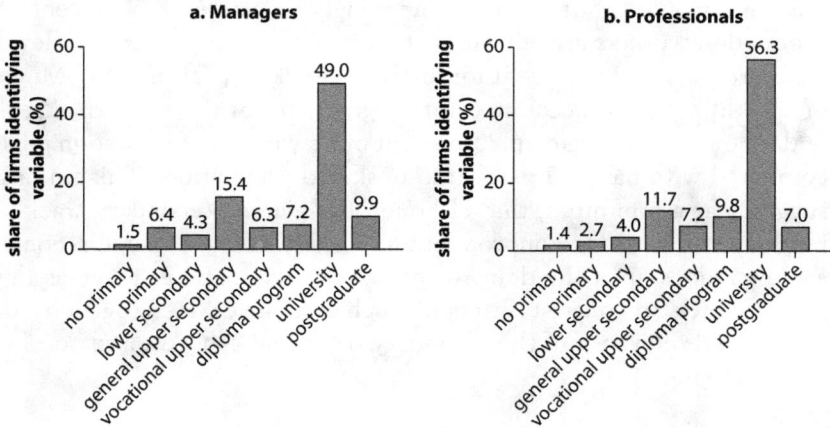

a. Managers

b. Professionals

Source: Indonesia Employer/Employee Survey of Skills/Labor Demand and Job Vacancies 2008, Employer Module.

Figure 2.17   Average Education Levels of Administrative and Sales Workers Recruited in 2007

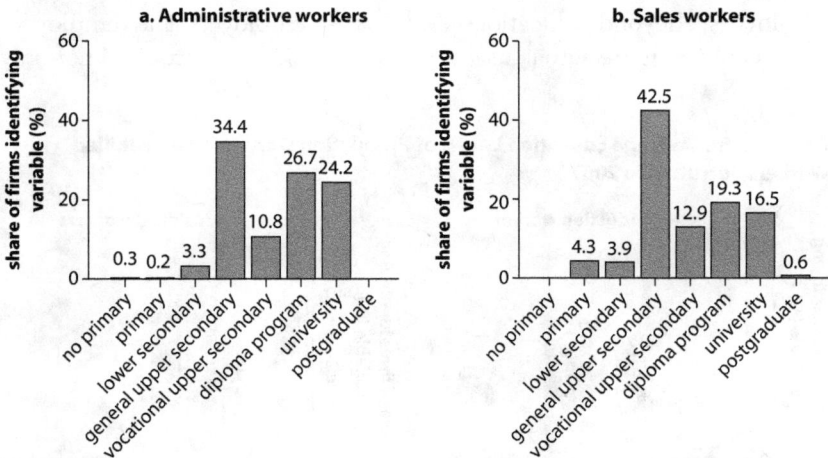

a. Administrative workers

b. Sales workers

Source: Indonesia Employer/Employee Survey of Skills/Labor Demand and Job Vacancies 2008, Employer Module.

significant share of university graduates in this type of occupation confirms some job overqualification, likely caused by a combination of slow top-job creation and heterogeneous quality and relevance of tertiary and secondary graduates.

At the level of production and unskilled workers, one finds, as expected, that production workers are more educated overall than unskilled workers, but not overwhelmingly so. Some 58.5 percent of production workers are educated at least at the upper-secondary level compared with 42.6 percent for unskilled workers (figure 2.18). Much of this difference is accounted for by graduates of the vocational secondary track, who make up 23 percent of new hires in production jobs, compared with barely 5 percent in unskilled occupations. This finding suggests, at a minimum, that although the general secondary track is more appreciated for nonproduction workers, the vocational secondary track does open the door to specialized occupations, whereas the general track, in contrast, offers no such assurances. Heterogeneity in quality and relevance of the secondary track again suggest a reason for this outcome.

Demand for "Actual Skills": Looking beyond Educational Attainment

What are the actual skills, both generic and technical, that employers look for in their employees? And what are the skills most needed according to employees? Beyond education levels, what employers and employees really care about are actual, usable skills. Such skills are acquired not only

Figure 2.18   Average Education Levels of Production Workers and Unskilled Workers Recruited in 2007

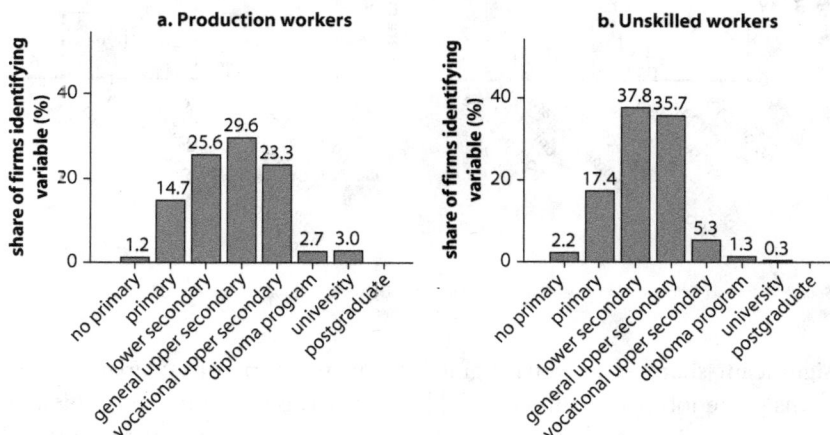

Source: Indonesia Employer/Employee Survey of Skills/Labor Demand and Job Vacancies 2008, Employer Module.

through education but also through other channels, such as on-the-job exposure.

As far as job-specific (or technical) skills are concerned, employers assess the quality of workers by considering their actual knowledge rather than by looking at their degrees obtained, as is illustrated by the importance given to practical and theoretical knowledge, which is higher than the importance given to the degrees themselves (table 2.2).

The way in which firm executives assess applicants' skills also reveals a less than perfect alignment between schooling and job-relevant skills. Interviews and probation periods are the most popular assessment methods, ahead of education level as attested by diplomas (table 2.3). This finding also points to a possibly important constraint in job matching, which is the lack of adequate skill certification.[12]

Theoretical knowledge and practical knowledge are considered equally important (with a slight edge for practical knowledge). What this finding suggests is the need to maintain balanced curricula irrespective of the tracks: that is, more practical knowledge should be included in the general secondary track, and conversely, vocational education should retain a solid transversal core.

As for experience, a high premium is put on job-relevant experience as opposed to general or diversified exposure. In other words, the qualities of workers, as assessed by employers, appear to be determined as much by their training (or the extent of practical content in their training) as by hands-on exposure to a certain activity.

Table 2.2   Importance of Job-Specific Skills and Education

Variable	Share of firms rating variable as very important (%)
Primary education	43
General upper-secondary education	27
Local university degree	21
Diploma program or vocational training	12
Foreign university degree	4
Grades	17
Theoretical knowledge	44
Practical knowledge	51
Experience in same field	46
Experience in different field	12
General experience	20

Source: Indonesia Employer/Employee Survey of Skills/Labor Demand and Job Vacancies 2008, Employer Module.

Table 2.3   Method of Assessing Applicants' Skills

Method	Share of firms responding	
	Noneducation services	Manufacturing
Interview	0.9	0.8
Educational institution	0.7	0.5
Recommendations	0.4	0.3
Proof of degree	0.4	0.3
Transcripts	0.4	0.4
Probaticn period	0.5	0.4
Written test	0.3	0.3
Education level	0.7	0.7

Source: Indonesia Employer/Employee Survey of Skills/Labor Demand and Job Vacancies 2008, Employer Module.

This result is mirrored in the employee skill survey, which gives a more nuanced picture, depending on the professional categories. As expected, on-the-job experience is particularly valuable for workers. For administrative and sales workers, however, training takes precedence, albeit with a preference for job-specific rather than academic programs. For managers and professionals, the inverse criteria apply: school-based training is the most important source of skills, even if job-specific training and on-the-job experience remain valuable assets (figure 2.19).

Predictably, a disaggregation of job-specific skills by type of occupation shows that theoretical and practical knowledge of the job appears to be more important for managers and professionals than for skilled workers. The relative importance of general versus vocational education as a source of skills also varies according to types of occupations. For managers and professionals, the general track is considered preferable to the vocational track at the secondary level as a source of skills, and this preference is even more pronounced at the tertiary level. The opposite is true of skilled workers, although the contrast at the tertiary level is not as stark.

When these results are disaggregated by sector, service firms also appear to put greater emphasis on actual skills across the board, irrespective of whether they are acquired in the classroom or on the job. The relative ranking is similar across sectors, although theoretical knowledge appears to be somewhat more important in the service sector.

The survey also confirms that primary education remains the building block of worker quality. Primary education remains central as a basis for

Figure 2.19   Most Important Sources of Skills for Current Job, as Perceived by Employees

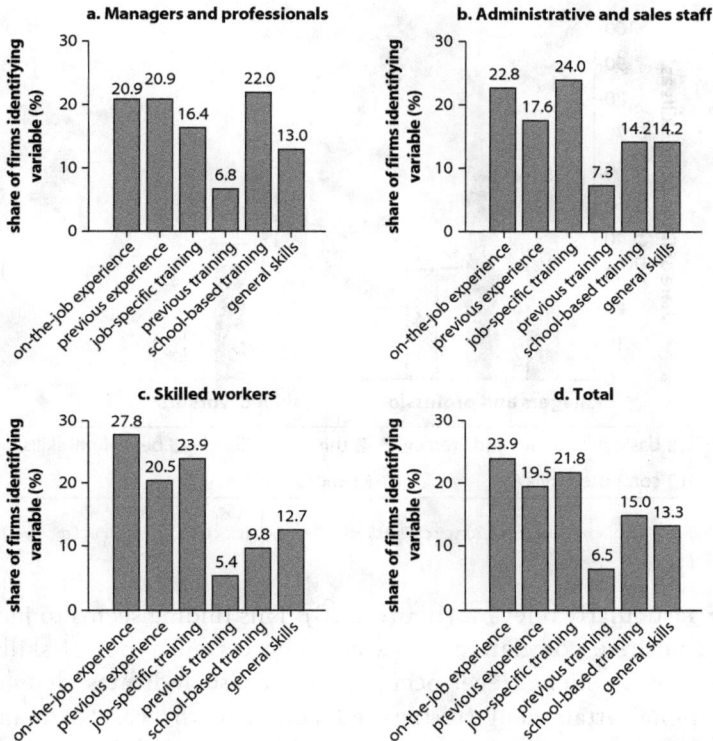

Source: Indonesia Employer/Employee Survey of Skills/Labor Demand and Job Vacancies 2008, Employee Module.

the acquisition of any further skills across all occupations and sectors, as indicated by the high importance attributed to this education level across the board.

Finally, the employer skill survey confirms that core skills (generic or subject based) are very important for the Indonesian workforce, particularly for the service sector, where behavioral skills are given particular preeminence, and for managers and professionals. Across job categories, core skills—particularly basic math and literacy but also generic skills such as thinking and behavioral skills—are valued above narrower (more specialized) skills such as familiarity with computers or English proficiency.[13] This finding is accentuated for managers and professionals, for whom thinking and—to a lesser extent—behavioral skills appear

Figure 2.20   Share of Firms Rating Skills of Managers, Professionals, and Skilled Workers as Very Important

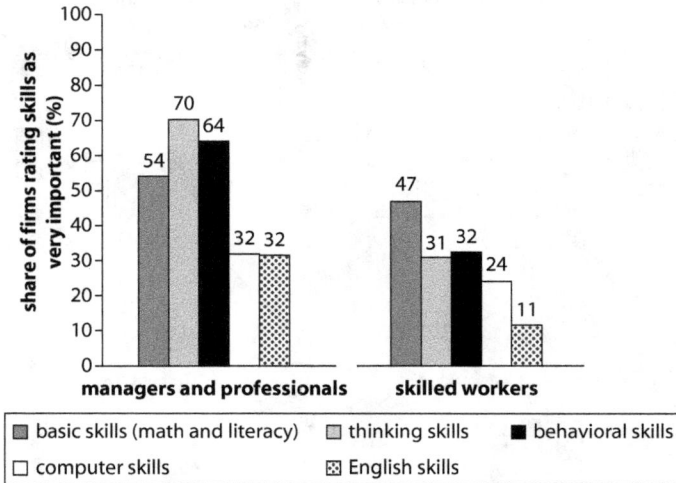

Source. Indonesia Employer/Employee Survey of Skills/Labor Demand and Job Vacancies 2008, Employer Module.

to be particularly relevant (figure 2.20). This finding seems to indicate that a positive correlation exists between certain types of skills and promotion to higher-level occupations. It also indicates that higher educational attainment (tertiary education in the case of managers and professionals) is used to signal higher generic skills beyond job-specific ones. In the future, core skills are expected to matter more than experience and, in the case of services, more than personal attributes[14] (figure 2.21). They are also particularly relevant in the service sector, whose managers and skilled workers are expected to score higher on behavioral skills (relative to workers in the manufacturing sector) and whose workers are expected to perform better on skills across the board (figure 2.22).

A closer look at behavioral skills shows that expectations here also differ according to positions and across sectors. Although managers and professionals are logically held to higher standards than skilled workers on measures of behavioral skills, one exception exists: team orientation is considered relatively less important for managers and professionals but the most important quality in skilled workers (figure 2.23). Communication skills and ability to work independently are particularly

Figure 2.21   Types of Skills Likely to Matter in the Future, by Sector

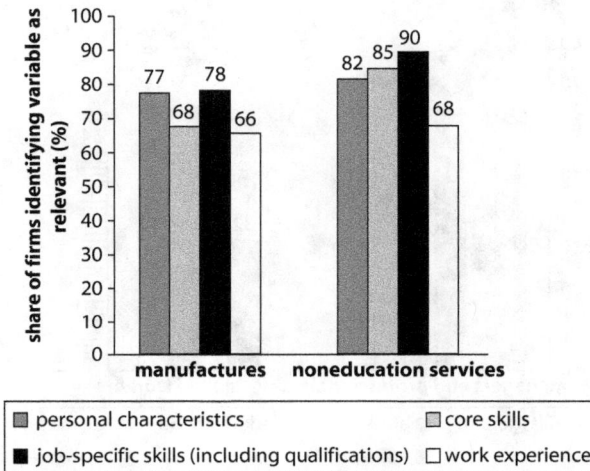

Source: Indonesia Employer/Employee Survey of Skills/Labor Demand and Job Vacancies 2008, Employer Module.

Figure 2.22   Share of Manufacturing and Noneducation Service Firms Rating Workers' Skills as Very Important

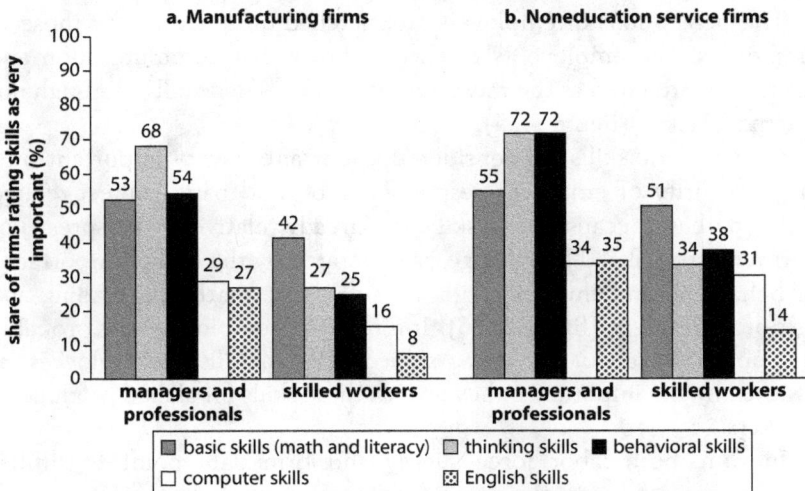

Source: Indonesia Employer/Employee Survey of Skills/Labor Demand and Job Vacancies 2008, Employer Module.

Figure 2.23   Share of Firms Rating Behavioral Skills of Managers, Professionals, and Skilled Workers as Very Important

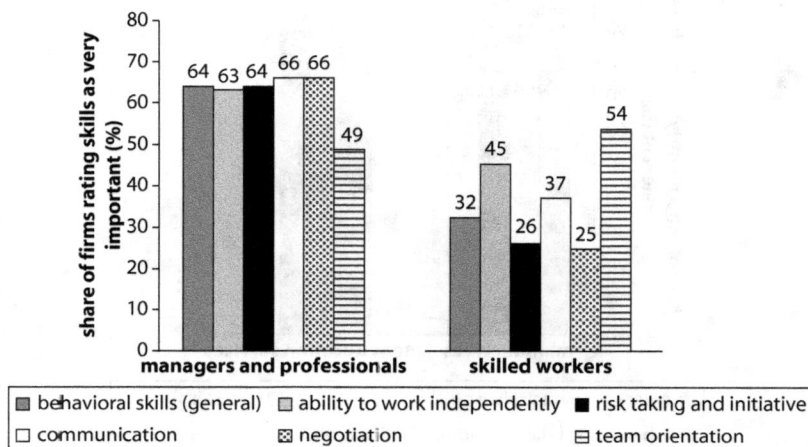

Source: Indonesia Employer/Employee Survey of Skills/Labor Demand and Job Vacancies 2008, Employer Module.

important across the board. Behavioral skills, for managers and workers alike, matter more in the service sector than in manufacturing, with a difference across sectors in the importance of communication skills particularly striking for skilled workers (figure 2.24).

The perceptions of employers are matched quite closely by those of employees. The employee skill survey shows that communication and team skills are rated as the most important or needed skills, although not the most lacked (figure 2.25).

Core generic skills are considered important or very important by a large majority of employee respondents, beyond basic subject-related skills (perhaps because these skills are already relatively widespread) or narrower specialized knowledge, as illustrated by the higher importance of behavioral and thinking skills vis-à-vis basic math and reading and use of computers (figure 2.26). Interestingly, employers are probably less optimistic about the basic subject-related skills of employees, as assessed by the importance they give to these skills for skilled production workers.

In sum, both labor force survey and firm data point to similar conclusions. There is clear evidence of sustained demand for skills, which is stronger in the service sector and is reflected in the demand for educational attainment, rather than in skilled work occupations.

Figure 2.24   Share of Manufacturing and Noneducation Service Firms Rating Behavioral Skills of Workers as Very Important

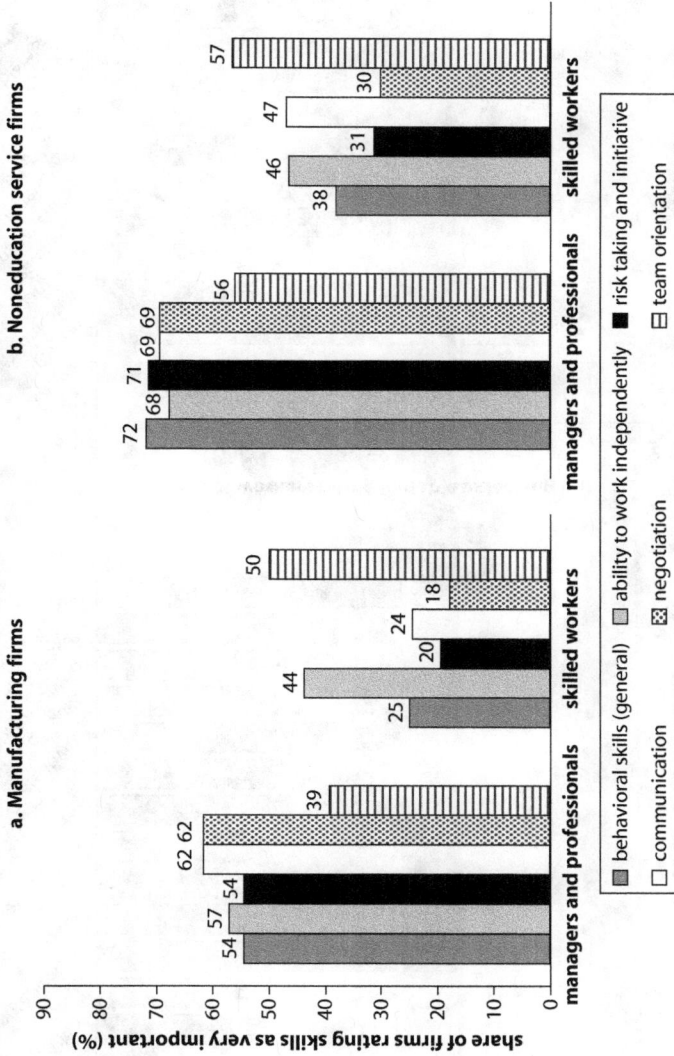

a. Manufacturing firms

b. Noneducation service firms

share of firms rating skills as very important (%)

managers and professionals

skilled workers

managers and professionals

skilled workers

■ behavioral skills (general)   ☐ ability to work independently   ■ risk taking and initiative
☐ communication   ▨ negotiation   ▤ team orientation

Source: Indonesia Employer/Employee Survey of Skills/Labor Demand and Job Vacancies 2008, Employer Module.

Figure 2.25   Most Important and Most Lacked Skills as Perceived by Employees

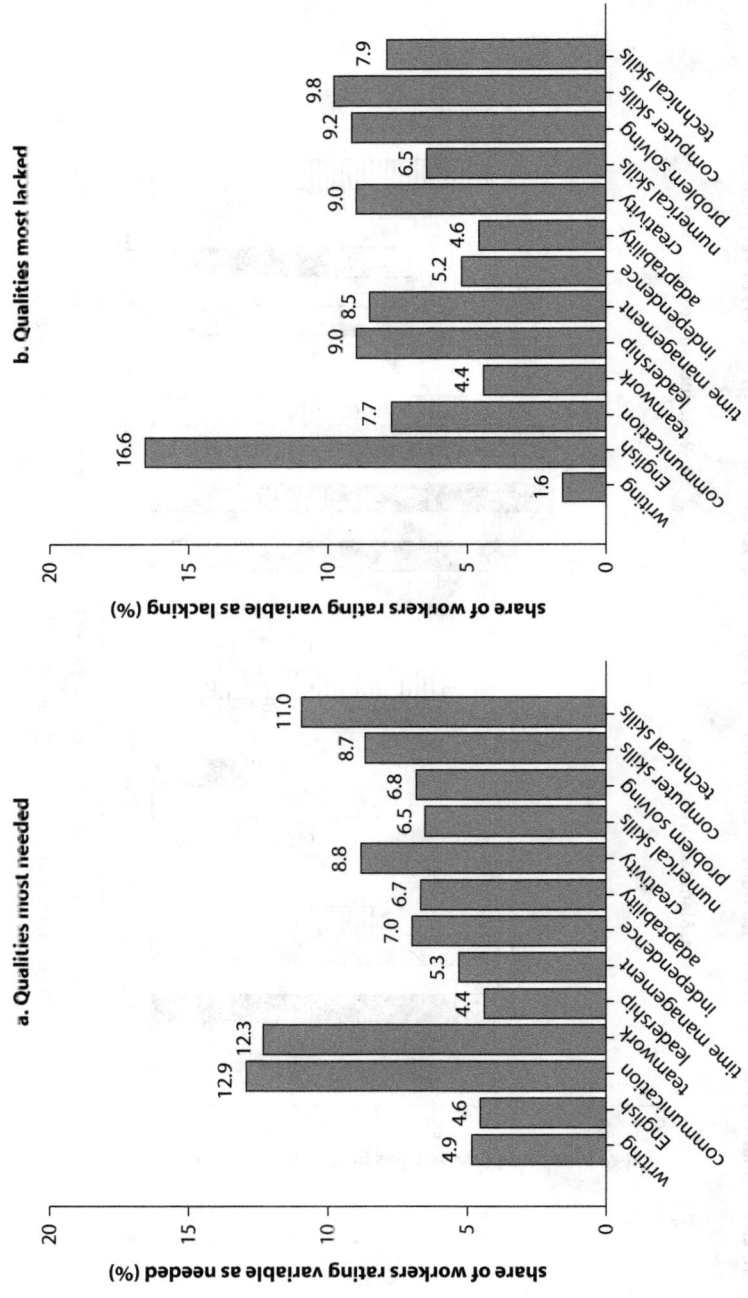

a. Qualities most needed

share of workers rating variable as needed (%)

Variable	Value
writing	4.9
English	4.6
communication	12.9
teamwork	12.3
leadership	4.4
time management	5.3
independence	7.0
adaptability	6.7
creativity	8.8
numerical skills	6.5
problem solving	6.8
computer skills	8.7
technical skills	11.0

b. Qualities most lacked

share of workers rating variable as lacking (%)

Variable	Value
writing	1.6
English	16.6
communication	7.7
teamwork	4.4
leadership	9.0
time management	8.5
independence	5.2
adaptability	4.6
creativity	9.0
numerical skills	6.5
problem solving	9.2
computer skills	9.8
technical skills	7.9

Source: Indonesia Employer/Employee Survey of Skills/Labor Demand and Job Vacancies 2008, Employee Module.

Figure 2.26   Importance of Various Skills on the Job as Perceived by Employees

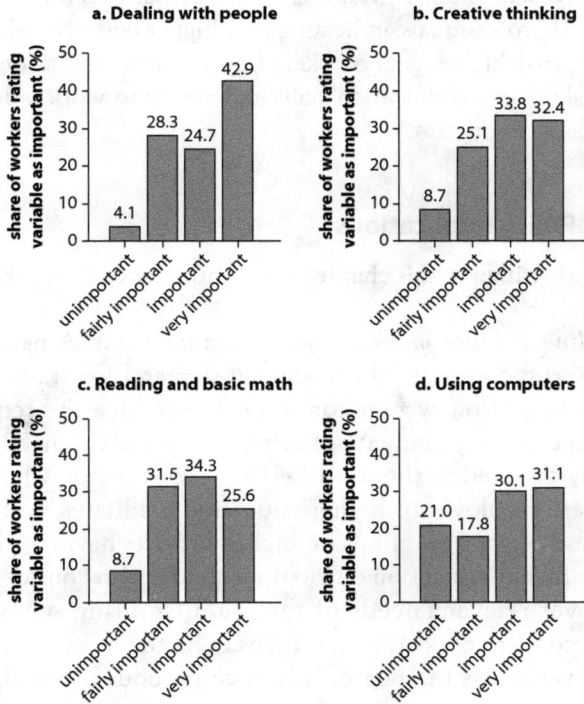

a. Dealing with people

b. Creative thinking

c. Reading and basic math

d. Using computers

Source: Indonesia Employer/Employee Survey of Skills/Labor Demand and Job Vacancies 2008, Employee Module.

(This differentiated trend also explains the relative wage compression.) Overall, the rise in education levels appears to be much stronger in the service sector, which is very much focused on hiring higher education and, to a lesser extent, secondary vocational graduates, followed by general track graduates (who still outpace vocational graduates overall). New hires in manufacturing are largely lower-secondary and general secondary graduates.

Nevertheless, actual knowledge appears to be more important than education levels themselves, highlighting the need for direct measures of functional skills, emphasizing both theoretical and practical knowledge of the job. Employers and employees alike consider on-the-job experience particularly valuable. Also notable is that core generic and subject-based skills (not only basic math and literacy[15] but also generic skills such as thinking and behavioral skills) are considered very important for and by the Indonesian workforce. This finding is particularly true for the service sector (where behavioral skills are given particular preeminence) and for managers and professionals, indicating that higher educational attainment is used to signal higher generic skills beyond job-specific ones. Among behavioral skills, communication skills and ability to work independently are particularly important.

Emerging Policy Implications

The trends identified in this chapter have a number of policy implications:

- *Responding to labor-market demand is important.* A need exists to continue responding to the sustained demand for skills by making sure the education system continues to produce the required secondary and tertiary graduates. Higher education will need to be continuously targeted to the needs of the service sector, which is by far the largest employer of higher-education graduates, and this focus will include strong emphasis on higher-order behavioral skills. However, the higher-education curriculum should also consider the more limited yet relevant needs of the manufacturing sector. General upper-secondary education continues to be the most important education level across the board. It is in continuous demand, but some preliminary evidence indicates deficiencies in its relevance to labor-market needs. These deficiencies must be addressed. This finding is mirrored by a need to improve the quality and relevance of vocational education, particularly in relation to the needs of the manufacturing sector.

- *Subject-based, generic, and job-specific skills should be integrated.* Ensuring a good integration of subject-based, generic, and job-specific skills in the curricula of all education levels (at the respective expected standard) is important. Overall, the findings of this chapter point to the importance of ensuring a strong core curriculum that supports literacy and math as well as analytical and creative thinking. More group-based, student-centered pedagogy is needed, with practical exercises and activities, and students should have more opportunities to interact with the workplace. Informal education should also be designed to achieve a well-integrated curriculum between subject-based, generic, and job-specific skills; it has particular potential for developing generic and job-specific skills.

- *A balanced curriculum in secondary education is needed.* The combined importance of practical and theoretical knowledge suggests the need to maintain a balanced curriculum in secondary education regardless of the track a student chooses, general or vocational. More practical knowledge should be included in the general secondary track, and conversely, vocational education should retain a solid transversal core.

- *General secondary education must meet the needs of the service sector.* More practical knowledge in general secondary schools may make them more appealing to the service sector, which over 2008 hired relatively few of these students compared to the manufacturing sector and its enrollment share. Increasing focus on skills particularly useful in the service sector, such as communication, computing, and English-language skills, may also be useful.

- *Vocational secondary education must meet the needs of the manufacturing sector.* Very limited employment of TVET graduates in manufacturing suggests a need for better targeting of the vocational curriculum to the needs of the manufacturing sector or increased interaction between manufacturers and TVET schools (part II of this book has more on this subject). A similar conclusion may seem to hold for higher-education graduates in manufacturing, where fewer but probably still valuable employment opportunities exist. Targeting the selected manufacturing subsectors with higher demand for skills may be a good option.

- *Opportunities for job-specific experience and school-to-work transition should be increased.* The fact that experience in the same field is extremely valued as a means to acquire job-specific skills raises school-to-work transition issues for young graduates that will need to be addressed (see chapter 4 and part II for more details on this issue).

- *Skill modules should be added to existing firm and labor force surveys.* Collecting information on skills most needed, skill gaps, the relationship between skills and labor-market outcomes, and the like would help researchers monitor how demand for skills changes over time and therefore policy makers can respond to such changes.

Notes

1. The decreasing trend may indicate some emerging constraints in the ability of the economy to absorb educated workers.

2. In Latin America, rates of return for tertiary education fluctuate between 14 percent and 28 percent (see di Gropello 2006).

3. Cambodia's high education premium is likely to reflect a still very low education level.

4. Most of the skilled workers are also going to the service sector in absolute terms, following the increasing GDP and employment share of the sector (notwithstanding slower-than-expected employment growth).

5. This possibility is also indicated by a rate of return on these skills higher than in the service sector.

6. These results control for parental wealth.

7. The highest unemployment rate for Indonesia shown in the regional comparison can be explained by a different cutoff point of the active population adopted for all countries (15 to 60 years of age). The youth unemployment rate is much higher than the average unemployment rate in Indonesia.

8. The two are likely to be at least partly related.

9. Most of the results reported here are statistically significant.

10. The upgrade is, however, higher for general secondary graduates than vocational graduates in terms of net hires (discussed later in this chapter).

11. In Indonesia, vocational upper-secondary schools offer seven specific majors: health, business management, agriculture, community welfare, tourism, arts and handicrafts, and technical skills.

12. This situation, as will be seen in part II, is improving, however.

13. At the same time, it may be significant to point out that although basic knowledge of computers and English is relatively less important for skilled workers, a good number of firms (respectively, 24 percent and 11 percent) still consider these skills very important.

14. Personal attributes are also defined as noncognitive skills in some skill literature. It is nonetheless notable that personal attributes—such as reliability, hard work, adaptability, and honesty—still matter so much. This fact alone deserves further analysis.

15. This fact reflects the finding that primary education remains the building block of worker quality across the board.

References

di Gropello, Emanuela, ed. 2006. *Meeting the Challenges of Secondary Education in Latin America and East Asia: Improving Efficiency and Resource Mobilization*. Washington, DC: World Bank.

di Gropello, Emanuela, and Chris Sakellariou. 2010. "Industry and Skill Wage Premiums in East Asia." Policy Research Working Paper 5379, World Bank, Washington, DC.

di Gropello, Emanuela, Hong Tan, and Prateek Tandon. 2010. *Skills for the Labor Market in the Philippines*. Washington, DC: World Bank.

OECD (Organisation for Economic Co-operation and Development). 2007. *Education at a Glance 2007*. Paris: OECD.

CHAPTER 3

Drivers in the Demand for Skills in Indonesia

What are the factors and the dynamics that influence demand for skills in Indonesia? This chapter delves deeper into understanding the demand for skills by investigating its various drivers (see figure 3.1). The analysis allows a more in-depth look at what skills are needed to respond to changing labor-market needs and to support economic development more broadly while making some predictions about expected demand. The chapter makes comprehensive use of both longitudinal and cross-section firm data and combines the quantitative analysis undertaken from the existing data with more qualitative insights from the employer skill survey, which also hints at differences across the industrial and service sectors (not captured in the existing firm surveys).

Although the evidence is not always straightforward to interpret, the data point to the relevance of technology, a more competitive business environment, some changes in work organization, and openness to trade and investment in explaining firms' demand for skilled labor. The relationship between skills, technological change, and competitiveness is fleshed out in this chapter.

Figure 3.1   Skill Drivers

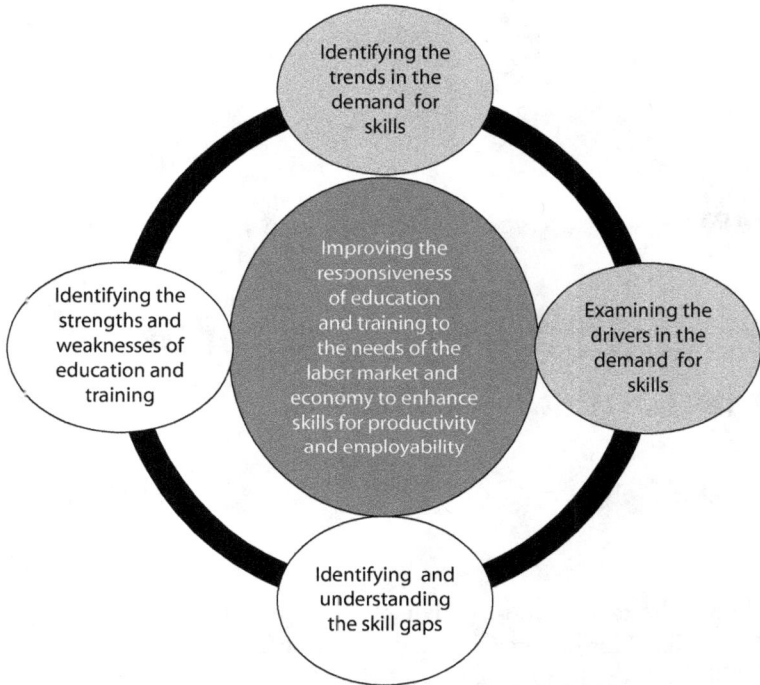

Source: Authors' representation.

Quantitative Evidence from the Manufacturing Sector (Firm Surveys)

This section describes evidence gathered from the manufacturing sector. This evidence derives from two sources: Indonesia's Manufacturing Survey of Large and Medium-Size Firms (Survei Industri, or SI) and the World Bank–led Investment Climate Surveys (ICSs) of firms in various East Asian countries.

In the three decades between 1975 and 2005, almost no increase occurred in the share of skilled labor as proxied by the share of nonproduction workers[1] in manufacturing employment or the total wage bill. According to the manufacturing survey, the respective employment share and relative wage skill premium of nonproduction and production workers in Indonesia in the manufacturing sector have stayed quite stable over the 1975 to 2005 period. This finding suggests that demand for skilled labor has remained rather flat over that period in the manufacturing sector, and it confirms the evidence described in chapter 2 for the trend in occupations and erratic skill premium. However, when one looks at subperiods and subsectors of activity, one can distinguish changes in these variables, as shown in figures 3.2 and 3.3. Manufacturing subsectors experienced different trends in demand over the time period—increasing, for instance, in nonmetallic mineral production; decreasing in paper products and printing; and remaining stable in chemicals (see table A.4 in appendix A). This variation and the interplant variation, which the data also capture, allow assessment of the drivers of demand for skills through decomposition and regression techniques.

Decomposition Analysis

Table 3.1 shows the decomposition of the aggregate change in the shares of skilled workers in total employment and in the wage bill for four main periods (corresponding to different phases of economic and policy development) into (a) within-industry shifts and (b) between-industry shifts following Pavcnik (2003). The objective is to understand whether an increase (or decrease) in the skilled labor share in a given period is driven by an increase (or decrease) in the skilled labor share within industries or

Figure 3.2   Employment Share of Skilled Labor in Manufacturing Firms, 1975–2005

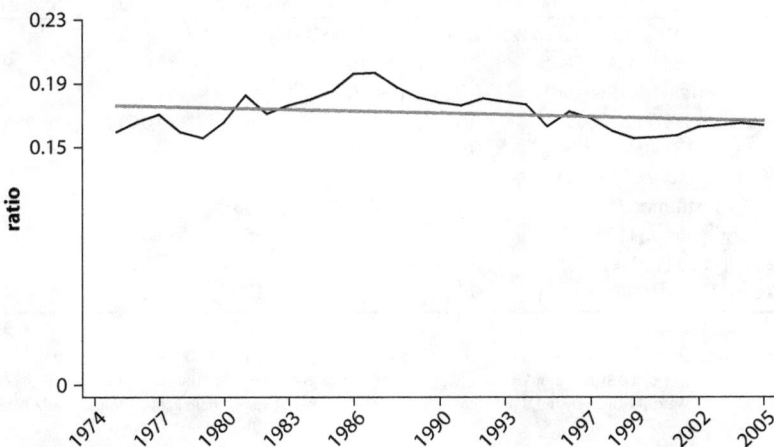

Source: Fernandes and Sundaram 2008.
Note: The figure shows the ratio of the total number of nonproduction workers (obtained as the sum from all manufacturing plants) to the total number of all workers (obtained as the sum from all manufacturing plants) in each year.

Figure 3.3   Wage Premium for Skilled Labor in Manufacturing Firms, 1975–2005

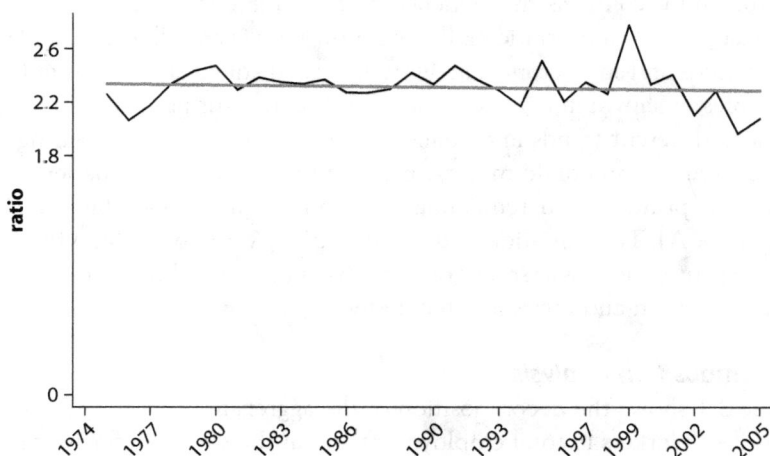

Source: Fernandes and Sundaram 2008.
Note: The figure shows the ratio of average wage paid to nonproduction workers (obtained as the ratio of total wages to skilled workers divided by total number of skilled workers in any year) to the average wage paid to production workers (obtained as the ratio of total wages to unskilled workers divided by total number of unskilled workers) in each year.

Table 3.1   Decomposition of Changes in Employment Shares and Wage Bill Shares of Skilled Labor

Indicator	Total	Within		Between	
		Value	Share (%)	Value	Share (%)
A. Employment share of skilled workers					
Import substitution (1975–86)	0.032	0.026	81	0.006	19
Export orientation (1986–96)	−0.023	−0.005	21	−0.018	79
Financial crisis (1996–2000)	−0.027	−0.017	64	−0.010	36
Postcrisis (2000–05)	0.016	0.004	23	0.012	77
B. Wage bill share of skilled workers					
Import substitution (1975–86)	0.059	0.058	98	0.001	2
Export orientation (1986–96)	−0.046	−0.024	51	−0.023	49
Financial crisis (1996–2000)	0.015	0.014	95	0.001	5
Postcrisis (2000–05)	−0.037	−0.048	130	0.011	−30

Source. Fernandes and Sundaram 2008.
Note: The total change in skilled labor employment (wage bill) shares is calculated as the difference in the weighted averages of the skilled employment (wage bill) shares of three-digit (Standard Industrial Classification) industries, with weights given by the three-digit industry's employment (wage) share in total employment (wage).

by the reallocation of labor resources toward industries with higher (or lower) average skilled labor share. If the majority of the change in skilled labor demand occurs within industries, then the most likely explanation for the change would be capital deepening or skill-biased technology shocks, which affect all industries more or less to the same extent (skill-biased technical change). If most of the change in skilled labor demand occurs between industries, then the traditional trade argument that industries with comparative advantage grow (both in terms of output and employment) as a result of increases in international trade is the more likely explanation.

Although differences exist among subperiods, most of the changes in the share of skilled labor in employment and wage bill have occurred between, rather than within, industries, pointing to the importance of shifts across industries of different skill intensity to explain changes in demand for skills. During the import substitution period, 81 percent of the increase in the employment share of skilled workers and 98 percent of the increase in the wage bill share of skilled workers were caused by increases in the share of skilled labor within industries. Given the closed nature of the Indonesian economy during that period, the emphasis of the government on investment in heavy industries, and the complementarity between capital and skills, the logical conclusion is that most of the increase in the share of skilled labor during this period in three-digit (Standard Industrial Classification) industries resulted from capital deepening.

The fortunes of skilled employment changed dramatically after Indonesia opened its economy to international trade in 1986. Between 1986 and 1996, the share of skilled employment *decreased*, and 79 percent of this decrease was driven by the reallocation of employment toward three-digit industries with a lower average share of skilled employment. The decrease in the wage bill share of skilled labor was split more evenly, with 51 percent occurring within and 49 percent between industries. Luckily, this pattern of change is consistent with the predictions from trade theory: as the economy was opened to international exchanges, it specialized following Indonesia's comparative advantage, which in the middle of the 1980s was in labor-intensive light-manufacturing industries, particularly garments, textiles, footwear, and wood products and furniture.

The employment share of nonproduction workers in manufacturing also decreased during the financial crisis. At the same time, the wages for unskilled labor declined more during the financial crisis than those for skilled labor in manufacturing, causing the wage skill premium to reach its highest level in 1999, immediately following the crisis. Thus, the wage bill share for skilled labor increased very slightly throughout the crisis period. The majority of the shift in skilled employment was driven by declines in skilled employment shares within industries as skilled labor exited from all three-digit industries and moved into different sectors, such as agriculture, informal small-scale industries, or informal services.

The postcrisis period presents a mixed picture. The bulk of the *increase* in the employment share of skilled labor is driven by the real-locaticn of labor toward three-digit industries with a higher average share of skilled labor employment, but—rather surprisingly—all of the *decrease* (more than 100 percent) in the wage bill share of skilled labor is driven by decreases in the wage bill share within three-digit industries. The negative relationship between the components of the change in the wage bill share of skilled workers indicates that a reallocation of labor occurred toward industries with a higher average wage bill share of skilled workers. The labor reallocation of the postcrisis period could in part be explained by a shifting structure of exports toward somewhat higher-skilled sectors—in particular, illustrated by an increasing relative weight in exports of chemicals and exports of machinery and equipment over that period.

Regression Analysis
Going one step further, looking at plant-level data, one finds that openness to trade and investment (as predicted by theory) results in important compositional changes within industries through a reallocation of labor and capital toward plants with higher efficiency or quality. Moreover, openness to trade is also likely to lead to an upgrading in the quality of plants as plants in import-competing sectors try to match competitors by improving their own efficiency and quality. With this knowledge as a given, the crucial issue is whether the compositional changes within industries as a result of trade openness (pushing plants to higher efficiency) translate into higher demand for skilled labor. The industry-level analysis undertaken here allows derivation of the net effect on the demand for skills of within-industry skill upgrading and reallocation of labor across high- and low-skill-intensive industries. However, it does not allow measurement of the extent of skill upgrading within plants that may have occurred following trade and investment openness—in particular, increased foreign ownership, which is associated with direct technological transfer to subsidiaries, or imports of intermediate inputs, which can bring about learning from embodied technologies. Additionally, making observations at the plant level increases variability and, therefore, the reliability of econometric estimations of the effects of openness on demand for skills. (Appendix B discusses the econometric framework

used to investigate the effect of various openness channels, as well as the effect of capital deepening on the demand for skilled labor at the plant level.)

Preliminary correlations between demand for skilled labor and openness to international trade and investments indicate that plants that are internationally integrated through foreign ownership, exports, or imported inputs exhibit, on average, a higher share of skilled workers in their total employment and in their total wage bill (table A.5). However, multivariate analysis is needed to disentangle the effects of openness variables while controlling for the other plant factors. The results of the demand for skills equation (reported in appendix B), which pools the data for all years in the 1990–2005 period, are reported in table 3.2 using the share of skilled workers in total employment as the dependent variable in columns (1) to (3) and the share of skilled workers in the total wage bill as the dependent variable in columns (4) to (6). Both ordinary least squares (OLS) and plant fixed-effect estimations—to control for time-invariant plant characteristics—are shown.

Overall, the coefficient on the ratio of capital to value added is positive and significant, suggesting the presence of capital-skill complementarity in Indonesian manufacturing. Plants that are more capital intensive employ a higher share of skilled labor, and they pay these workers a greater share of their wage bill, relative to less capital-intensive plants.

Evidence suggests that plants that import material inputs demand more skilled labor, whereas plants that are more export oriented demand less skilled labor. Evidence is less clear-cut on foreign direct investment (FDI). The coefficients on FDI and imported inputs are positive and significant at the 1 percent confidence level in all OLS regressions, and this result is also fully confirmed when one controls for plant fixed effects for imported inputs. In other words, evidence shows that plants that import their material inputs tend to hire more skilled workers and pay a larger share of their wage bill to skilled workers relative to plants that use only domestic material inputs. The loss of significance of FDI in column (3) of table 3.2 suggests that plants that are partially or fully foreign owned pay a larger share of their wage bill to skilled workers than do plants that are domestically owned, but the former do not necessarily hire more skilled workers. Finally, the coefficient on the exports dummy is negative and significant also at the 1 percent confidence level in all OLS regressions and at least one of the regressions of plant fixed effects, suggesting that exporting manufacturing plants use relatively fewer skilled workers (at least as measured in terms of nonproduction workers).

Table 3.2　Skilled Labor Share Regressions

Indicator	Dependent variable is employment share of skilled workers			Dependent variable is wage bill share of skilled workers		
	OLS (1)	OLS (2)	Plant fixed effects (3)	OLS (4)	OLS (5)	Plant fixed effects (6)
log(capital/value added)	0.0174*** [0.0002]	0.0171*** [0.0002]	0.0021*** [0.0006]	0.0235*** [0.0006]	0.0235*** [0.0006]	0.0041*** [0.0016]
log(value added)	0.0223*** [0.0002]	0.0208*** [0.0002]	-0.0003 [0.0006]	0.0350*** [0.0006]	0.0339*** [0.0006]	0.0022 [0.0017]
Foreign direct investment dummy	0.0065*** [0.0016]	0.0043*** [0.0016]	-0.0023 [0.0019]	0.0290*** [0.0044]	0.0266*** [0.0043]	0.0172*** [0.0049]
Exports dummy	-0.0269*** [0.0009]	-0.0249*** [0.0009]	-0.0023*** [0.0008]	-0.0135*** [0.0019]	-0.0105*** [0.0019]	0.0024 [0.0016]
Imported materials dummy	0.0045*** [0.0009]	0.0018** [0.0009]	0.0023** [0.0010]	0.0227*** [0.0024]	0.0180*** [0.0024]	0.0104*** [0.0023]
Plant fixed effects	No	No	Yes	No	No	Yes
Industry fixed effects (2 digit)	Yes	No	No	Yes	No	No
Industry fixed effects (3 digit)	No	Yes	No	No	Yes	No
Year fixed effects	Yes	Yes	Yes	Yes	Yes	Yes
Province fixed effects	Yes	Yes	No	Yes	Yes	No
Number of observations	225,699	222,632	225,965	220,219	217,275	220,475
R^2 (adjusted)	0.17	0.19	0.01	0.24	0.26	0.01

Source: Fernandes and Sundaram 2008.

Note: The results are based on data for 1990–2005. Robust standard errors are in brackets. *, **, and *** indicate significance at a 10 percent, 5 percent, and 1 percent confidence level, respectively. OLS = ordinary least squares.

Some transfer of skill-biased technology to Indonesian plants appears to occur through imported material inputs, but this channel for skill upgrading has remained limited and is declining. Although this channel does contribute to an increase in the employment and wages of skilled labor, the rather stagnant share of plants importing intermediate inputs (table A.6) and the concomitant increase in exporting plants suggest that only limited potential exists for skill upgrading through imported technology in Indonesia. Additionally, regression analysis by subperiod[2] shows the positive effect of imports on demand for skills to be declining in the postcrisis period.

Finally, this section quickly discusses some results based on the ICS.[3] The main advantage of the ICS data in relation to typical country firm censuses is the availability of a variety of measures of skilled labor, including measures of skilled and unskilled workers and educational attainment, beyond a large set of variables related to the degree of openness to trade and investment as well to technology and innovation. The main disadvantage of these data, however, is that they consist of a cross-section of plants and thus can provide evidence (or lack thereof) of only a *correlation* between openness variables and the relative demand for skilled labor.

ICS results on a sample of eight East Asian countries show evidence of a robust positive correlation between FDI, technological innovation, and share of educated workers, as well as an ambiguous effect of exports. The overall pooled results of regressions (controlling for country, industry, and size fixed effects) for the eight countries of the demand for skills show an ambiguous or even negative relation between exports and share of workers with at least secondary education[4] but a robust positive relation between skills, FDI, and measures of technological innovation or adoption,[5] which is consistent with skill-biased foreign ownership and other technology adoption in East Asia (table A.7).

The same results for only Indonesia confirm the ambiguous effect of FDI found in the census analysis but show a positive relationship between exports and educated workers. The relationship between technology and skills found at the regional level is generally confirmed and quite in line with that between imports and skill demand in the census analysis. When considering the results individually for Indonesia, however (see table 3.3 for a synthesis of results on the main variables of interest by country based on the regressions shown in table A.8), the ambiguous effect of foreign ownership on demand for skills found in the census regression is somewhat confirmed, but the relationship between exports and demand

Table 3.3   Regression Coefficients of Critical Variables, by Country Level

Country	Variable		
	Export	Foreign ownership	Technological innovation
Cambodia	1.531***	0.628	−0.161
China	−0.406***	0.191***	0.342***
Indonesia	0.388**	−0.118	0.247*
Korea, Rep.	0.015	0.419***	0.051
Malaysia	0.336	0.131	0.007
Philippines	−0.028	−0.231	0.497***
Thailand	0.142**	0.012	0.134**
Vietnam	−0.050	0.400***	0.055

Source: Table A.8 in appendix A.
Note: *, **, and *** indicate significance at a 10 percent, 5 percent, and 1 percent confidence level, respectively.

for skills turns positive. The positive association between technological innovation or adoption found at the regional level is confirmed, although somewhat less strongly than in other countries, confirming both the positive relationship between imports and skills highlighted in the census analysis (imports are one of the main channels for technological transfer[6]) and the somewhat recent declining effect of imports on demand for skills also highlighted previously.

The discrepant results in the relationship between exports and skills across the firm census and the ICSs could have many possible reasons. First, although the cross-section regression controls for as many observable and unobservable variables as possible, its small sample size and cross-sectional nature make it a much less favorable framework for analyzing causality and controlling for heterogeneity, thus raising the possibility of a spurious relationship. Second, however, the dependent variable is different across the two analyses, and the relationship between educational attainment and exports may, in fact, not be as visible when using occupations as a proxy for skills. This possibility is particularly likely in the context of Indonesia, where a less than perfect alignment exists between occupations and educational attainment (made worse in the firm census data, where only a rough distinction between nonproduction and production workers is available) and the occupation structure has remained relatively stable (lack of variability). Overall, manufacturing exporting firms may employ more educated workers, but this factor may not necessarily translate into more highly skilled occupations or a higher proportion of nonproduction workers.

Qualitative Evidence from the Service and Manufacturing Sectors: Skills, Export Orientation, Technology, and Other Factors

This section reviews the main evidence on drivers of demand for skills arising from the employer skill survey. The results of the survey need careful assessment because they generally report only simple comparisons across sectors and trade orientation, which do not take into account many different observable and unobservable factors.[7] Nonetheless, the results provide an interesting, more qualitative account of the dynamics behind demand for skills at the firm level; offer insights into the service sector; suggest new potential drivers of demand; and allow for easy interactions between different potential drivers (for example, technology and trade orientation or workplace organizational changes and economic sectors).

Overall, the employer skill survey results confirm the somewhat positive relationship between technology and demand for skills, with much more focus on product innovation or higher-quality standards (not captured by the analysis of quantitative data) than on process innovation (captured under the technology and, to a lesser extent, the import variable). These results are in line with the somewhat weak results of the technology variable in the regressions. The survey results also confirm the higher role for technology variables in the exporting sector and in some manufacturing subsectors with high value added, and they show some emphasis on the role of computer use (as a measure of process innovation), particularly in the service sector. To the extent that technology plays a larger role in the exporting sector, one can expect that sector to have relatively higher value added or at least be subject to higher competition than would the nonexporting sector, leading to a positive correlation with demand for skills. This result is what the skill survey finds: the exporting sector (which, beyond the role of technology-related variables, also emphasizes the competitive environment as a driver of demand) is confirmed in general to employ more educated workers and to put more emphasis on generic skills. This evidence—notwithstanding all its caveats—seems to be more in line with the ICS analysis, which indicates a positive within-sector effect of exports on the share of educated workers because of higher competitive pressure, but it does not contradict completely the census evidence, which also points to an increase in the relationship between exports and skills in the latest period, probably because of higher value added (as also illustrated by the positive simple correlations).

Additionally, the relationship between export orientation and education levels is found to be clearly stronger in the service sector than in the manufacturing sector, pointing to the higher sophistication and drive to compete of the exporting service sector compared with its manufacturing counterpart. Finally, the survey points to the importance of other overall drivers of demand for skills not directly tested in the regressions, such as the overall more competitive business environment (second in importance to higher product quality standards), the supply of skills itself, and changes in work organization (such as more teamwork and client orientation).

Staffing changes appear to be driven by changes in demand for products in both sectors, although to a much larger extent in manufacturing. Product innovation is another important factor across the board, although more significant for exporters. This finding is likely to be correlated with the economic cycle, which also explains many of employers' hiring and firing decisions. However, other factors, such as demand for higher-quality products and demand for new products (both requiring new sets of skills from employees), are also identified as relevant by a large number of respondents in both sectors (figure 3.4). These factors, which are proxies

Figure 3.4   Main Reasons for Staffing Changes, Noneducation Service and Manufacturing Firms

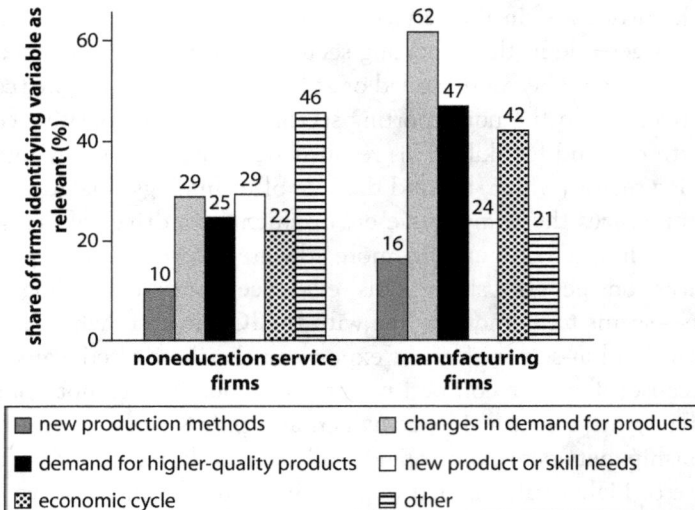

Source: Indonesia Employer/Employee Survey of Skills/Labor Demand and Job Vacancies 2008, Employer Module.

for product innovation and adoption, appear accentuated in the case of exporting firms. Over half of respondents cite demand for higher-quality products as a relevant reason for staffing changes (figure 3.5).[8] Interestingly, exporters also consider changes in demand to be important, but less so than among manufacturers generally. Maybe surprisingly, new production methods, proxying for process innovation, do not appear to be a significant factor affecting staff changes (although they are a bit more significant in the exporting sector).

The importance of technology is echoed in the assessment by business executives of the factors behind their own firm's demand for skills, but with significant caveats. A more competitive business environment is a key driver of demand for skills across the board. The role of export orientation is not clear-cut. Although a very large majority of respondents (90 percent and 78 percent, respectively, in the manufacturing and service sectors) cite higher-quality standards as a key determinant (figure 3.6)—proxying somewhat for product innovation—the effect of new technology (a better proxy for process innovation) appears relatively less important. Imported technology, in particular, seems less important; it is considered relevant by 20 percent and 14 percent of respondents in the manufacturing and service sectors, respectively. In a not entirely

Figure 3.5   Main Reasons for Staffing Changes, Nonexporters and Exporters

Source: Indonesia Employer/Employee Survey of Skills/Labor Demand and Job Vacancies 2008, Employer Module.

Figure 3.6   Drivers of Firms' Increased Use for Skills, Manufacturing and Noneducation Service Firms

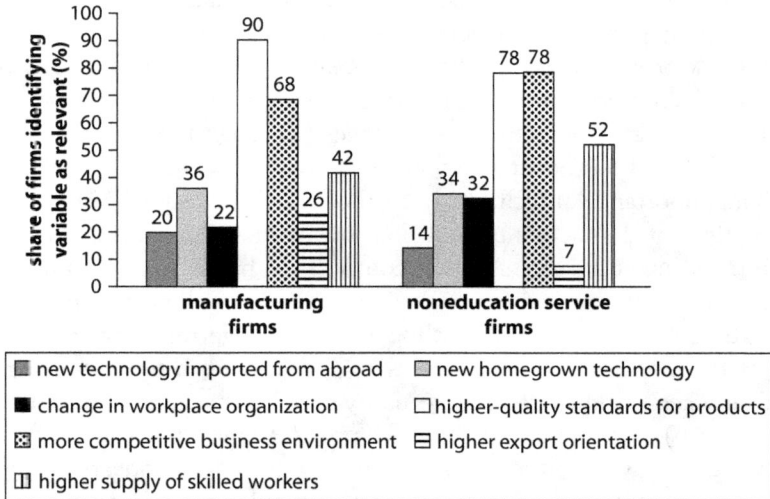

Source Indonesia Employer/Employee Survey of Skills/Labor Demand and Job Vacancies 2008, Employer Module.

surprising finding, process innovation is less of a driver of demand for skills than product innovation (as suggested by international experience). This relatively low effect confirms the lesser role of the technology variable (which proxies for process innovation) in driving demand for skills in Indonesia than in other countries in the region, including the decline in the effect of imports. Export orientation is shown as being rather unimportant. This finding is not totally unexpected given the ambiguous regression results. However, the data do not disqualify the theory that links openness to a higher need for skills when the survey response of executives whose firms realize a positive share of their sales abroad[9] is isolated: then, a more familiar pattern emerges[10] (figure 3.7).

Virtually all drivers take heightened significance for firms engaged in the export markets, with higher relative relevance for export orientation and homegrown technology. The fact that homegrown technological change continues to dwarf imported technology probably reflects the types of exports that Indonesian firms realize, as well as a somewhat declining import orientation. As anticipated, export orientation appears much more important to exporting firms, probably in correlation with competition and quality standards, which a large majority of respondents

Figure 3.7   Drivers of Firms' Increased Use for Skills, Nonexporters and Exporters

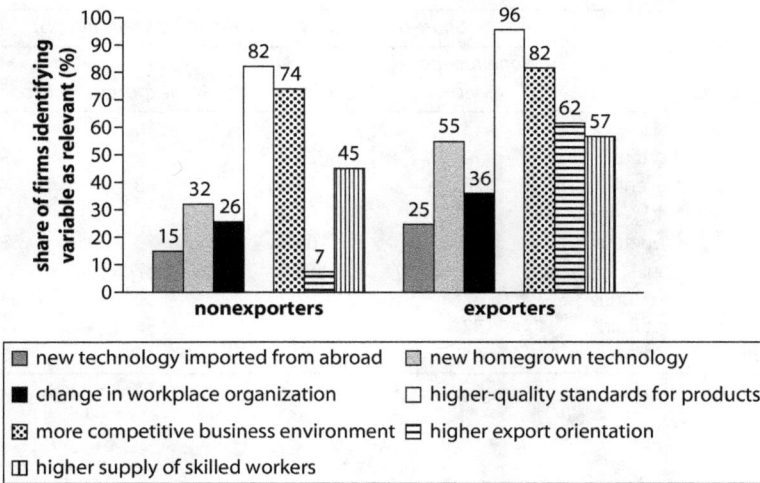

Source: Indonesia Employer/Employee Survey of Skills/Labor Demand and Job Vacancies 2008, Employer Module.

in exporting firms (respectively, 82 percent and 96 percent) rate as relevant to their firms' need for skills (figure 3.7).

Because of the sample size, looking at the industrial and service subsectors can give only an indicative insight. In general, we find that the subsector analysis confirms the predominance of product standards and the business environment as key drivers of demand for skills. However, although significant homogeneity exists across the service subsectors, more variation is seen across the industrial subsectors, with a stronger role for new imported or homegrown technology in subsectors such as coal and petroleum, fabricated metals, computing machinery, and electrical machinery. This finding is not surprising in these higher-value-added subsectors.

Looking at the changes in work organization that affect employers' demand for skills confirms a role for technological factors but also points to deeper transformations in the way that business is being conducted. A critical mass of respondents cites more innovation and greater use of computers as key determinants,[11] with greater use of computers particularly important in the service sector and, especially, the export-oriented sector (table 3.4). The relative importance of computer use highlights the role that simple technology adoption can have on the demand for

Table 3.4   Changes in Work Organization Likely to Drive Demand for Skills, by Sector and Export Orientation

	Share of firm identifying variable as relevant (%)			
Type of change	Noneducation services	Manufacturing	Nonexporters	Exporters
Less routine tasks	13	19	16	18
Less specialist duties	24	22	19	29
Greater client orientation	70	82	78	74
More teamwork	71	83	78	80
More flexible structure	52	63	58	58
More innovation	65	69	67	62
More managing duties	45	57	52	54
Increased job rotation	37	43	38	52
Greater use of computers	44	55	46	68

Source: Indonesia Employer/Employee Survey of Skills/Labor Demand and Job Vacancies 2008, Employer Module.

skills. However, it is also striking to see that greater client orientation and teamwork top the list in both sectors of activity and for exporters and domestic producers alike.

What do these findings imply for the types of skills that employers demand? The deep changes in work organization and culture outlined in this section seem to suggest that core generic skills will take on heightened importance. Indeed, thinking and behavioral skills come at the head of the list (of narrower specialized skills) for professional staff members and immediately after basic skills in the case of skilled workers (figure 3.8).

No one specific skill appears to matter particularly to exporting firms, but all skills seem to take on heightened significance. Exporting firms are generally associated with a higher education profile, although results are more clear-cut in the service sector. Although the difference in the relative importance of skills is not huge, some of the biggest gaps between exporters and nonexporters (more than 25 percentage points difference in responses) are in thinking, computer, and English-language skills for managers and professional staff and basic skills for skilled workers. Therefore, that exporting firms tend to expect a different educational profile for their prospective employees and to recruit at higher levels of education is hardly surprising (see figures 3.9 and 3.10 for net hires). However, the effects of integration vary substantially across sectors. Among manufacturing firms, exporters put a clear premium on education but not overwhelmingly so (figure 3.9), perhaps because some of these

Figure 3.8   Share of Firms Rating Workers' Skills as Very Important, by Type of Occupation and Export Orientation

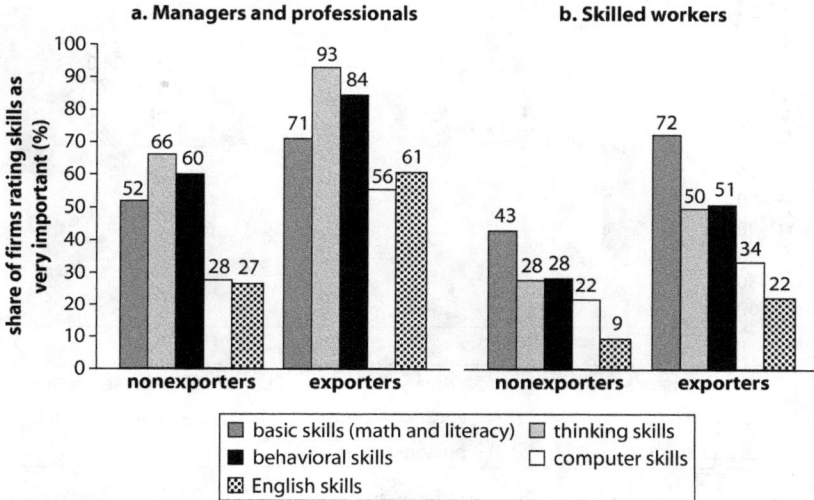

Source: Indonesia Employer/Employee Survey of Skills/Labor Demand and Job Vacancies 2008, Employer Module.

Figure 3.9   Education of Net Hires in the Manufacturing Sector

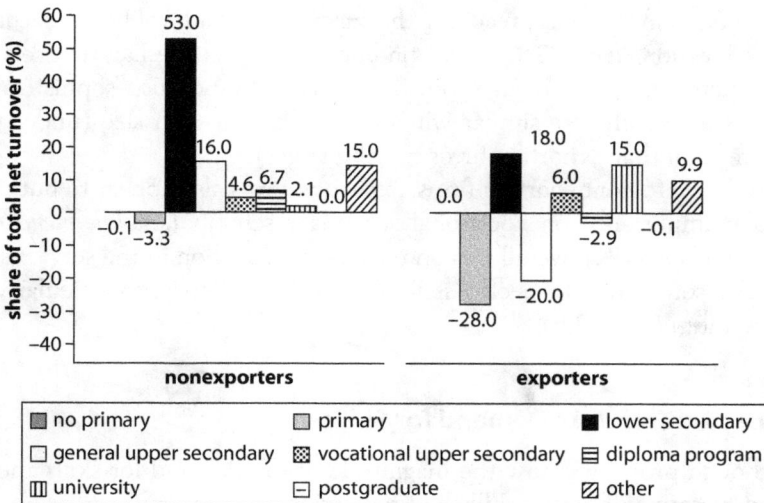

Source: Indonesia Employer/Employee Survey of Skills/Labor Demand and Job Vacancies 2008, Employer Module.

Figure 3.10   Education of Net Hires in the Service Sector

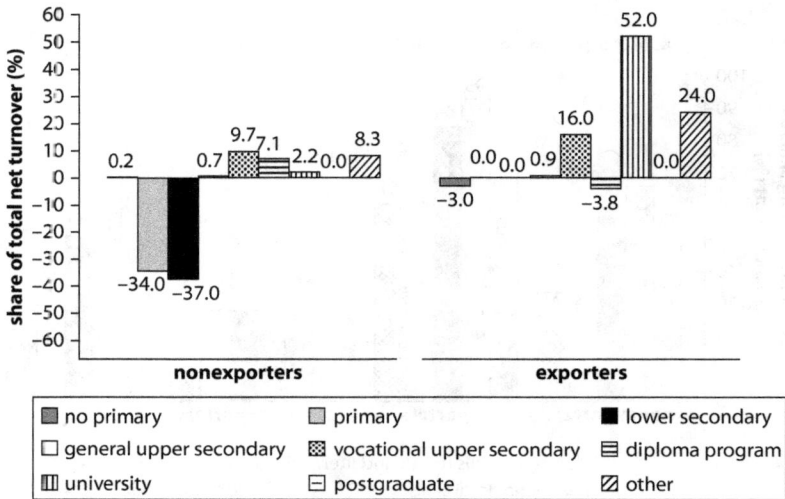

Source: Indonesia Employer/Employee Survey of Skills/Labor Demand and Job Vacancies 2008, Employer Module.

firms still rely on labor-intensive and low-skilled production methods, which is in line with some of the quantitative analysis shown in the regression section. However, in service sector exporting firms, barely any job created in the year preceding the survey was at a level below secondary education (figure 3.10). This finding may reflect the fact that service exporters are typically in sophisticated activities or use sophisticated processes. Results are similar when controlling for firm size (under the assumption that exporting firms may be larger).

Relative to nonexporting firms, exporting firms also appear to put particular importance on vocational secondary schools (*sekolah menengah kejuruan,* or SMK) overall and on university education in the service sector as a source of job-specific skills. Practical knowledge is particularly at a premium (table 3.5).

Expected Trends in Demand for Skills

Although projecting how the magnitude of the demand for skills, measured in terms of actual skills and education and training, will evolve is difficult, this book can cast some light on broad future trends by looking at the trends of a few critical variables: FDI, exports, imports, and services.

Table 3.5   The Importance of Job-Specific Skills and Education

Variable	Share of firms rating variable as important (%)	
	Nonexporter	Exporter
Primary education	41	51
General upper-secondary education	26	33
Vocational upper-secondary education	25	44
Local university degree	20	24
Diploma school or vocational training	13	11
Foreign university degree	4	3
Grades	15	26
Theoretical knowledge	43	51
Practical knowledge	48	66
Experience in same field	45	53
Experience in different field	12	12
General experience	20	27

Source: Indonesia Employer/Employee Survey of Skills/Labor Demand and Job Vacancies 2008, Employer Module.

Indonesia has continued to make significant efforts to open its economy in recent decades and, despite some sharp fluctuations, remains an open emerging economy. Average levels of import protection have declined since the major reforms of the 1980s, and most sectors receive quite low levels of state protection. Despite severe macroeconomic shocks since the reforms, most notably in the late 1990s and 2009, recovery in basic indicators of openness is expected. Figure 3.11 presents evidence of historical estimates of the ratio of FDI to GDP, exports to GDP, and imports to GDP and gives some idea of historical trends, as well as some insight into future projections.

Although FDI as a percentage of GDP plunged in the immediate aftermath of the Asian economic crisis in the late 1990s, reaching a low of −2.76 percent of GDP in 2001, FDI has gradually recovered. In 2005, it reached 2.92 percent of GDP, but since then, FDI has slowly decreased, albeit remaining above 0 percent. International Monetary Fund (IMF) projections speculate that FDI will likely be between 0.5 percent and 0.6 percent of GDP through 2014 (marking a very slight increase).

After reaching a high of nearly 60 percent of GDP in 2000, exports as a share of GDP have gradually declined. In 2003, they stood at 35.5 percent of GDP, and in 2010 they declined to 20 percent. Projections, however, indicate that export levels will rise again, albeit slowly, in the near term and reach 28 percent of GDP in 2014.

Figure 3.11   FDI, Exports, and Imports as a Share of GDP, 1997–2014 (Projected)

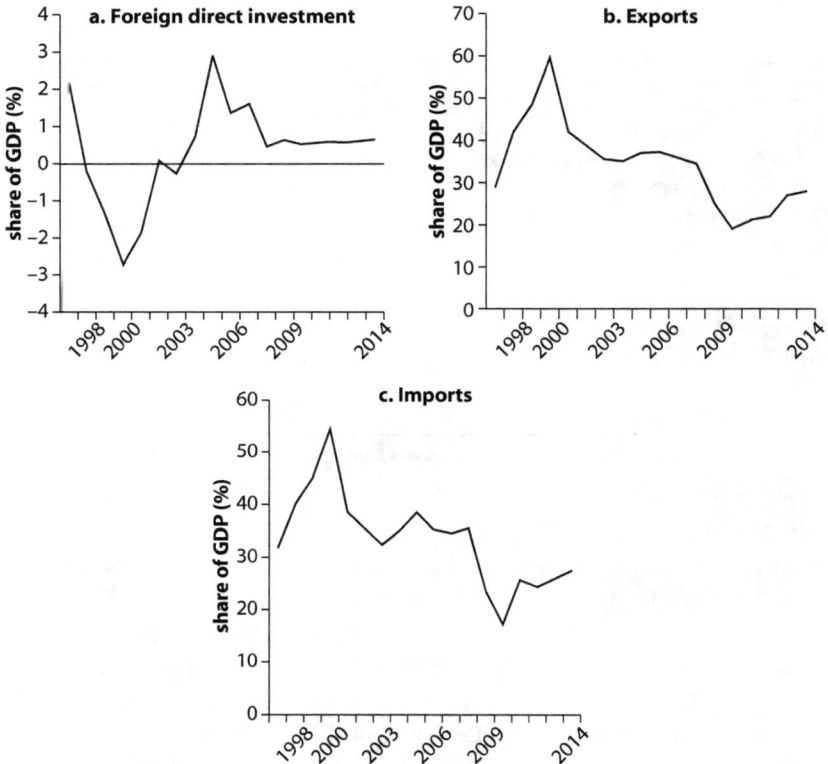

Sources: Global Financial Statistics database 2009; projections based on IMF Article IV Medium-Term Expenditure Framework Data.

When examining historical trends related to imports, one observes a similar pattern: high volumes of imports in 2000, followed by a gradual decrease, and then a sharp plunge as a result of the global economic slowdown. However, in 2014, imports are expected to recover to 28 percent of GDP.

Recent trends in openness and economic structure indicators will drive up demand for skills. About 50 percent of the manufacturing firms surveyed in the 2003 ICS had introduced a new technological process (through adaptation or innovation) in Indonesia, making that process an important driver of demand for skills in the country (notwithstanding some of the caveats on the relative importance of process and product innovation). Predicting the future pace of technological innovation is difficult, but if the latest IMF projections are right about FDI and, particularly, imports, and if one assumes that technology transfer from abroad has an important role, then one can deduce that the demand for skills will increase by 2014. Clearly, the effect will be stronger if such technology transfer from abroad is accompanied by further domestic investment in research and development. Similar conclusions are valid with respect to exports. If one assumes that the gradual upward trend is confirmed and that exports will remain associated with higher needs for skills, this trend will also imply an increase in demand. Finally, if the recent behavior of the service sector in terms of GDP and employment is confirmed, this trend will also translate into increased demand. Overall, combined with the need to foster higher value added in manufacturing, this evidence suggests that Indonesia should very actively invest in building a strong skill basis. The question of which skills will be most in demand is addressed in the section of this chapter on emerging policy implications.

In sum, the combination of the regressions and the more qualitative results provides some evidence that openness (imports and exports); a competitive business environment; technology; the role of computers (in particular, in the service sector); and some changes in work organization, such as more teamwork and client orientation, are determinants of demand for skills in Indonesia. Although the evidence is strong for product innovation, a competitive environment, and technology within the exporting sector and some high-value-added subsectors, it is not overwhelming for the other factors; in particular, the role for process innovation is possibly weak, and the role of exports is ambiguous. Notwithstanding these findings, one can probably say that firms that have introduced product innovation and some process innovation, such as more intensive use of computers, tend to demand more skilled labor across the board and that, in more specific settings, such as the exporting and higher value-added sectors, process innovation more generally is also associated with higher demand for skills. Along these lines, one can probably also say that exporting sectors (in particular, the exporting service sector) tend to hire more highly skilled workers in terms of educational attainment while putting particular emphasis on thinking, negotiating, computer, and language skills; practical knowledge; and vocational education. Recovering upward trends in FDI, imports, and exports are likely to be associated with increasing demand for skills in the future.

The relationship identified between adaptation of new technologies, product innovation, and skills is also important, because (at least in this study's cross-section settings where no causality can be inferred) it goes both ways. Firms with higher shares of highly skilled labor (at a university level) are more apt to innovate. Similarly, firms with higher shares of skills at the university or, to a lesser extent, vocational level are more prepared to compete internationally. Skills make an even bigger difference for manufacturing subsectors with higher value added, such as electrical and computing machinery, fabricated metals, and communication equipment, where being innovative and maintaining competitiveness are particularly crucial to the survival of the sector. Unfortunately, in some of these subsectors, finding the right skills is particularly difficult (see chapter 4).

Finally, all generic skills (including thinking and behavioral skills) appear to take on heightened significance for the exporting sector, suggesting that at an intermediate or advanced level they are some of the key skills that the sector needs to face international competition and that it looks for when hiring workers at certain education and qualification levels. Generic skills will also be central to supporting technological innovation and adaptation—as is shown in part II—accompanied by the provision through advanced degree levels of certain fields of education, such as science and technology, math, natural sciences, and electronics.

Emerging Policy Implications

The trends identified in this chapter have the following policy implications:

- *Skills-technology complementarities.* The importance of skills-technology complementarities makes it all the more imperative to ensure that adequate numbers of tertiary and upper-secondary graduates with adequate skills are available to be absorbed in the technology-intensive sector and make a real difference. Critical skills to address these needs are creative and critical thinking, a command of information and communication technology skills, proactivity and curiosity, and a broad-based understanding of company operations and industry knowledge, as well as other skills further examined in chapter 5.

- *Skills for the exporting sector.* Exports are likely to remain a significant driver of demand for skills, which stresses the need for an adequate number of tertiary and upper-secondary graduates with adequate skills. These graduates can be expected to quickly find work within the sector and help in its expansion. Critical skills for the export sector that will need to be provided through the education and training system include thinking, negotiation, computer, language, and practical knowledge skills.

- *Strong generic skills across the board.* Overall, the need for strong generic skills, including behavioral ones such as communication, negotiation, and client orientation, and the ability to work independently, will remain important in the future because of the growing share of services (the other and probably most important key driver) and the ongoing changes in organization of work that require more skills as the workplace becomes more client and teamwork oriented. The education and training sector, combined with job experience, will be the most important provider of these skills.

Notes

1. Educational attainment in terms of schooling levels and years achieved is higher for nonproduction workers than for production workers.
2. See regression results across periods in Fernandes and Sundaram (2008).
3. ICSs are World Bank–led firm surveys undertaken in most countries and mostly focused on the manufacturing sector.
4. Most of this effect is due to China. When China is excluded from the sample—with the caveat that the sample becomes significantly smaller and thus results lose some reliability—the effect of exports on the demand for skills becomes positive and significant (see table A.8).
5. The technology variable refers to firms having "introduced a new technology that substantially changed the way the main product was produced in the three years prior to the survey" (definition adopted in the ICSs). This definition leaves room for both (a) adaptation of an existing technology developed domestically or imported from abroad and (b) innovation within the firm.
6. In fact, when imports are controlled for, the relationship between technology and demand for skills in the regional pooled regression weakens significantly.
7. Size, however, has generally been taken into account in the comparisons of exporting and nonexporting firms, and there are no significant differences in results.
8. This finding may in part reflect the recent shift toward higher-value-added exporting subsectors.
9. *Exporters* is used here as a proxy for firms integrated in the world economy.

10. The discrepancy could come from the fact that Indonesian firms overall have remained relatively inward looking despite the opening of the economy to trade and capital flows; perhaps even more likely is that the survey sample covers too few open sectors.

11. The use of computers is also a key determinant of demand for skills in the regional regressions on demand for skills, when robustness to different technology-related variables is analyzed (see table A.9).

References

Fernandes, Ana, and Ramya Sundaram. 2008. "Skill Demand and Openness in Indonesia." Background paper prepared for this book, World Bank, Washington, DC.

Pavcnik, Nina. 2003. "What Explains Skill Upgrading in Less Developed Countries?" *Journal of Development Economics* 71 (2): 311–28.

CHAPTER 4

A Skill Mismatch?

Are any skill gaps emerging? What are they, and where are they? This chapter investigates the question of whether rising demand for skills, despite increasing supply, has resulted in a skill gap at the national and sectoral levels (figure 4.1). Gaps can be assessed in various ways. This book uses two main definitions. One is based on gaps in relation to the expectations of employers (and employees), and the other, when available, is based on comparing gaps to some international average or even to levels found in higher-income countries. The first definition follows a demand-side approach and is often the only way available to measure gaps in higher-level skills. The second definition uses a supply-side approach (standardized international testing) and is still available only up to lower-secondary education and, therefore, for more basic skills—mostly, though not solely, academic skills. In the context of an analysis of workforce skills, this chapter focuses on the first definition of *gap*, whereas chapter 5 on education and training also deals with the second definition. Beyond some general measures of skill bottlenecks according to employers, this chapter seeks to understand some of their causes, with particular emphasis on the role of quality and relevance gaps (looking at the alignment—or lack thereof—between those actual skills that graduates acquire in the course of their studies and those that

Figure 4.1 Skill Gaps

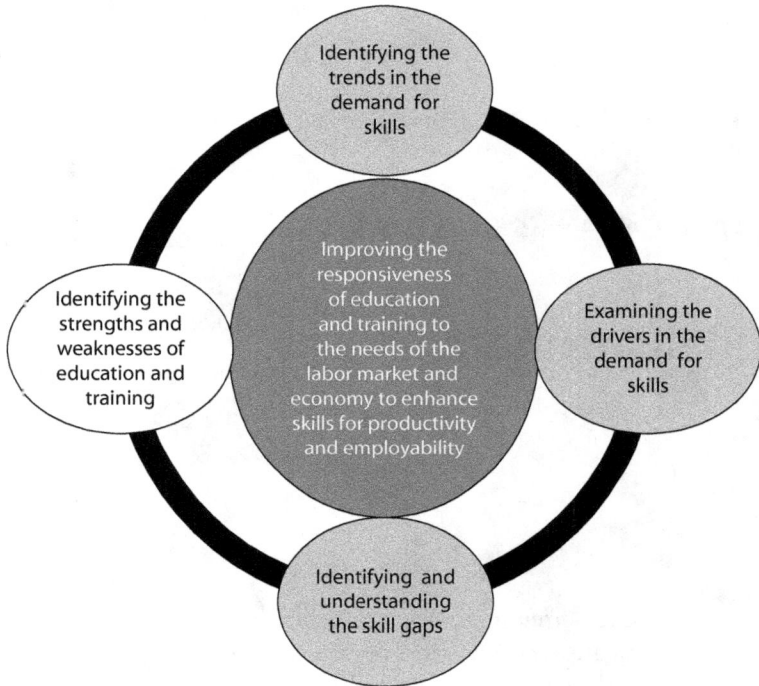

Identifying the trends in the demand for skills

Identifying the strengths and weaknesses of education and training

Improving the responsiveness of education and training to the needs of the labor market and economy to enhance skills for productivity and employability

Examining the drivers in the demand for skills

Identifying and understanding the skill gaps

Source: Authors' representation.

employers particularly demand). This chapter also investigates more specifically skill issues in young workers. The chapter relies mostly on the employer and employee skill surveys.

Overall, the chapter points to relevance and quality concerns more than quantity concerns regarding workforce skills, with some other labor-market-related causes also explaining matching difficulties. Quality is a particularly critical issue for upper-secondary education graduates (general and vocational) in both the manufacturing and service sectors, where evidence indicates serious gaps in generic and technical skills. Young workers are in a particularly critical situation.

Macro Trends

At the more macroeconomic level, the employer survey tends to suggest that skills are not yet a binding constraint to business development.

Among a set of 14 suggested bottlenecks to their firms' activity, respondents ranked workers' skills and education fourth from last position (table 4.1). Only 7 percent of respondents considered workers' skills and education to be a "moderate" or "major" obstacle to their activity, well below variables such as macroeconomic instability (49 percent), corruption (36 percent), or cost of finance (33 percent).

Although other factors gain more importance in subsamples of firms with certain characteristics, such as size, export orientation, certification by the International Organization for Standardization (ISO), and foreign direct investment (FDI), the importance of skills as a bottleneck also increases. Isolating in the data those firms that realize some of their sales abroad (a proxy for export orientation and integration in world markets) yields a significant difference, albeit not a strong one. Whereas other differences are much more striking (such as the perceived quality of infrastructure or fiscal and regulatory policies), skills do appear to be more of a constraint for export-oriented firms (table 4.2).

The same conclusions hold when looking at firm size or proxies for firm institutionalization such as ISO certification. Larger and more established firms are more likely to consider skills an obstacle. Skills are reported to be a constraint by 11 percent of respondents of ISO-certified firms (the share goes up to 13 percent in the sample of manufacturing firms) and by 9 percent of respondents from the largest firms compared

Table 4.1   Main Bottlenecks to Business Development

Obstacle	Share of firms identifying obstacle as moderate or major (%)
Access to finance	23
Cost of finance	33
Quality of telecommunications	5
Quality of roads	13
Quality of electricity	19
Tax rates	10
Business licensing	5
Labor regulations	4
Worker skills	7
Uncertainty on regulation	27
Macroeconomic instability	49
Corruption	36
Organized crime	26
Contract violation	19

Source: Indonesia Employer/Employee Survey of Skills/Labor Demand and Job Vacancies 2008, Employer Module.

Table 4.2   Main Bottlenecks to Business Development, Nonexporters and Exporters

Obstacle	Share of firms identifying obstacle as moderate or major (%)	
	Nonexporters	Exporters
Access to finance	18	6
Cost of finance	25	23
Quality of telecommunications	4	9
Quality of roads	10	18
Quality of electricity	14	31
Tax rates	7	17
Business licensing	4	3
Labor regulations	2	12
Worker skills	5	8
Uncertainty on regulation	19	27
Macroeconomic instability	32	38
Corruption	31	32
Organized crime	23	22
Contract violation	18	14

Source: Indonesia Employer/Employee Survey of Skills/Labor Demand and Job Vacancies 2008, Employer Module.

to 3 percent in the smaller firms (respectively, highest and lowest quartile by size of the labor force).

Finally, skills become much more of a constraint in a sample of manufacturing firms with most of these attributes combined. This finding is evident from the results of the Indonesia Investment Climate Survey, where large, export-oriented, and foreign-owned manufacturing firms are overrepresented. The survey indicates that about 40 percent of firms identify skills as at least a moderate obstacle (figure 4.2). At the regional level, this number is large, which also indicates that the survey conducted for this book provides a lower-bound (conservative) estimate of demand for skills and skill gaps in the country.

Difficulties Finding Skills

Although skills do not yet appear to be a binding constraint for the economy, the skills-for-needs issue does not appear trivial. In fact, skills are already a significant driver of staff changes, even ranking second in order of importance in the service sector (figure 4.3).

Additionally, subjective assessments of difficulties of matching needs with available skills provide further evidence that skills are becoming an

Figure 4.2   Skill Bottlenecks in East Asia

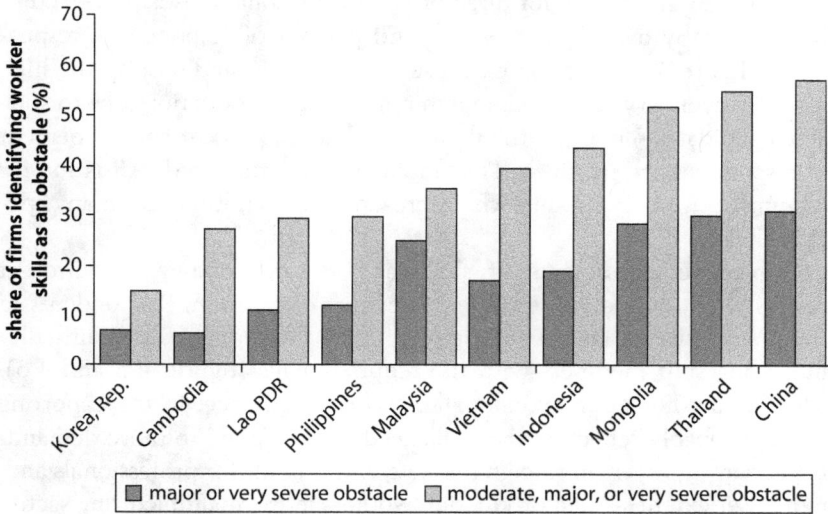

Source: Almeida 2009, using ICSs (various years).

Figure 4.3   Main Reasons for Staffing Changes, Manufacturing and Noneducation Service Firms

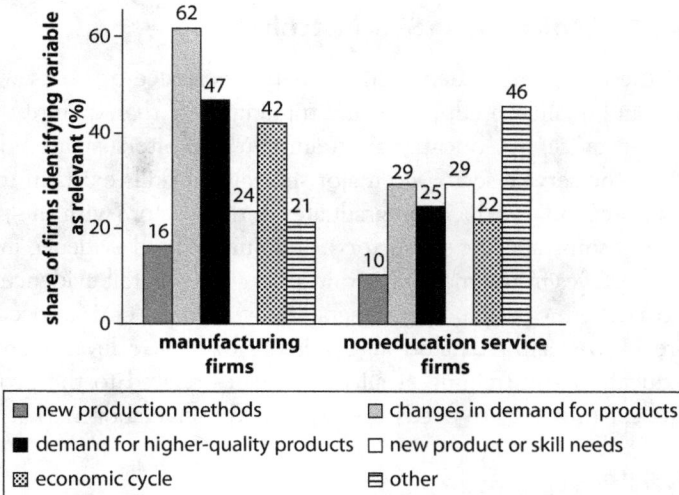

Source: Indonesia Employer/Employee Survey of Skills/Labor Demand and Job Vacancies 2008, Employer Module.

issue in Indonesia. Although unskilled positions are logically easy to staff, finding the right profile for director and professional jobs is perceived to be difficult by over 80 percent and 60 percent of respondents, respectively (figure 4.4). In between those two extremes and despite the high level of secondary schooling, matching sales and production jobs to suitable candidates remains difficult according to 27 percent and 26 percent of respondents, respectively. This finding is in contrast to the situation for administrative occupations, which presumably do not require many specific skills.

Subjective assessments of skill gaps generate somewhat different results when one looks at sectors or export orientation. Respondents in the manufacturing and exporting sectors tend to report greater difficulty in finding staff members with the required skills (figures 4.5 and 4.6). This finding holds for virtually all categories of worker in the exporting sector, probably reflecting the skills needed to respond to more demanding clients or buyers in foreign markets, and it holds for professionals and, to a lesser extent, skilled production workers in the manufacturing sector.

The relationship between difficulties in finding the right skills and export orientation observed in Indonesia is very much attuned with findings in other East Asian countries. A comparative analysis of firm surveys reveals a positive relationship between export orientation and skills as a bottleneck (figure 4.7).

Reasons for Difficulties in Skill Matching

Most of the empirical evidence confirms the existence of issues with the relevance and quality of education and training more than quantity, as captured, for instance, by educational attainment. Despite sustained demand for skills in the service sector, no major shortage of skills exists in terms of higher- and secondary education graduates in that sector (with the possible exception of some specific subsectors), and only limited evidence indicates possible shortages in the manufacturing sector. The overall evidence in fact points to a dynamic of "education upgrading" within the current occupation structure. However, the data do suggest issues with the relevance and quality of education and training at all levels, issues related to the process of matching existing skills to needs, and some additional labor-market issues.

Employers' Perceptions

Employers' perceptions point to a distinction between quantity of training supplied and quality of training and highlight other reasons as

Figure 4.4   Degree of Difficulty of Matching Needs with Available Skills

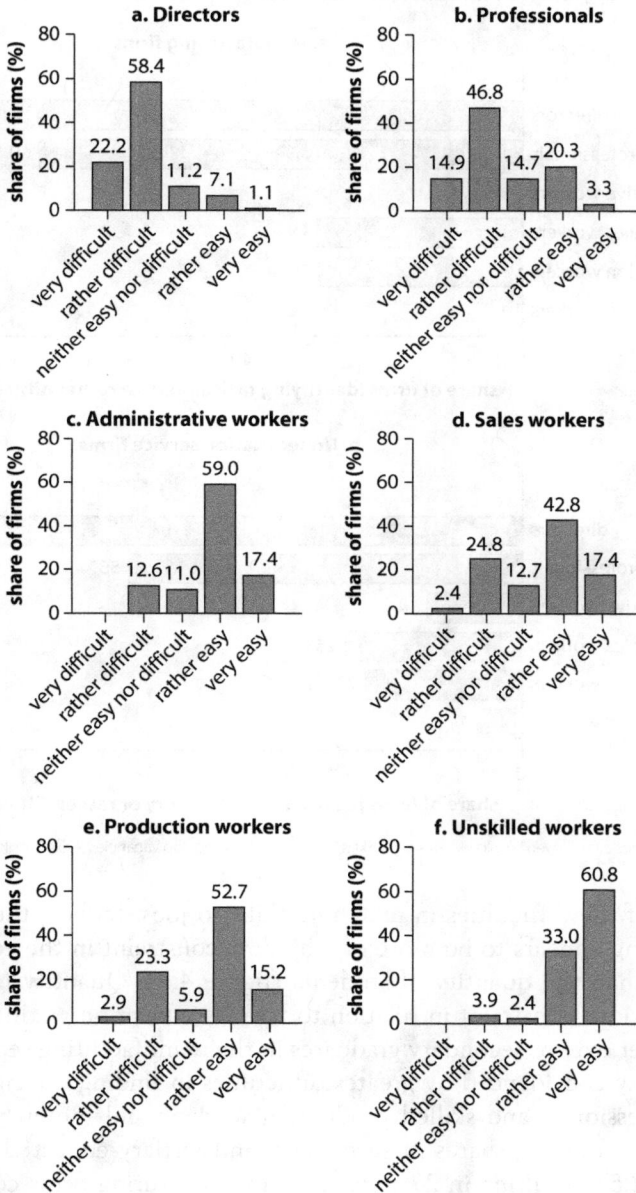

a. Directors

b. Professionals

c. Administrative workers

d. Sales workers

e. Production workers

f. Unskilled workers

Source: Indonesia Employer/Employee Survey of Skills/Labor Demand and Job Vacancies 2008, Employer Module.

Figure 4.5   Degree of Difficulty of Matching Needs with Available Skills, Manufacturing and Noneducation Service Firms

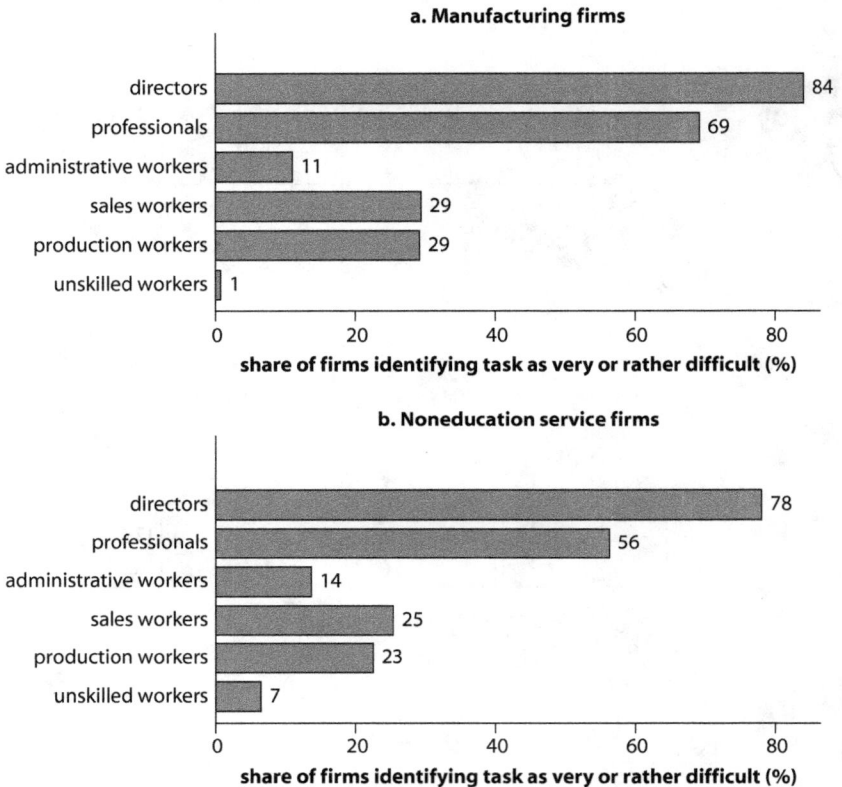

a. Manufacturing firms

Category	Value
directors	84
professionals	69
administrative workers	11
sales workers	29
production workers	29
unskilled workers	1

share of firms identifying task as very or rather difficult (%)

b. Noneducation service firms

Category	Value
directors	78
professionals	56
administrative workers	14
sales workers	25
production workers	23
unskilled workers	7

share of firms identifying task as very or rather difficult (%)

Source: Indonesia Employer/Employee Survey of Skills/Labor Demand and Job Vacancies 2008, Employer Module.

causes of the difficulties in matching skills to jobs. Indeed, the quality of training appears to be more of a binding constraint in the education system than the quantity of students (figure 4.8). Quantity may be a more serious constraint in relation to tertiary education graduates and, to a lesser extent, secondary graduates in the manufacturing sector. This possibility is evidenced by greater difficulties in finding the right skills for professionals and skilled production workers and somewhat rising returns and falling shares of secondary- and tertiary-educated workers (figure 2.5), resulting in 27 percent of manufacturing firms complaining about quantity issues. In contrast, quantity appears to be an issue in only a few specific subsectors in services. At the same time, reasons behind perceived shortages in skills do not all relate to education or

Figure 4.6 Degree of Difficulty of Matching Needs with Available Skills, Nonexporters and Exporters

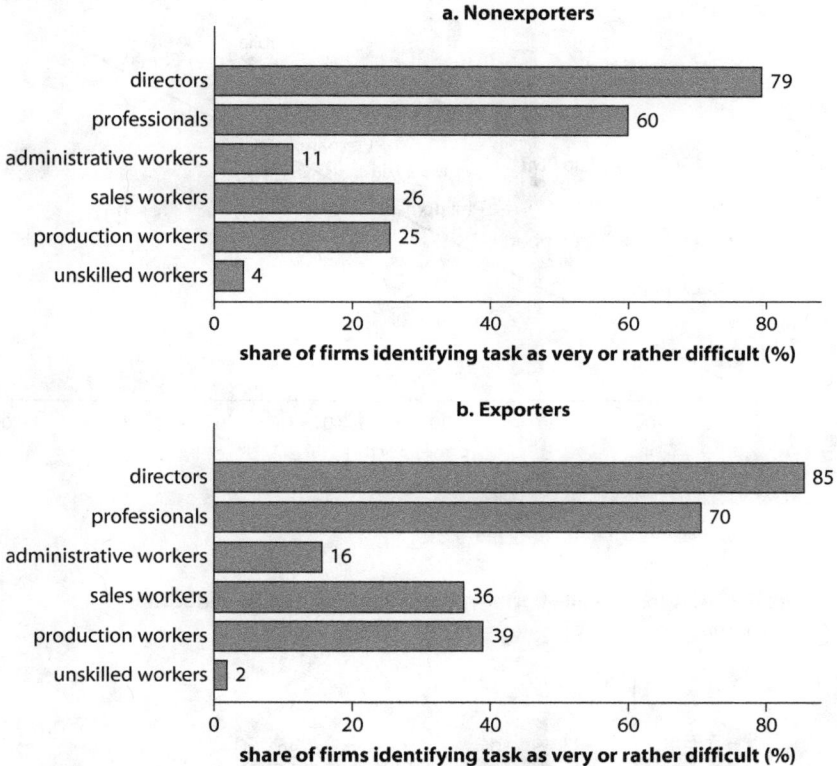

a. Nonexporters

Category	Value
directors	79
professionals	60
administrative workers	11
sales workers	26
production workers	25
unskilled workers	4

share of firms identifying task as very or rather difficult (%)

b. Exporters

Category	Value
directors	85
professionals	70
administrative workers	16
sales workers	36
production workers	39
unskilled workers	2

share of firms identifying task as very or rather difficult (%)

Source: Indonesia Employer/Employee Survey of Skills/Labor Demand and Job Vacancies 2008, Employer Module.

training: in fact, low starting wages and high job turnover appear equally, if not more, important (in manufacturing) than education-related issues.

At the subsector level, although quality continues to be more of an issue, both quantity and quality of locally trained students are at the forefront of employers' concerns in the paper, coal and petroleum, nonmetallic minerals, machinery, and furniture industries, as well as in the hotel and real estate subsectors (and, to a lesser extent, transport and financial services). These results are generally in line with the combined behavior of rates of return and share of skilled workers by subsector shown in figure 2.6, with the caveat that somewhat different subsector classifications do not make for perfect comparisons.

Figure 4.7   Skill Constraints and Export Orientation: Share of Firms Identifying Workforce as an Obstacle

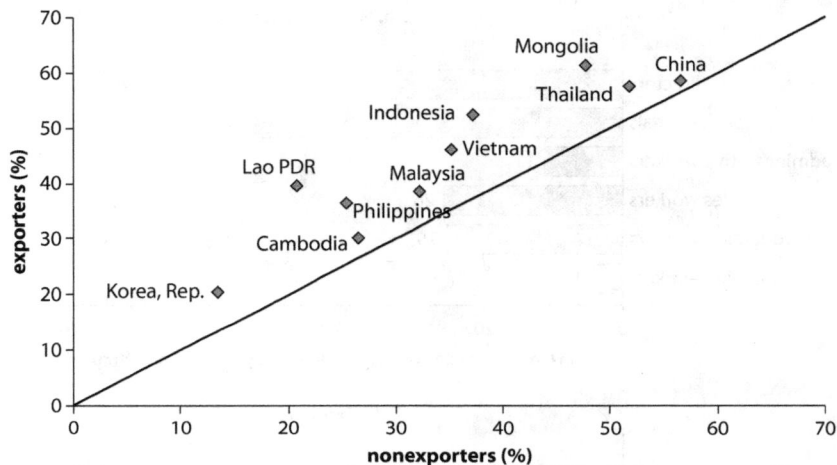

Source: Almeida 2009, using ICSs (various years).

Figure 4.8   Causes of Skill Shortage, Manufacturing and Noneducation Service Firms

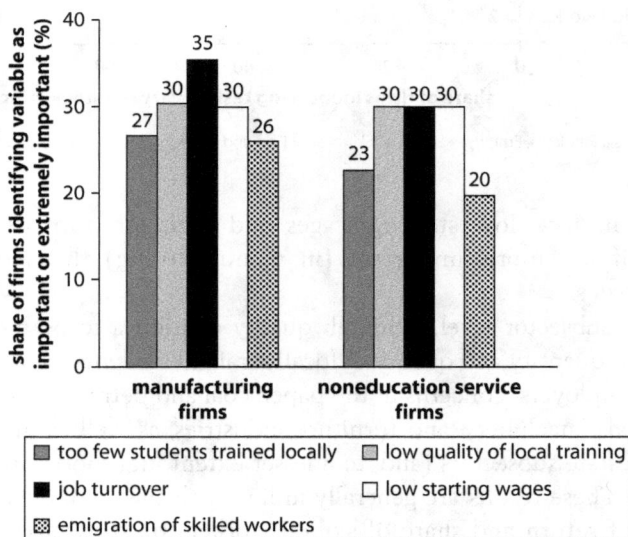

Source: Indonesia Employer/Employee Survey of Skills/Labor Demand and Job Vacancies 2008, Employer Module.

Recruitment Practices

Beyond skill and labor-market-related characteristics such as high job turnover and low wages for skilled workers, difficulties in finding the right skills for certain positions may simply stem from a failure to match existing skills efficiently with demand. Some evidence has already been presented on the former reasons, but the latter is also at play in Indonesia. The predominance of private networks and contacts as means for employers to identify recruits and for employees to find suitable opportunities is a clear indication of frictions in the matching process[1] (table 4.3). (The perfect equivalence between employers' and employees' opinions is also quite noticeable here—compare table 4.3 and table 4.4).

The sluggish nature of the job-matching process in Indonesia is further exemplified in the alternative methods that employers use to fill positions (table 4.5). The very low prevalence of recruitment from other firms or from other regions (let alone overseas) appears symptomatic of a job market that is not liquid enough.

What Does Vacancy Analysis Reveal?

The employer skill survey provides detailed data on vacancies, which can be used to further document and understand possible skill mismatches while also zooming in on specific occupations, sectors or subsectors, and trade orientations.

The data on vacancies strengthen the point that quantity—at least in terms of skilled occupations—is not a significant issue in Indonesia.

Table 4.3   Normal Methods by Which Employers Fill Vacancies

Method	Share of affirmative responses from firms (%)
Newspaper ad	30
Vacancy notice posted outside firm	20
Internet	10
Job fair	1
Employee recommendation	50
Private network	80
Public employment service	1
Private employment service	10
Recruiter	10
Contact with schools	10
Internal promotion	20

Source: Indonesia Employer/Employee Survey of Skills/Labor Demand and Job Vacancies 2008, Employer Module.

Table 4.4   Main Methods by Which Employees Find Jobs

Method	Share of affirmative responses from employees (%)
Newspaper ad	17
Vacancy notice	16
Internet	8
Employer recommendation	36
Private network	47
Employment service	4
Job fair or school	9
Internal promotion	8

Source: Indonesia Employer/Employee Survey of Skills/Labor Demand and Job Vacancies 2008, Employee Module.

Table 4.5   Alternative Methods of Filling Vacancies

Method	Share of affirmative responses from firms (%)
Training current staff	47
Recruiting from other firms	11
Recruiting from other regions	8
Recruiting from overseas	1
Hiring and training undergraduates	11
Subdividing work and hiring	47
Assigning more tasks	74
Leaving position vacant	17

Source: Indonesia Employer/Employee Survey of Skills/Labor Demand and Job Vacancies 2008, Employer Module.

Looking at the dynamics of the vacancy-filling process in 2007, one sees, on the one hand, that the numbers of applicants are well in excess of vacancies for all job categories and, on the other hand (and more important), that after the first screening process (which in Indonesia is about checking minimum educational attainment, title, and experience), more qualified candidates are still available than vacancies, thus allowing practically all vacancies to be filled (figure 4.9).[2] At most, the low share of qualified applicants in relation to total applicants indicates that many workers do not fulfill minimum requirements and still apply because of limited vacancies related to overall limited employment creation.

These findings are fairly similar across sectors; however, a higher proportion of candidates apply for positions in the service sector. The service sector tends to attract more applicants for fewer positions, allowing it to make a broader choice, which then leads to a similar ratio between qualified candidates and vacancies (figure 4.10).

Figure 4.9   Vacancies by Job Title, 2007

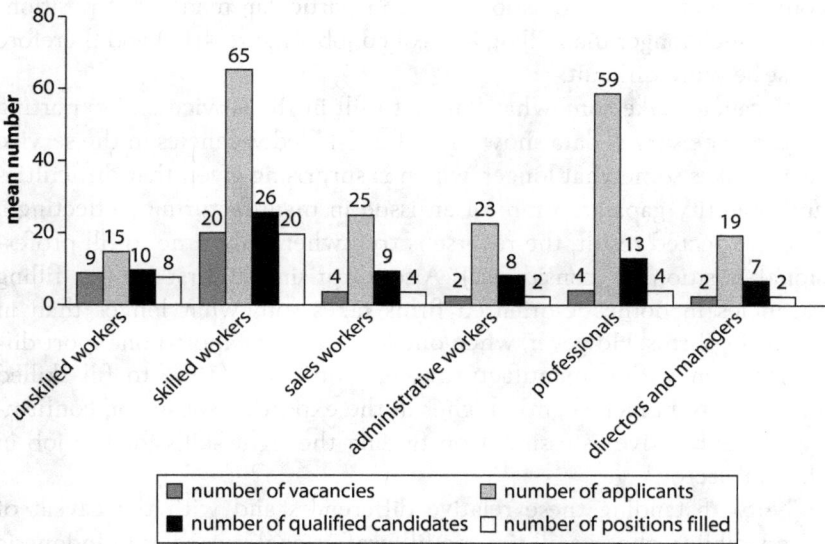

Source: Indonesia Employer/Employee Survey of Skills/Labor Demand and Job Vacancies 2008, Employer Module.

Figure 4.10   Skilled Vacancies, 2007

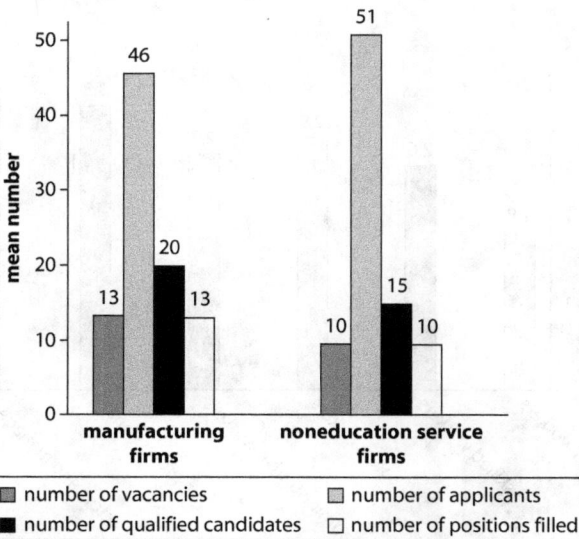

Source: Indonesia Employer/Employee Survey of Skills/Labor Demand and Job Vacancies 2008, Employer Module.

Measures of time spent by prospective employers to fill open positions confirm that filling professional and, in particular, managerial positions takes much longer than filling less skilled jobs (figure 4.11) and therefore must be more difficult.

Vacancies take somewhat longer to fill in the service and exporting sectors. The survey data show that filling skilled vacancies in the service sector takes somewhat longer, which is surprising given that difficulties and quantity gaps are more of an issue in manufacturing (reflecting a more expected result, the reverse is true when only time to fill professional positions is considered). Also surprising at first glance, filling vacancies in domestic-oriented firms takes somewhat longer than in exporting firms. However, when one looks at the export-nonexport differentiation within manufacturing, one finds that time to fill skilled vacancies is, in fact, slightly higher in the exporting subsector, confirming the subjective assessment on finding the right skills for the job in that subsector.[3]

Notwithstanding these relative differences and with the caveat of comparability, the overall time to fill professional vacancies in Indonesia is still on the low side in East Asia, which likely confirms that a sufficient

Figure 4.11   Average Number of Weeks to Fill Vacancies

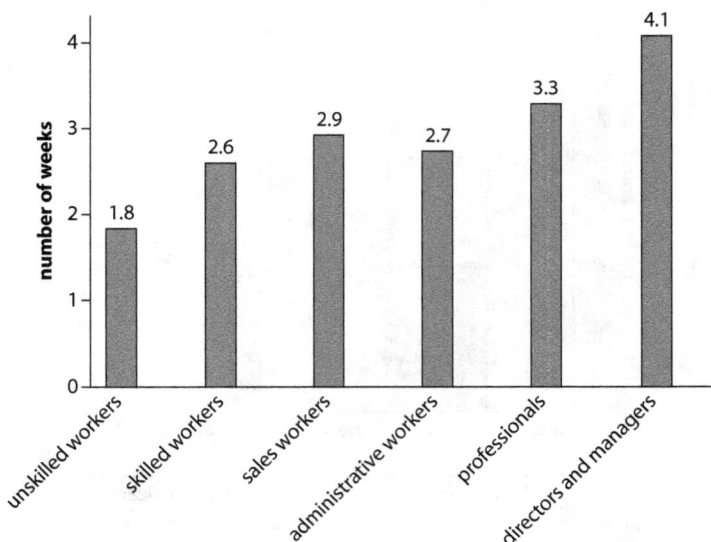

Source: Indonesia Employer/Employee Survey of Skills/Labor Demand and Job Vacancies 2008, Employer Module.

Figure 4.12 Time to Fill Professional Vacancies in East Asia

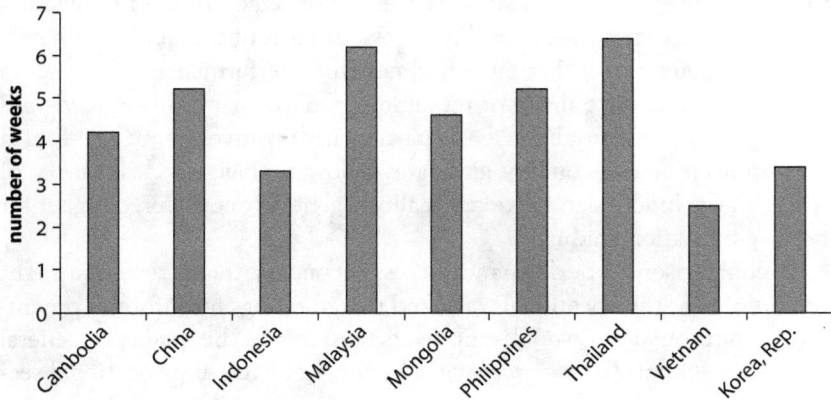

Sources: ICSs (various years); Employer Skill Surveys (various years).

quantity of at least minimally qualified workers exists for skilled positions.[4] Filling professional vacancies in Indonesia takes a bit more than three weeks, whereas it takes six weeks or more in Malaysia and Thailand and more than five weeks in China and the Philippines (figure 4.12).

In contrast, the methods adopted for assessing the skills of the qualified candidates in view of the hiring decision suggest that, beyond a minimum needed, educational attainment and titles are not considered as a particularly good proxy of actual job-relevant skills in Indonesia, thus confirming issues with the quality and relevance of education and training. As seen in chapter 2, the data indicate that interviews and probation periods are the most popular methods to assess skills, far ahead of educational institution attended, transcripts, and grades attained (table 2.3). This finding indicates possible weaknesses in the process of skill certification in Indonesia that also help complicate the skill-matching process.

Toward a Better Understanding of Quality and Relevance Gaps

This section aims at better understanding quality and relevance concerns by looking at performance using different skill measures, with particular focus on gaps in functional skills and the population of newly hired graduates and young employees. It finds evidence of significant quality and relevance gaps.

Employers' Perspectives on the Quality of Newly Hired Graduates

Quality and relevance are issues even in the selected group of individuals who are finally employed. Employers' assessments of the quality of newly hired graduates reveal that most find new hire performance only "fair." In light of the need for training or retraining (in particular of secondary graduates), "fair" should not be taken as particularly positive. About one-fourth of employers find secondary graduates below average—a close proxy of "poor" in the Indonesian context. Quality is generally considered higher for tertiary-education graduates.

A comparison of performance across secondary tracks reveals a slight preference for the vocational track and mixed ratings for informal preemployment programs. Overall, employers tend to rate the quality of general secondary schools (*sekolah menengah umum,* or SMU) and vocational secondary schools (*sekolah menengah kejuruan,* or SMK) equally, with a slight edge for the latter, whose graduates elicit fewer "poor" ratings and more "very good" ones (figure 4.13). As for informal preemployment programs, they tend to produce more "very poor" students, but they also manage to generate a not indifferent share of "very good" graduates,[5] suggesting a strong heterogeneity in the quality of informal institutions or students.

Quality is generally higher at the tertiary level, with results a bit more heterogeneous in universities than in tertiary vocational institutes. Results are lower across the board for informal postsecondary vocational institutions. Universities generate more "below average" students than do vocational tertiary institutions but also more "very good" students, pointing to higher variance in results (figure 4.14). Informal postsecondary vocational institutions[6] elicit generally less positive assessments across the board.

Perceptions on the quality of graduates differ across sectors (figures 4.15 and 4.16). Interestingly, whereas opinions on general secondary education graduates are fairly similar across sectors, perceptions on the quality of vocational secondary graduates are significantly more negative in the service sector than in the manufacturing sector, notwithstanding the higher number of vocational graduates who work in the latter, which may point to issues with curriculum balance and strength of generic skills, which are likely to be particularly pertinent to the service sector (see part II). In general, vocational graduates have more of an edge in the manufacturing sector, given their relative strengths in specific skills, but this edge does not necessarily translate into more hiring. The manufacturing sector also tends to have a slightly more positive perception of

Figure 4.13   Quality of Secondary-Cycle Recruits Hired in the 12 Months Preceding the Survey

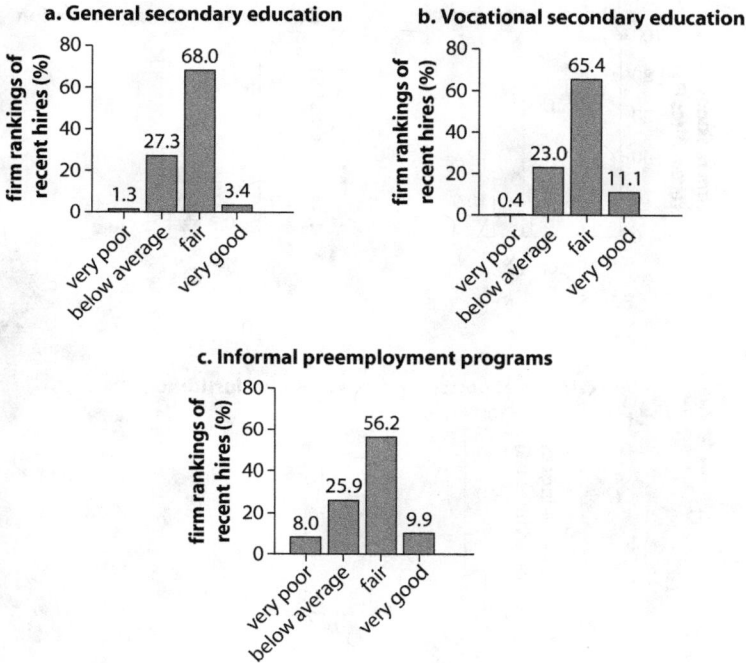

a. General secondary education

b. Vocational secondary education

c. Informal preemployment programs

Source: Indonesia Employer/Employee Survey of Skills/Labor Demand and Job Vacancies 2008, Employer Module.

university graduates than the service sector, judging from the higher proportion of "very good" graduates, but "below average" graduates are also higher, making the results not that clear-cut. The situation is reversed for vocational higher education, where more variance of opinions exists in the service sector.

Retraining Needs

Skill gaps of newly hired graduates are confirmed by the need for training or retraining. Employers report significant training needs for their staff, which is particularly acute for younger workers in skilled occupations. On average, the survey data indicate that employers rate 30 percent of their employees between 30 and 45 years of age as in need of training, and the share increases to almost 50 percent in employees under age 30. This finding is consistent with the already noted quality gap, inefficient skill-matching process, and importance of practical knowledge and job-specific

Figure 4.14   Quality of Tertiary-Cycle Recruits Hired in the 12 Months Preceding the Survey

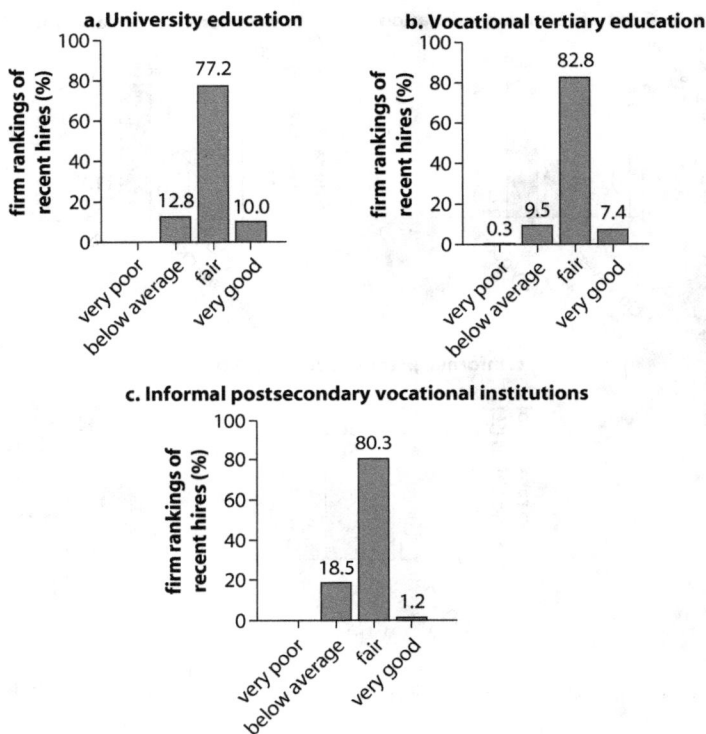

a. University education

b. Vocational tertiary education

c. Informal postsecondary vocational institutions

Source: Indonesia Employer/Employee Survey of Skills/Labor Demand and Job Vacancies 2008, Employer Module.

experience. Interestingly, skills are perceived to be missing most acutely for skilled production workers (table 4.6), who are largely trained at the secondary level, confirming the gravity of quality gaps in secondary education (and possibly insufficient opportunities or quality of on-the-job training and scarce relevant prior work experience).

Educational background is a weaker predictor of training needs, although needs are confirmed to be greater at the secondary level. Need for training is lowest for staff members with incomplete primary education and for those with postgraduate degrees. Although the perceived need for skills is slightly higher among graduates of the general upper-secondary track (as opposed to the vocational upper-secondary track), the reverse is true at the tertiary level. Needs for training are higher for secondary graduates across the board, followed by graduates of diploma

Figure 4.15 Quality of Secondary-Cycle Recruits Hired in the 12 Months Preceding the Survey, Manufacturing and Noneducation Service Firms

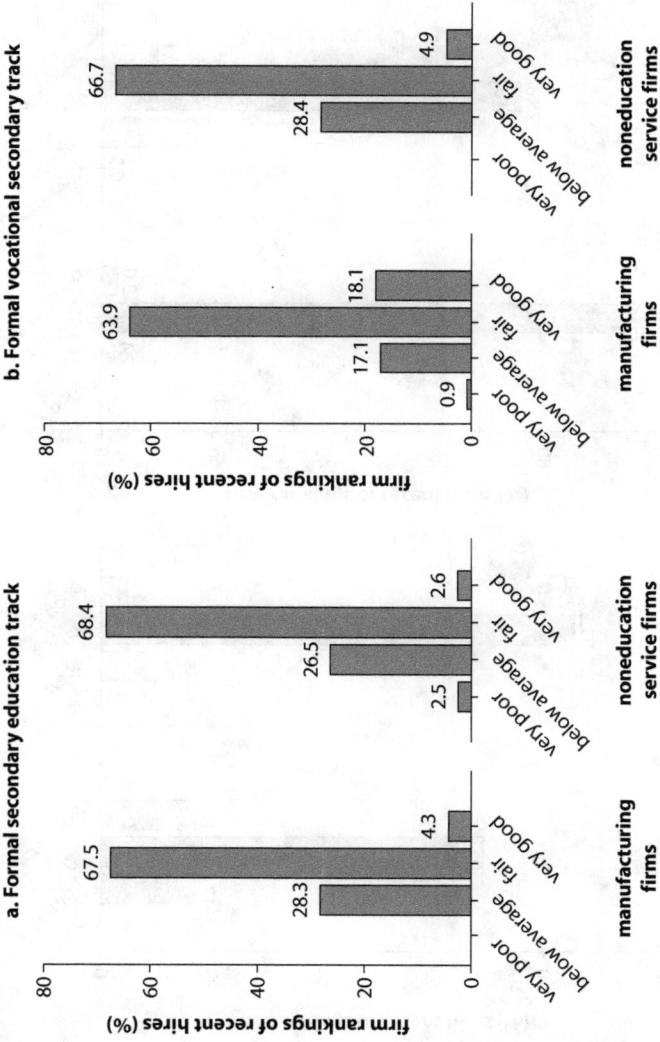

a. Formal secondary education track

b. Formal vocational secondary track

Source: Indonesia Employer/Employee Survey of Skills/Labor Demand and Job Vacancies 2008, Employer Module.

Figure 4.16 Quality of Tertiary-Cycle Recruits Hired in 12 Months Preceding the Survey, Manufacturing and Noneducation Service Firms

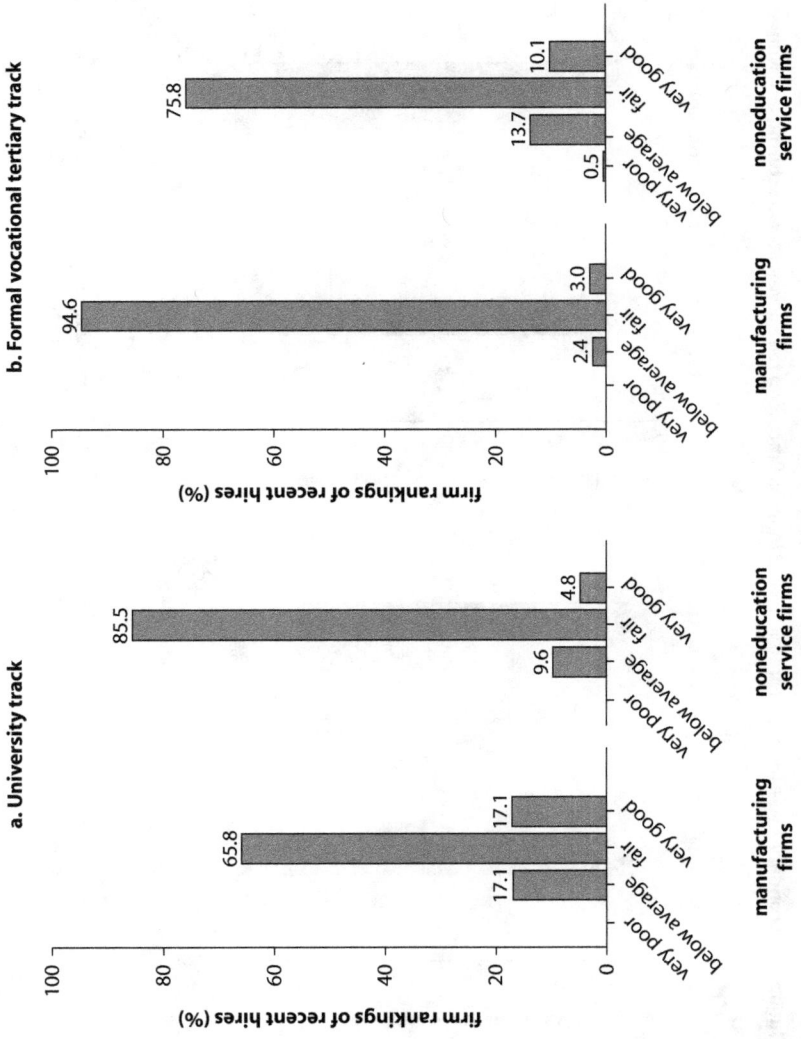

a. University track

b. Formal vocational tertiary track

Source: Indonesia Employer/Employee Survey of Skills/Labor Demand and Job Vacancies 2008, Employer Module.

Table 4.6   Share of Staff in Need of Training, by Professional Category

Professional category	Share of staff identified by firms as in need of training (%)
Directors	21.06
Professionals	22.13
Administrative workers	29.03
Sales workers	26.59
Skilled production workers	38.71
Unskilled workers	11.14
Permanent workers	27.40
Temporary workers	16.83

Source: Indonesia Employer/Employee Survey of Skills/Labor Demand and Job Vacancies 2008, Employer Module.

Table 4.7   Share of Staff in Need of Training, by Schooling Level

Schooling level	Share of staff identified by firms as in need of training (%)
Primary (incomplete)	5.36
Primary (complete)	18.47
Lower secondary	22.17
General upper secondary	32.22
Vocational upper secondary	28.90
University	21.37
Diploma program	25.85
Postgraduate	5.90

Source: Indonesia Employer/Employee Survey of Skills/Labor Demand and Job Vacancies 2008, Employer Module.

programs (table 4.7). Although slightly lower, the high percentage of vocational secondary graduates who need retraining is a rather worrying finding considering the more practical and job-oriented nature of the programs and their generally higher costs, which suggests serious quality or relevance deficiencies. In part, the need for retraining of vocational upper-secondary graduates may be in generic skills.

Gaps in Personal Attributes and Functional Skills

Beyond education levels and occupations, the employer and employee surveys also allow exploration of the main gaps in actual functional skills. This analysis provides critical insights on what lies behind the insufficient quality of graduates[7] and skilled employees, as well as on the mechanics of skill acquisition. This section provides an analysis for overall employees, followed by a further look at young employees.

With respect to personal characteristics, employers highlight weaknesses in staff commitment and honesty and, to a lesser extent, reliability and adaptability (figure 4.17). These weaknesses are highlighted for managers and professionals as well as skilled workers, although the last tend to perform worse on almost all attributes. Some of these personal attributes should have the potential to be shaped somewhat by the education and training system and on-the-job experience.

For generic and subject-based skills, the widest gaps across professional profiles are for English and computer skills, followed by thinking and behavioral skills (figure 4.18). By contrast, subject-based skills do not appear to be a major problem (at least according to employers, who may not be as good a judge of this type of skill). In a comparison of the evidence on the importance of skills with skill gaps, if 30 or 40 percent of firms mention gaps in thinking skills, clearly it is very relevant given the absolute or relative importance attributed to these skills. The same reasoning applies to a somewhat lesser extent to behavioral skills. Although these skills were not generally considered critical, the significant gaps in English and computing skills remain very relevant in the export and technologically intensive sectors, where demand for such skills tends to be higher. In particular, both skills are reported as more important in the export sector.

Figure 4.17   Share of Firms Rating Personal Characteristic as Weakest

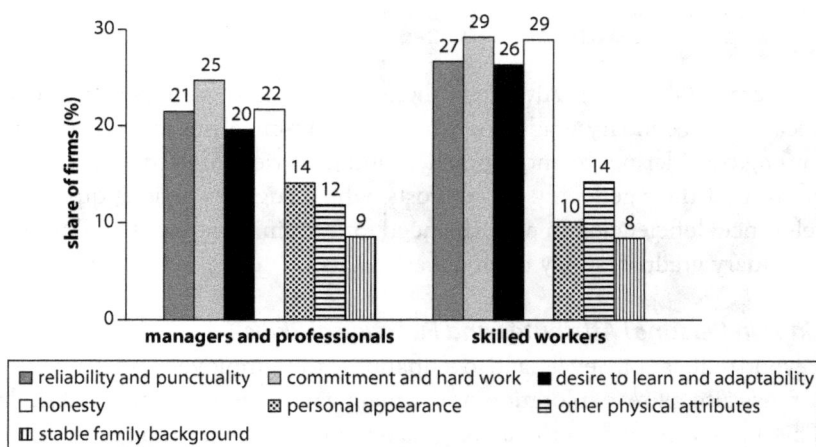

Legend:
- reliability and punctuality
- commitment and hard work
- desire to learn and adaptability
- honesty
- personal appearance
- other physical attributes
- stable family background

Source: Indonesia Employer/Employee Survey of Skills/Labor Demand and Job Vacancies 2008, Employer Module.

Figure 4.18 Share of Firms Identifying a Gap in Given Staff Skills

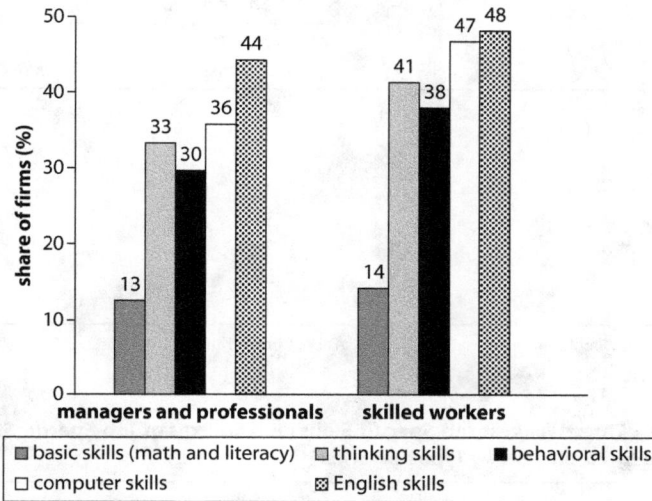

Source: Indonesia Employer/Employee Survey of Skills/Labor Demand and Job Vacancies 2008, Employer Module.

Zooming into each set of skills—basic, thinking, and behavioral—one does not find important contrasts except in the case of behavioral skills, where leadership, team orientation, and ability to work independently are considered particularly weak. The survey data show that Indonesian workers may possibly be relatively less strong in math than in reading and writing, but no real differences are seen within thinking skills. Looking at behavioral skills, one sees that leadership is considered to be particularly weak for managers and professionals, while independence and team orientation are particularly weak in the case of skilled workers (table 4.8). Team orientation and ability to work independently are also the two most critical skills for skilled workers.

Finally, significant gaps exist in theoretical and practical knowledge of the job, in line with the evidence on the most important skills. The finding provides some further evidence that skill acquisition is the result of a complex process involving the cumulative effect of schooling and other factors such as on-the-job training and work experience. Overall information on gaps is not available for job-specific skills, but when one reviews evidence on the weakest skills according to employers, in conformity with the evidence on the importance of skills, both theoretical knowledge and

Table 4.8   Share of Firms Identifying a Gap in Behavioral Skills, by Type of Worker

	Share of firms identifying gap (%)	
Skill	Managers and professionals	Skilled workers
Behavioral skills	30	38
Ability to work independently	28	49
Risk taking	27	38
Communication	33	39
Negotiation	32	37
Team orientation	26	44
Organization	35	40
Leadership	41	36

Source: Indonesia Employer/Employee Survey of Skills/Labor Demand and Job Vacancies 2008, Employer Module.

Table 4.9   Three Weakest Job-Specific Skills (and Sources of Job-Specific Skills) Identified by Employers, by Type of Worker

Skill or source of skill	Managers and professionals (%)	Skilled workers (%)
Diploma program	3.5	3.5
Foreign university	1.0	0.5
General work experience	11.0	11.0
Grades	4.0	4.0
Local university	9.0	3.0
Practical knowledge	18.0	18.0
Previous experience in a different field	5.5	5.5
Previous experience in the same field	18.0	17.0
Primary education	4.5	7.0
Vocational upper-secondary education	3.0	6.6
General upper-secondary education	3.5	5.5
Theoretical knowledge	17.5	16.0

Source: Indonesia Employer/Employee Survey of Skills/Labor Demand and Job Vacancies 2008, Employer Module.

practical knowledge of the job appear to be weak for all categories of workers (table 4.9). The emphasis on university for managers and professionals and secondary education for skilled workers likely reflects the education level most often possessed by these categories of workers and the related standards expected to be achieved for these education levels, rather than absolute weaknesses.[8] In general, these findings confirm that actual job-specific skills are more important than specific education level and degrees. Although such skills are related to educational attainment, they also somewhat transcend them by being the result of the cumulative educational experience (that is, from early childhood to postgraduate education); its quality; and informal education programs, on-the-job training, and work experience. This conclusion relates back to the need for additional assessments and probation periods to assess skills and to the need for additional training to fill the gaps (which, as shown in chapter 6, is focused on both job-specific and generic skills).

Needs for Expatriate Staff (or Job-Specific Skills)

An additional illustration of the quality or relevance gap is given by the number of firms in both the manufacturing and the service sectors that have to resort to hiring expatriates.[9] Almost 5 percent of firms in the manufacturing sector resorted to hiring expatriate staff and slightly less (3.5 percent of firms) in services, presumably to fill a gap in a specific narrow subset of professional skills unavailable locally.

Gaps in Functional Skills and Employment Outcomes and Youth

In the future, given the government of Indonesia's very strong focus on youth employment, focusing on the skill profile of younger workers makes sense to see to what extent it may play a role in influencing labor-market outcomes. Although the employer survey provides little possibility of age-specific disaggregation of actual core skills, such analysis can be done with the employee survey (which, however, covers a smaller random sample[10]). Following is a brief analysis of skill gaps in the population of younger workers (defined here to be 27 years of age or younger) in the employee survey.[11] About 51 percent of these young workers are female, and 85 percent have at least a lower-secondary education.

Because Indonesia has made concerted efforts to expand access to all levels of education in recent decades, youth are, not surprisingly, disproportionally more educated up to the diploma level. However, higher educational attainment is not synonymous with adequate skills. Data from the National Socioeconomic Survey (Survei Sosial Ekonomi Nasional, or SUSENAS) indicate that people older than 55 years of age, the official retirement age, make up 56 percent of those who are unschooled; those under 30 years of age account for only 6 percent of the unschooled. People between 31 and 55 years of age make up more than half of those with less than primary education; in contrast, 61 percent of those under 30 years of age achieve at least a lower-secondary education, a positive consequence of the expansion of basic education to include lower-secondary school, and 50 percent have at least upper-secondary education. Although educational attainment has significantly increased, Indonesian youth still have profound skill gaps that increase the challenges they face in their employment prospects.

With respect to the workers' perceived need for skills, differences occur across age groups that may be attributable to differences in occupations (including level of responsibility) as well as more profound generational shifts.[12] For instance, younger workers perceive a greater need for team skills and adaptability and inversely less of a need for communication, leadership, or independent thinking (figure 4.19). Other important skills for youth are creativity, computing, and technical skills. Surprisingly, English skills are not considered more relevant by youth and remain quite low in importance overall.

Younger workers appear to put less emphasis than their senior colleagues on dealing with people, perhaps reflecting their lesser involvement in management roles (figure 4.20). In contrast, creative thinking and computer proficiency score relatively highly in the new generation (figures 4.21 and 4.22).

The perceived gaps in creativity, computing, and some technical skills are particularly critical for young workers at this time. English is the largest gap across the board. Although English may not be considered that relevant, it is perceived as the most serious gap by younger and older workers alike, matching employers' perceptions. The other most important gaps reckoned by young workers are in leadership, problem solving, creativity, computing, and some technical skills—of which creativity, computing, and technical skills are the most critical at this time, given the need for such skills (figure 4.23). Writing skills are not seen as an important gap.

More worrisome, young workers seem to experience a lower sense of preparedness or qualification for their job or for professional life in general (figure 4.24). Along these lines, survey data show that more than 40 percent of young workers very much agree that additional skills would improve their performance. This evidence is consistent with the findings on retraining by age group, which show a much higher need to be trained for those under 30 years of age.

Perhaps reflecting the importance of experience, the survey data also show that more senior workers also exhibit greater confidence that their skills allow them to meet changing market needs.

Finally, youth have a much higher unemployment rate and tend to be employed in fairly unskilled occupations. Beyond labor-market reasons, insufficient skills are likely to be part of the equation. Youth unemployment is reaching almost 25 percent in Indonesia, compared with 5 percent for the overall population, and it is particularly high for secondary school

Figure 4.19 Skills Most Needed by Younger and Older Workers

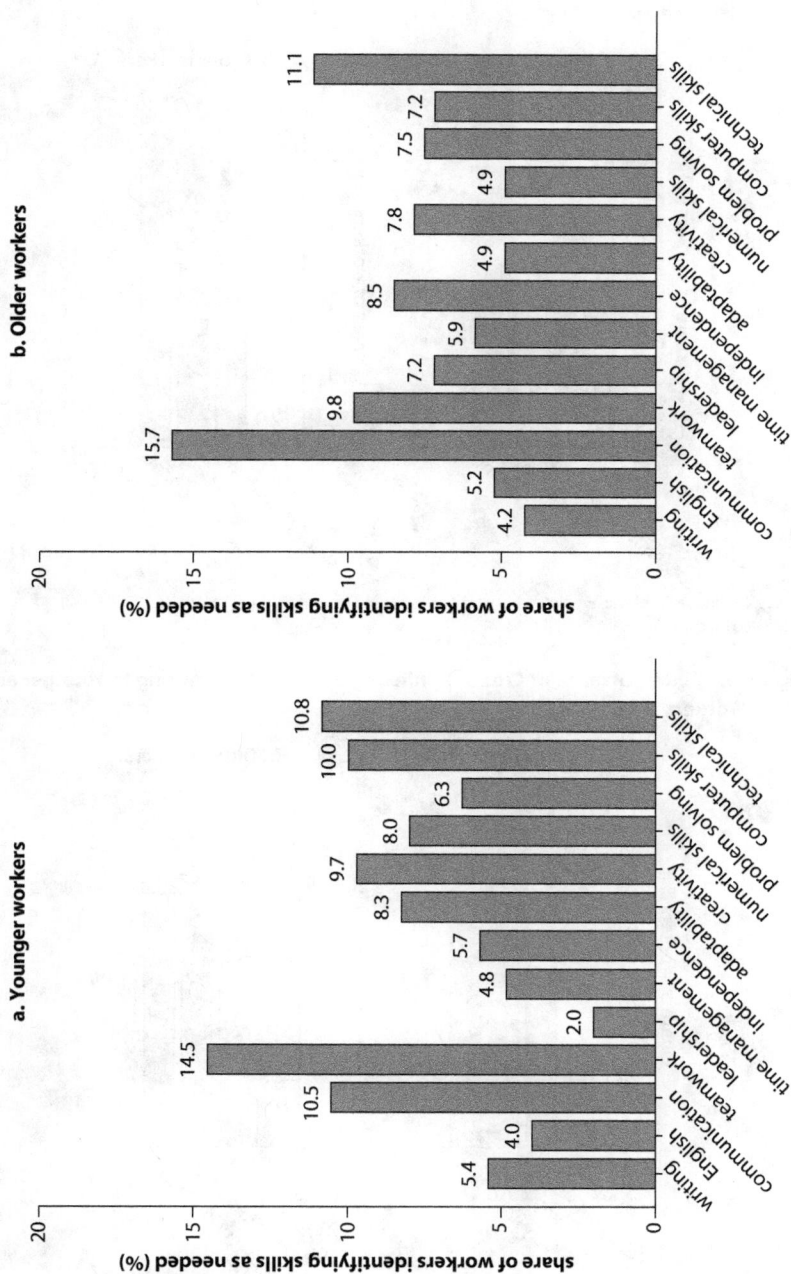

a. Younger workers

Bars (share of workers identifying skills as needed, %):
- writing: 5.4
- English: 4.0
- communication: 10.5
- teamwork: 14.5
- leadership: 2.0
- time management: 4.8
- independence: 5.7
- adaptability: 8.3
- creativity: 9.7
- numerical skills: 8.0
- problem solving: 6.3
- computer skills: 10.0
- technical skills: 10.8

b. Older workers

Bars (share of workers identifying skills as needed, %):
- writing: 4.2
- English: 5.2
- communication: 15.7
- teamwork: 9.8
- leadership: 7.2
- time management: 5.9
- independence: 8.5
- adaptability: 4.9
- creativity: 7.8
- numerical skills: 4.9
- problem solving: 7.5
- computer skills: 7.2
- technical skills: 11.1

Source: Indonesia Employer/Employee Survey of Skills/Labor Demand and Job Vacancies 2008, Employee Module.

Figure 4.20   Importance of Dealing with People on the Job, according to Younger and Older Workers

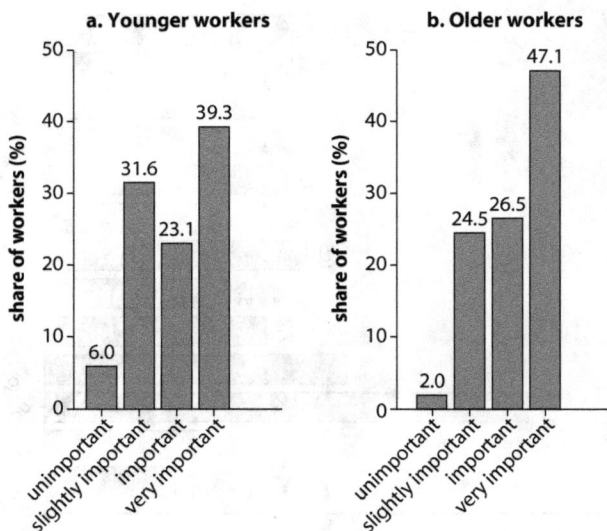

Source: Indonesia Employer/Employee Survey of Skills/Labor Demand and Job Vacancies 2008, Employee Module.

Figure 4.21   Importance of Creative Thinking on the Job, according to Younger and Older Workers

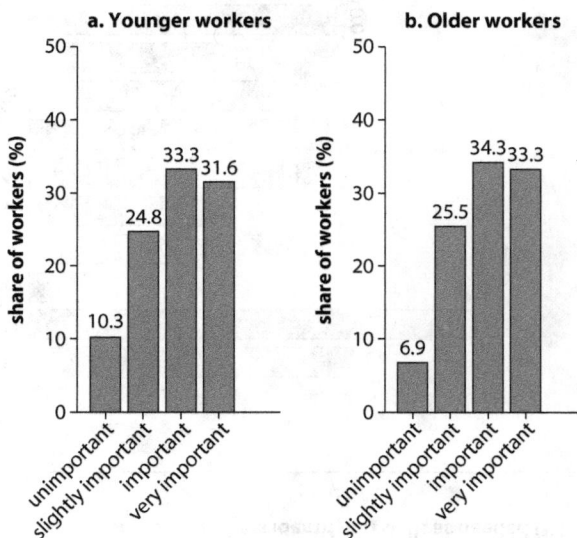

Source: Indonesia Employer/Employee Survey of Skills/Labor Demand and Job Vacancies 2008, Employee Module.

Figure 4.22 Importance of Using Computers on the Job, according to Younger and Older Workers

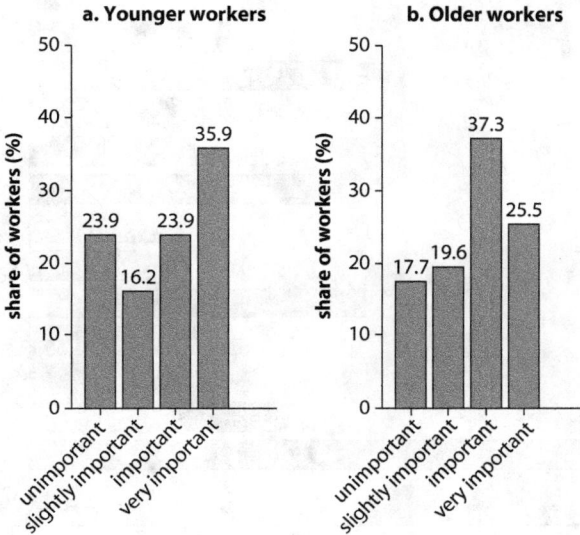

Source: Indonesia Employer/Employee Survey of Skills/Labor Demand and Job Vacancies 2008, Employee Module.

graduates (figure 4.25). These results, which come from regression analysis that controls for family wealth, are likely to a large extent owing to insufficient skills because of lack of previous experience (which, as has been seen, is a very important source of skills) and poor quality of schooling. For those lucky enough to become employed, the skill survey shows that, despite their higher relative educational attainment, they are largely used in occupations that do not match their qualifications.[13] Not surprisingly, these young workers appear less convinced than their older counterparts that their current job offers enough scope to use their skills (figure 4.26). Slow overall employment growth and the already noted misalignment between occupations and educational attainment are likely to explain, to an important extent, this poor employment situation. However, insufficient skills compared to the skill requirements of the labor market is another significant candidate—judging from the low quality of secondary education—that is likely to explain the particularly high unemployment rate[14] for these graduates,[15] the perception of insufficient preparedness, and the need for retraining in part caused by the high premium on job experience. This last factor is likely to lead employers to prefer workers who are more experienced in the absence of other incentives

Figure 4.23 Skills Most Lacked by Younger and Older Workers

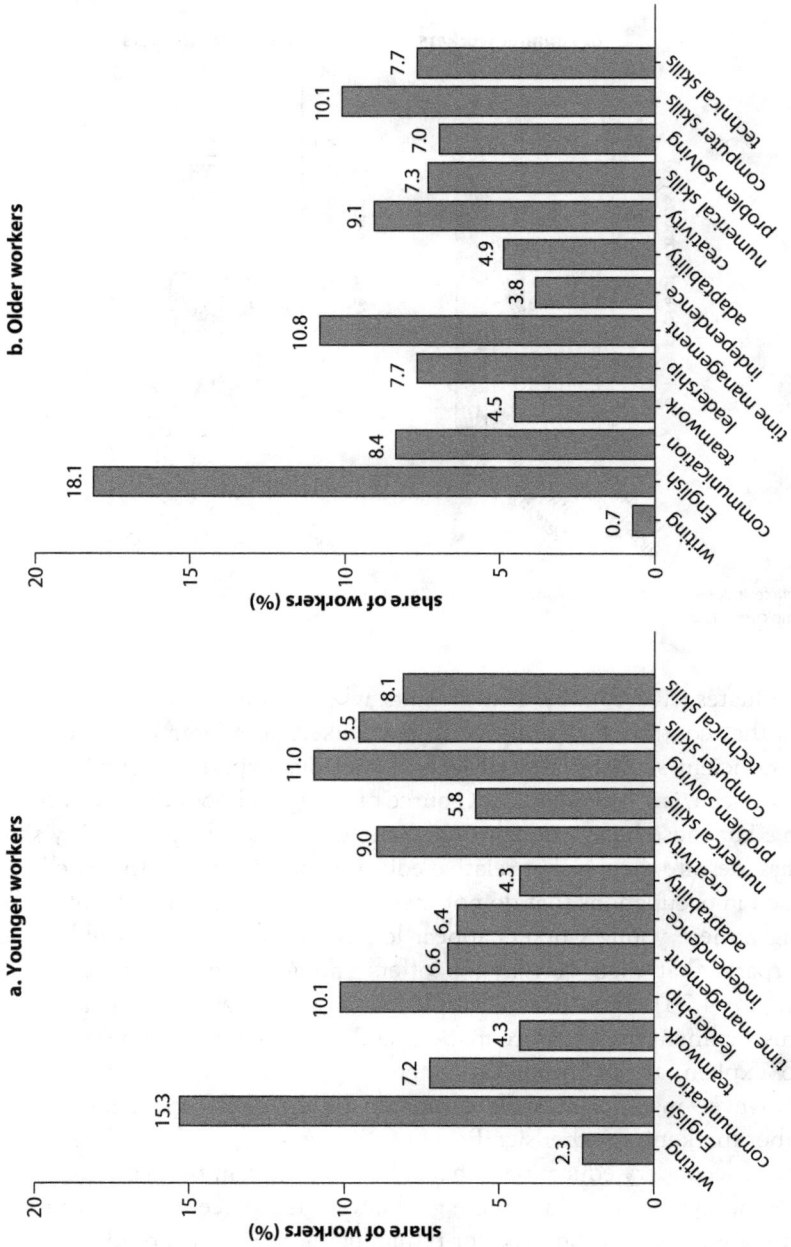

a. Younger workers

Skill	share of workers (%)
technical skills	8.1
computer skills	9.5
problem solving	11.0
numerical skills	5.8
creativity	9.0
adaptability	4.3
independence	6.4
time management	6.6
leadership	10.1
teamwork	4.3
communication	7.2
English	15.3
writing	2.3

b. Older workers

Skill	share of workers (%)
technical skills	7.7
computer skills	10.1
problem solving	7.0
numerical skills	7.3
creativity	9.1
adaptability	4.9
independence	3.8
time management	10.8
leadership	7.7
teamwork	4.5
communication	8.4
English	18.1
writing	0.7

Source: Indonesia Employer/Employee Survey of Skills/Labor Demand and Job Vacancies 2008, Employee Module.

Figure 4.24 Perception of Educational Preparedness for Jobs, according to Younger and Older Workers

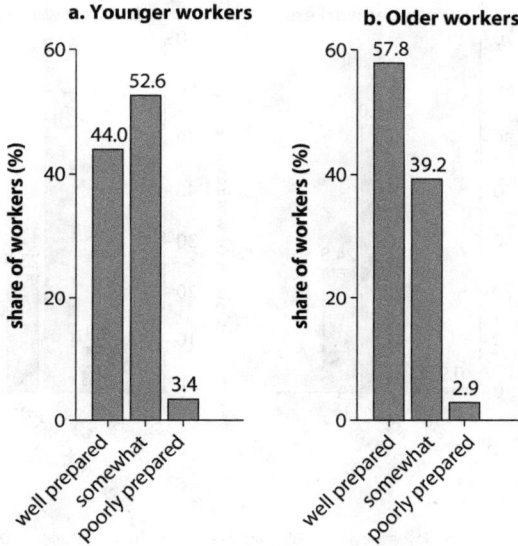

Source: Indonesia Employer/Employee Survey of Skills/Labor Demand and Job Vacancies 2008, Employee Module.

Figure 4.25 Predicted Probability of Being Unemployed, by Characteristic for 15- to 24-Year-Olds, 2006

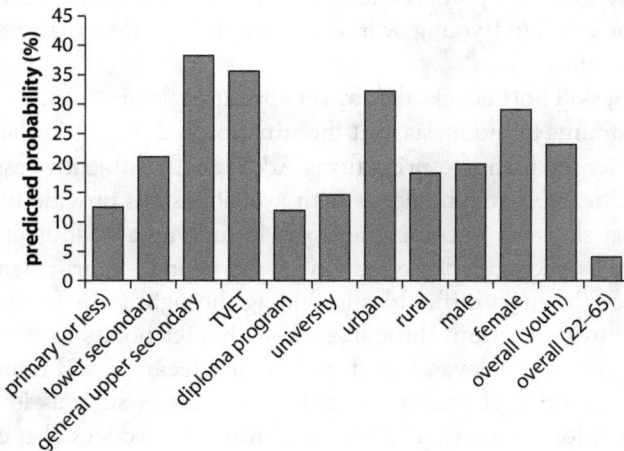

Source: SUSENAS 2006.
Note: Youth is defined as 24–35 years of age for tertiary education graduates.

Figure 4.26   Perception of Younger and Older Workers That Current Job Offers Scope to Use Skills

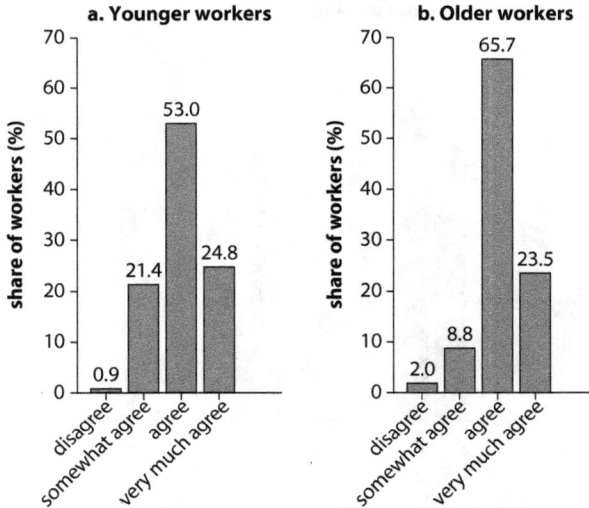

Source: Indonesia Employer/Employee Survey of Skills/Labor Demand and Job Vacancies 2008, Employee Module.

to hire young people. In sum, although sustained rates of return point to sustained demand overall for educated workers—even combined with some limited evidence of shortages—the job experience premium and more general lack of preparedness produce a somewhat stronger skill mismatch for educated young workers in the job market that needs to be urgently addressed.

In sum, skill bottlenecks do not yet appear to be one of the major business constraints in Indonesia, but the situation is different for larger, more export-oriented manufacturing firms. Additionally, subjective assessments of difficulties in matching needs with available skills provide further evidence that skills are becoming an issue in Indonesia. Manufacturing (for professionals and skilled production workers) and export-oriented firms experience the most difficulties in finding the right skills for the job, but services also face serious difficulties. The chapter points to the existence of issues with the relevance and quality of education and training more than the quantity of graduates, with other causes such as low starting wages, high job turnover, and poor recruitment practices also explaining matching difficulties. The evidence confirms, however, some limited shortages (caused more by relevance than by overall quantity issues) of secondary and tertiary graduates to fill professional and skilled production worker jobs in the manufacturing sector. Quantity is more of an issue in some specific higher-value-added manufacturing sectors and a couple of service subsectors.

Overall, according to employers, quality is a particularly critical issue for upper-secondary education graduates (general and vocational), in both the manufacturing and service sectors. However, the quality of newly hired tertiary education graduates also has room for improvement. Quality gaps are apparent from the need for retraining, which is particularly evident for secondary graduates and young workers. In measures of functional skills, the biggest gaps are in computing and English skills (which are not very important overall, except in the exporting sector and, to a minor extent, the service sector). Significant gaps in thinking skills also exist, which represent a major constraint across the board to growth and competitiveness. Gaps also exist within behavioral skills, in the ability to work independently and in teamwork for skilled workers and in leadership skills for managers and professionals. Thinking skills are seen as particularly important in both the service and manufacturing sectors, and teamwork is important in the new workplace environment. Overall, the perceived gaps in theoretical and especially practical knowledge are also worrisome because they are considered essential job-specific skills. Lack of job experience is also an issue, particularly for younger workers who say they are poorly prepared. Also critical are their perceived gaps in creativity, computing, English, and some technical skills. Finally, employment outcomes are all worse for Indonesian youth than for their older counterparts.

Emerging Policy Implications

The evidence presented in this chapter has several policy implications:

- *Fixing secondary education as the "weakest link."* Secondary education graduates are the weakest link in terms of quality and relevance, with gaps that are clear in both the general and vocational streams. Although performing slightly better than general secondary graduates, technical and vocational education graduates seem to be inadequate for both the service sector (perhaps because they lack generic skills) and the manufacturing one (where they are better considered but not hired, leading to difficulties in finding the right skills for skilled production workers). This finding suggests an urgent need for reform. The overall low quality of general secondary graduates is visible from the judgment of both sectors and also requires very serious consideration. The gaps in English, computing, thinking, and practical knowledge skills suggest some directions for improvement of the two streams, which are reconfirmed in part II.

- *Improving quality and relevance of higher education.* Although of generally better quality, the skills of higher-education graduates also need improvement, with particular emphasis on higher-order thinking skills, English, and job-specific skills. Fields of education must prepare students for the manufacturing and service subsectors, which are experiencing some shortages of or increasing demand for skilled workers.
- *Identifying skills for the exporting sector.* Identifying how to strengthen the skills needed in the exporting sector is crucial, given the importance of skill mismatches in that sector.
- *Implementing a comprehensive and complementary approach to skills.* Overall, beyond issues with formal secondary and tertiary education, the gaps in functional skills can be related to a cumulative education process, plus informal education programs, on-the-job training, and work experience. This problem highlights the need for a comprehensive approach to skills in which the different skill acquisition pathways complement each other.
- *Improving recruitment practices and skill signaling.* At the same time, considering and addressing the other not strictly quantity or quality skill-related reasons for skill mismatches, such as poor recruitment practices or issues of skill certification (poor skill "signaling"), is important.
- *Tackling the skills of youth at risk.* Finally, youth are really at risk in Indonesia, presenting serious overall skill gaps and a general lack of preparedness, which, together with a premium on job experience, contribute to particularly poor employment outcomes. How should this issue be addressed? An integrated approach seems warranted.

Notes

1. Care needs to be taken in interpreting these results given the cumulative nature of the answers.
2. The situation may be a little less clear-cut in terms of educational attainment given the level of "education upgrading" within occupations, as illustrated in figure 2.16.
3. The overall exporting-nonexporting differentiation was at least partly capturing the difference between the manufacturing and service sectors.

4. This conclusion relies on the assumption that the time to fill vacancies is more closely linked to quantity than to quality gaps.

5. These results need to be taken with care, given the limited number of observations on informal education in the survey.

6. These results need to be taken with care, given the limited number of observations on informal education in the survey.

7. A full picture of what lies behind quality gaps in formal education should also look in depth at gaps in subject-related lower- and upper-level skills. Chapter 5 does so in part.

8. Clearly, the data are not saying that skilled workers receive better university education, but rather that for them this level of education is not as relevant as secondary education as a source of job-specific skills.

9. Hiring expatriates is usually a last option given the lack of diversified recruitment practices.

10. The 200 interviewed employees were randomly sampled across as many firms as possible.

11. Workers 27 years of age or younger represent about 60 percent of the employee sample.

12. Comparisons among generations are made difficult by the possibility of selection bias ("survival of the fittest") and skill decay for older cohorts, two somewhat countervailing effects. Thus, such comparisons need to be made with care.

13. A recent report on youth and labor-market outcomes points out that younger workers have overall more access to new formal jobs than older generations, however (see World Bank 2010).

14. The unemployment rate for secondary education graduates is higher than that for university graduates, who have higher reservation wages and face a higher risk of job overqualification.

15. In addition, it may explain their lower access to formal paid jobs (World Bank 2010).

References

Almeida, Rita. 2009. "Does the Workforce in East Asia Have the Right Skills? Evidence from Firm Level Surveys." Background paper prepared for Regional Study on Skills, World Bank, Washington, DC.

World Bank. 2010. *Skills, Education, and Labor Market Outcomes for Youth in Indonesia*. Jakarta: World Bank.

PART II

An Overview of the Indonesian Skill Development System

Although education and training (in their formal and informal components) are not the only determinants of skill gaps and employability in Indonesia, given the importance of labor-market reasons and other channels through which skills can be acquired (such as work experience), they are clearly critical. They are the main source of academic skills and a key source of generic and technical skills, fundamental to the successful insertion of graduates into the labor market and to fulfilling the needs of the economy. Unfortunately, education and training are failing somewhat to fulfill this role adequately, as shown, among other indicators, by employers' perceptions of the quality of newly hired graduates and measures of actual skills.

As Indonesia looks to transition to a knowledge economy and increase competitiveness, growth, and employment performance, gaps in job-relevant and high-quality skills are increasingly being seen as significant obstacles. As a result, the nation's education and training system needs to be examined and improved to close these gaps. In this context, this part of the book provides an overview of the supply of skills in Indonesia and the institutions that provide them. It assesses how the country's educational system is performing and proposes some options to make it more responsive to growing labor-market needs. It looks at the supply of skills by the education and training sectors in Indonesia, investigating both formal and informal skill acquisition pathways. This part of the book addresses the following key questions: To what extent is the education and training sector providing skills relevant to the needs of the labor market and the economy? What are the main strengths, weaknesses, and challenges in the provision of skills? What are the possible measures to improve quality and responsiveness to the needs of the labor market and the economy? (See figure II.1.)

Some steps toward reform are already being taken. Indonesia has invested heavily in vocational and educational training, often substituting these systems for academic ones. At the same time, policy makers have begun to look for greater contributions to skill development from other subsectors of the education system. They are reconsidering how access to and quality and relevance of the secondary and tertiary subsectors could be improved to make the supply of skills more responsive to the demands and needs of employers. Addressing these issues of educational reform has been extremely difficult in the face of a dearth of data, information, and analysis on the outcomes and challenges for the sector. Policy makers need more and better information to identify priorities and policy options.

Figure II.1   Strengths and Weaknesses of Education and Training

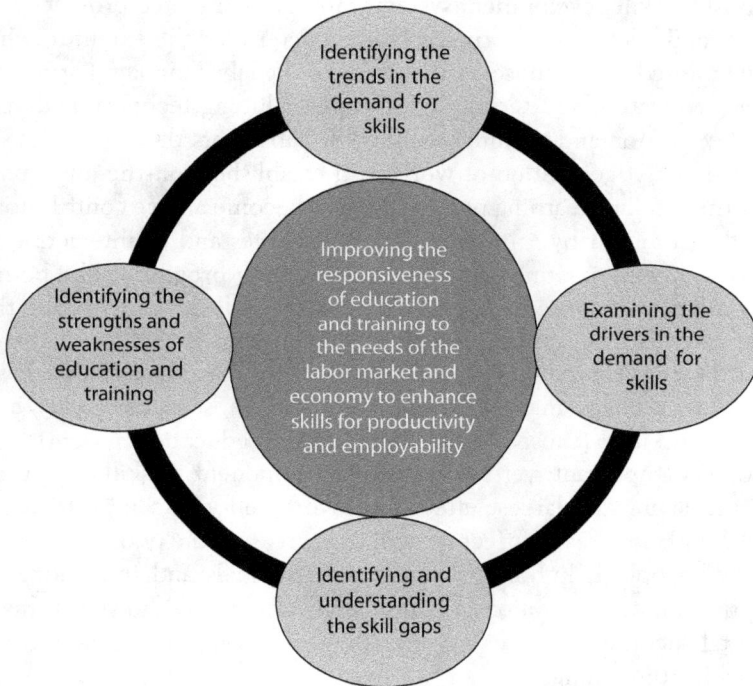

Identifying the trends in the demand for skills

Improving the responsiveness of education and training to the needs of the labor market and economy to enhance skills for productivity and employability

Identifying the strengths and weaknesses of education and training

Examining the drivers in the demand for skills

Identifying and understanding the skill gaps

Source: Authors' representation.

Conceptual Framework for the Supply of Skills

To address this gap, this part provides an overview of the characteristics, outcomes, and challenges facing the education and training sector in Indonesia, with particular focus on the secondary and tertiary subsectors,[1] making large use of the employer and employee skill surveys, as well as available evidence from household and labor force surveys, new country reports, and existing literature. A comprehensive approach is taken by also touching on the sector's capacity to provide skill development opportunities for the unskilled ("second-chance" programs) and on-the-job training. Thus, this part really emphasizes three core aspects of skill production: (a) the general ability of a system to produce a skilled labor force, (b) the ability to continue updating these skills over time, and (c) the ability to help unskilled young adults and adults gain skills.

Looking at these three interrelated dimensions necessarily leads one to consider skill development systems rather than isolated providers. The quality and relevance of formal schooling determine the extent to which newly minted graduates serve the needs of the labor market. Formal secondary education and tertiary education, including technical and vocational education and training, are the key subsectors that shape the skill set of the next generation of workers. If established, on-the-job training and other lifelong learning providers could become a large contributor to skill development by improving labor outcomes and counteracting the obsolescence of existing education and training programs. The boundaries of this dimension are not particularly well developed, but they cover any lifelong training and skill development activity—on the job or in the classroom—that would help workers keep their skills relevant to the needs of the market or simply enhance those skills. Finally, helping the unskilled (those left out of the formal education system) is the third very important, yet understudied, component of skill supply, and beyond having the largest effect on poverty, efforts to raise their skill level could also greatly affect growth by increasing the pool of educated, talented people; help fulfill rising demands for skills; and, in the long run, benefit multiple generations, because study after study shows that higher parental income improves the health, education, and economic outcomes for the young.

Although identifying the characteristics of effective systems is difficult, a benchmark can nonetheless be useful. Typically, a comprehensive skill development system would include the following components:

- Sufficient, high-quality, and relevant school-based formal education and training opportunities at all levels to provide the following skills:
  - Primary—basic academic and generic skills
  - Secondary—more advanced academic and generic skills, as well as some technical skills
  - Tertiary—higher-order academic, generic, and technical skills
- Quality informal education and training
  - To provide academic, generic, and technical skills to out-of-school groups
  - To complement formal education with additional generic or technical skills
  - To provide opportunities for updating academic and technical skills over time
- Sufficient firm training

Figure II.2   Players in and Policies for Supply of Skills and Components of the Benchmarking Approach

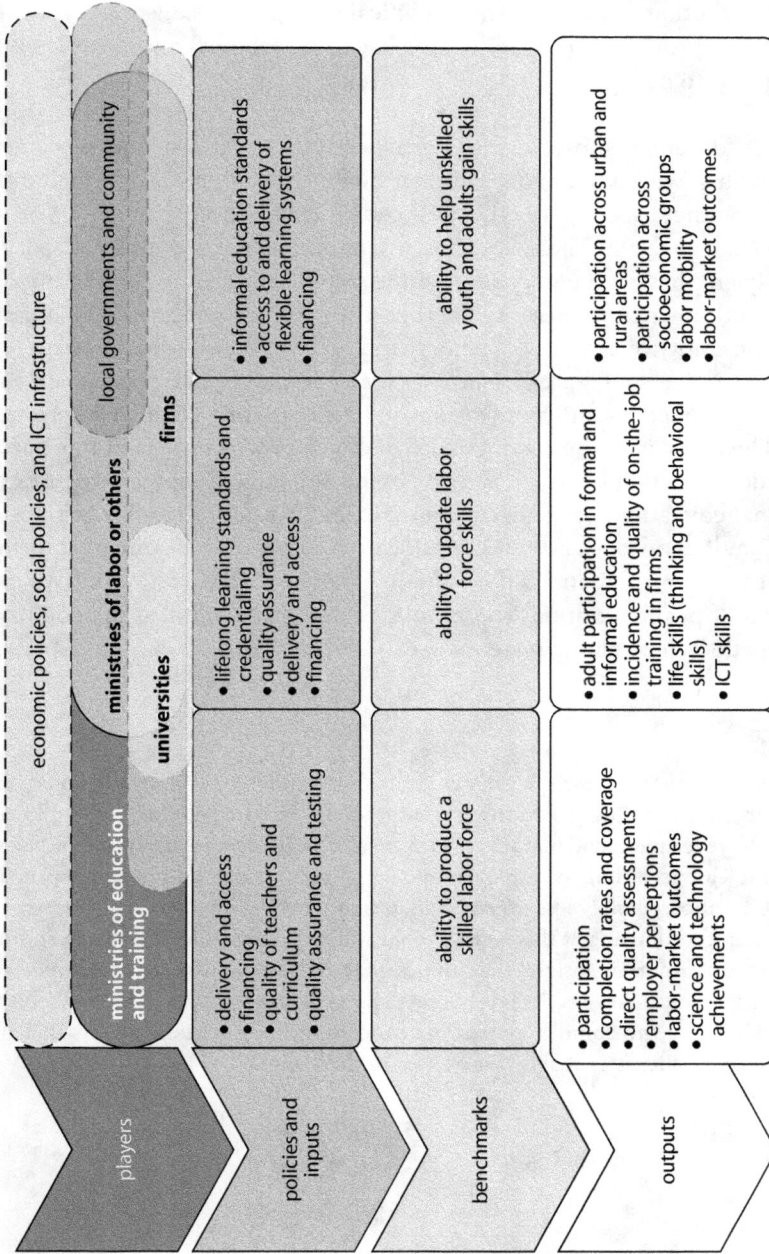

Source: Authors' representation.

Note: ICT = information, communication, and technology.

- To complement formal and informal education and training with additional (job-relevant) technical and generic skills
- To provide opportunities for keeping technical and generic skills up to date.

These different subsectors in turn need to be linked and integrated through a well-functioning national qualification framework, including, among other aspects, effective skill certification.

While analyzing these key dimensions and subsectors, this part particularly emphasizes a comparison of the public and private roles in providing and financing these skills (because skill development is a joint responsibility of a variety of actors) and highlights policy and market failures in doing so. Figure II.2 provides a basic conceptual framework that can be applied to this part (the shaded areas are of particular interest).

The analysis of the Indonesian skill development system in this part is divided into two chapters and five main sections. Chapter 5 focuses on formal education, particularly emphasizing broader outcomes of the system and secondary and tertiary education. Chapter 6 examines informal education and training and on-the-job training. Each section identifies a menu of possible options to improve the responsiveness of the country's education and training system.

Note

1. Skill acquisition starts in early childhood, and this book has already noted how important primary education continues to be in the eyes of employers. However, math and literacy seem to be at a fairly acceptable level in Indonesia (at least according to employers and employees), making a revision of primary education possibly less urgent. Still, primary testing may tell a different story; therefore, looking at this sector would still be worthwhile, perhaps in another report. Another insight that things may not be as rosy as employers and employees believe is the level of math and reading in lower-secondary schools, which, by the cumulative nature of the education process, suggests that primary quality is probably low as well in these areas.

CHAPTER 5

The Ability to Produce a Skilled Labor Force

An Overview of the Indonesian Formal Education Sector

This chapter provides an overview of the formal education system in Indonesia, emphasizing some of its main overall outcomes as well as the main characteristics and outcomes of secondary (both general and vocational) and higher education. The first section discusses the structure and basic outcomes of the education sector as a whole in terms of access, equity, and quality; the next section turns to the country's rapidly expanding system of technical and vocational education and training (TVET) and examines its place in providing the country's workforce with adequate and relevant skills; and the last section describes the main characteristics of the higher-education subsector and its main outcomes and challenges. The chapter uses the employer and employee skill surveys, complemented by a combination of (a) background papers prepared for this book and (b) other recent studies and reports.

In brief, the main findings of the chapter are the following:

- Equity of access remains a very serious concern in Indonesia.
- Subject-based skills have improved but are still below par in terms of international standards.

- The two tracks of secondary education have both advantages and disadvantages, and both are in serious need of improvement to become more responsive to labor-market needs.
- Universities need to become more adaptable to industry needs while increasing their focus on skills for innovation.

Structure and Basic Outcomes of the Formal Education System

This first section focuses on the basic structure and outcomes of the Indonesian education system, particularly the formal system, to further understand some of the constraints on the supply side. Emphasis is placed on past trends, when available, and current level of coverage, equity of access, and quality of the system to determine where the system is coming from, what its current state is, and where it may be heading in terms of these critical indicators. Quantity of skills does not appear to be an important constraint at this time (except in rather specific cases); therefore, drastic coverage changes are not required. The labor market, nonetheless, has the capacity to continue absorbing new graduates, as shown by the stable skill premiums, despite increasing educational attainment, thus justifying continued gradual growth. While expansion continues its pace, ensuring that the education system becomes more equitable is important so that the country can count on a wider talent pool to nurture the still insufficient quality of its human resources. Moreover, Indonesia needs to ensure that, at a minimum, its education system provides all students with strong core basic skills as a foundation for the further acquisition of higher-level, subject-based generic and technical skills within and outside the education system.

Structure

Indonesia's formal education system consists of four levels: preschool; basic, which consists of primary and lower secondary; secondary; and higher education (figure 5.1). The primary cycle is six years long, and students enter at seven years of age. Lower secondary is three years long, as is secondary. Within higher education, several degree and certificate paths are possible. They include the diploma, the duration of which can be from one to four years, depending on the field, and the internationally standard bachelor's, master's, and doctoral programs. TVET provides an alternative to general education. Students can enter TVET programs at the secondary or diploma level. To enter higher education, students must pass a secondary school graduating exam.

Figure 5.1   The Education System in Indonesia

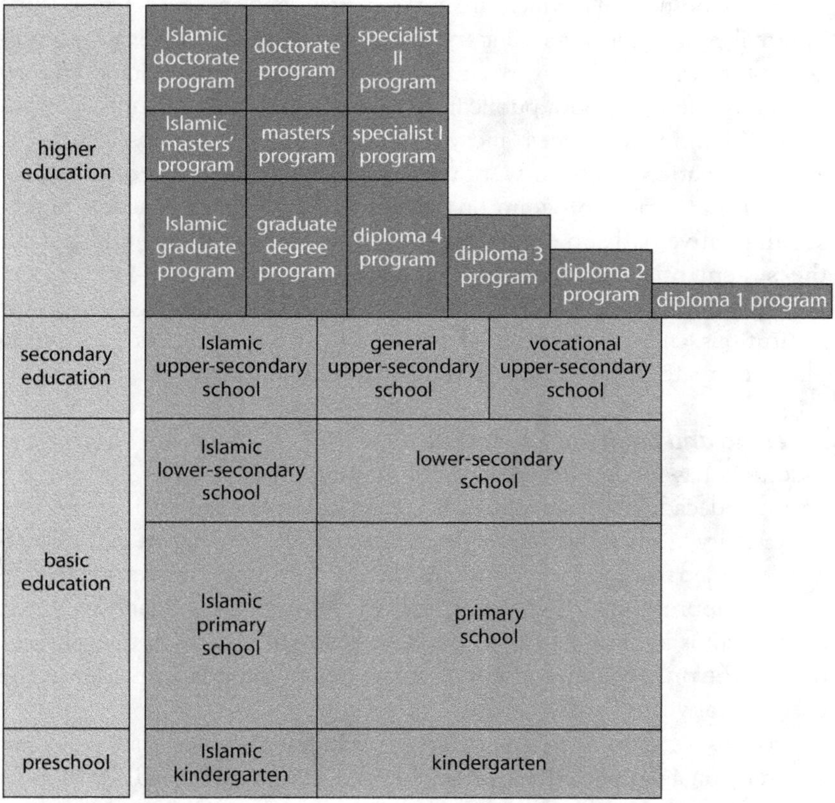

higher education	Islamic doctorate program	doctorate program	specialist II program				
	Islamic masters' program	masters' program	specialist I program				
	Islamic graduate program	graduate degree program	diploma 4 program	diploma 3 program	diploma 2 program	diploma 1 program	
secondary education	Islamic upper-secondary school	general upper-secondary school	vocational upper-secondary school				
basic education	Islamic lower-secondary school	lower-secondary school					
	Islamic primary school	primary school					
preschool	Islamic kindergarten	kindergarten					

Source: Embassy of the Republic of Indonesia 2000.

For each level of education, a separate Islamic track is available to students, which serves as an alternative to the general education system. These tracks are coordinated with the corresponding general educational track in terms of students' ages and length of study.[1] A large degree of flexibility exists between tracks, with students switching from Islamic education to general education, and vice versa, at all levels. In 2006, for example, more than 10 percent of new students in general and vocational upper-secondary schools entered from Islamic lower-secondary schools. In 2008, the distribution of students in secondary education was spread across the three categories of general, vocational, and Islamic education in an approximate ratio of 62:31:7 (Martawardaya 2008a).

The system also includes both formal and informal components. Informal components, which are further examined in chapter 6, include informal primary, lower-secondary, and upper-secondary equivalency programs (known as *Pakets* A, B, and C); preemployment vocational training programs offered by both public institutions (known as *balai latihan kerjas*, or BLKs) and private ones; and youth employment programs to support a more effective school-to-work transition, such as the new Education for Youth Employment program or the Kursus Para Profesi program to create alternative paths to employment. Beyond preemployment education, the system offers possibilities of postemployment on-the-job training both within firms and outside them, through public and private training institutions, and an occupational qualification framework has been put in place to create the seeds of a lifelong learning framework.

Access to and Equity of Education

Indonesia has made impressive gains in enrollment at all levels over the past two decades, but these gains have leveled off in the past few years. At the primary level, net enrollment reached just over 90 percent in 2003 and has remained near that level since. At the lower-secondary level, net enrollment is approaching 70 percent, and at the upper-secondary level, net enrollment is approximately 45 percent. Figure 5.2 shows net enrollment rates at the primary, lower-secondary, and upper-secondary levels over the past several years.

Indonesia's gross enrollment rates (GERs) at the secondary level are generally on a par with those of neighboring countries. The GERs of most countries in the region fluctuate at about 70 percent to 80 percent. The Indonesian GER is practically at the East Asia and Pacific regional average of 76 percent and, as can be expected, well below the Organisation of Economic Co-operation and Development (OECD) average of 101 percent (figure 5.3).

Indonesia has made relatively slower progress on increasing enrollments in higher education, although the GER at the tertiary level has continued to increase slowly over the past several years. In 2001, Indonesia's tertiary GER was 14.4 percent; in 2004, it was 16.5 percent; and in 2007, it stood at 17.4 percent.[2] The country's GER for higher education is lower than that of some of its neighbors (figure 5.4) and a bit lower than the East and Pacific regional average of 23 percent. It is, not surprisingly, much lower than the OECD average of nearly 70 percent.

Indonesia's enrollment gains over the past several years have done little to stem disparities in access for underrepresented groups. Gender, age,

Figure 5.2   Net Enrollment Rates at the Primary, Lower-Secondary, and Upper-Secondary Levels, 2003–06

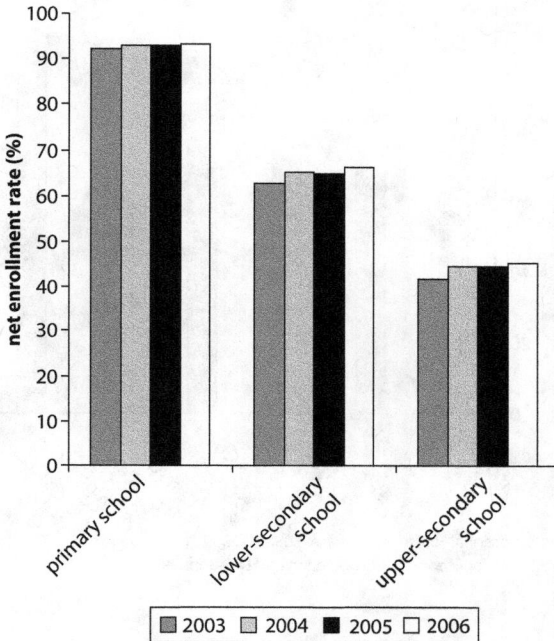

Source: National Socioeconomic Survey (Survei Sosial Ekonomi Nasional, or SUSENAS) (various years).

spatial, and income disparities exist in access to education, especially higher education, although rural-urban disparities are significantly larger than gender ones.

Overall, women have increased their levels of participation across all education levels, but disparities remain: 53 percent of those enrolled in primary education are female, and this ratio increases to 56 percent of those enrolled at the diploma level. However, although women make up approximately 49 percent of the population, the proportion of women with bachelor's degrees is much lower than that for men (43 percent compared with 57 percent). Significant gender disparity also exists in the distribution of men and women without schooling: women account for almost 70 percent of those who are unschooled. Current enrollments at the secondary level suggest that these distributions may change over time as more women continue to enroll in education. Figure 5.5 provides data on the gender balance at each level of education in Indonesia.

Figure 5.3   Secondary Gross Enrollment Rates in Selected Countries, 2007

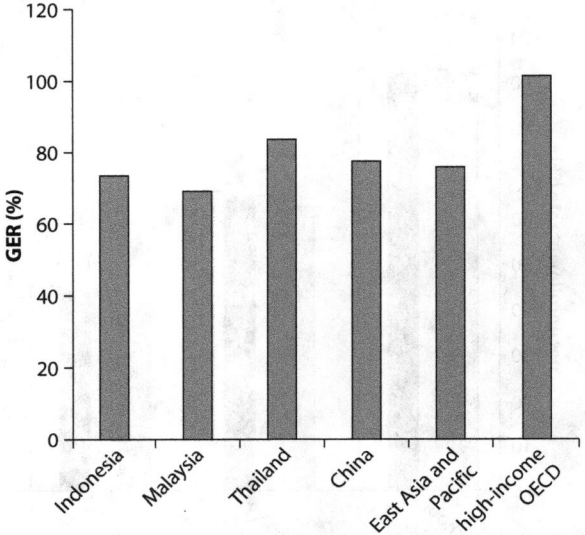

Source: World Bank's Educational Statistics Database (EdStats) 2009.
Note: OECD = Organisation for Economic Co-operation and Development.

Figure 5.4   Tertiary Gross Enrollment Rates in Selected Countries, 2007

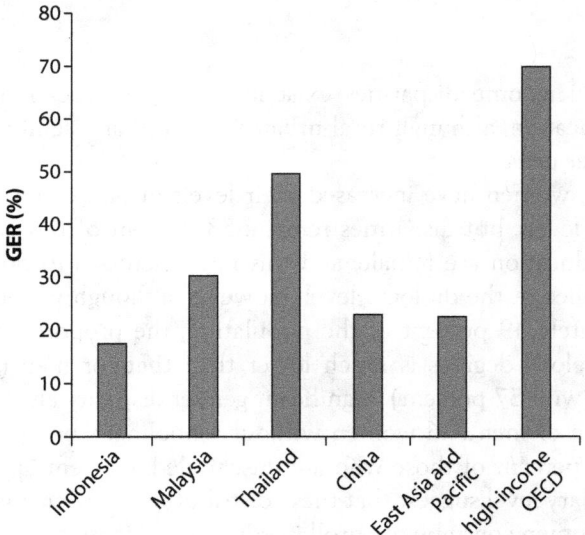

Source: EdStats 2009.
Note: OECD = Organisation for Economic Co-operation and Development.

Figure 5.5   Gender Balances at Various Education Levels

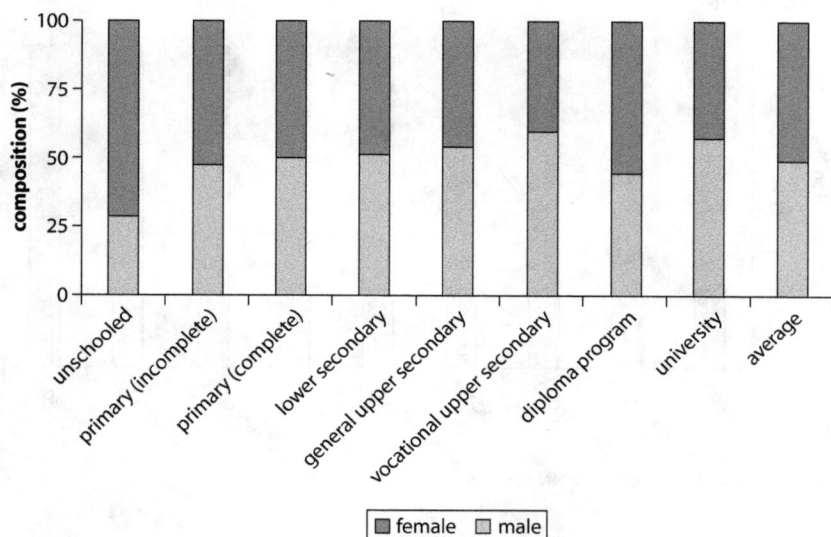

Source: SUSENAS 2007.

In addition to these disparities of gender and age, a significant disparity exists in access to education between urban and rural populations. The
urban population in Indonesia is significantly more educated, even
though the country's population is roughly split between rural and urban
areas. Of those without any education, 70 percent live in rural areas
(figure 5.6). Rural students make up only 30 percent of those studying
at the secondary or diploma level. Only 15 percent of those studying for
a bachelor's, master's, or doctorate degree are rural students.

Beyond the rural-urban divide, a significant spatial disparity clearly
exists in access among Jakarta and central Java, eastern Java, and eastern
Indonesia. Almost half the unschooled population lives in central and
eastern Java, even though only 35 percent of the population lives in these
areas. Residents of the eastern part of Indonesia are also overrepresented
among the unschooled. By contrast, Jakarta, western Java, and Sumatra
have much lower proportions of unschooled people in their populations.
Jakarta is the region with the highest concentration of highly educated
people; more than 70 percent of its population has an upper-secondary
school education (figure 5.7).

As in many other countries, systematic differences exist in access to
education between the rich and the poor across all levels. At the university

Figure 5.6   Proportions of Rural and Urban Students Enrolled at Each Level of Education

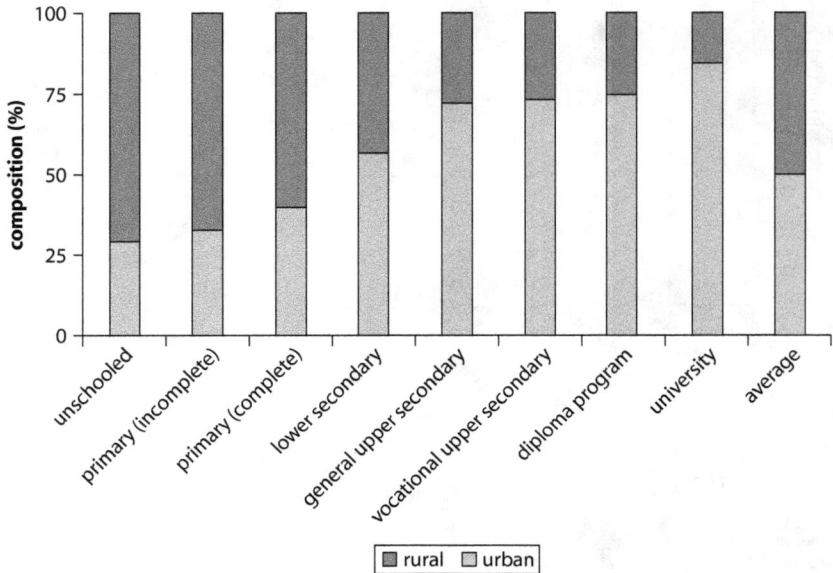

Source: SUSENAS 2007.

level, more than 70 percent of those enrolled are in the richest quintile of the population. At the diploma level, this figure is 60 percent. Students from the poorest three income quintiles make up only 10 percent of university graduates and 17 percent of diploma graduates (figure 5.8). In contrast, they make up about 80 percent of the unschooled and almost 75 percent of primary school graduates. Poverty and low educational attainment are strongly correlated. The poorest account for more than 33 percent of the unschooled and less than 1 percent of those enrolled in universities. Scholarships for the disadvantaged exist, mostly from alumni associations and the private sector, but their number and scope are limited. To spur demand among the poor, the government of Indonesia enacted a conditional cash transfer program called Program Keluarga Harapan (Hope for Family Program) in 2007. Under the program, poor families receive financial compensation if their children remain enrolled in primary school. At the tertiary level, the country has introduced a full and partial scholarship scheme, but the coverage is limited, and the scheme is fundamentally targeted to students already enrolled in tertiary education, thus ignoring high school leavers who do not have the

Figure 5.7   Geography and Access to Education

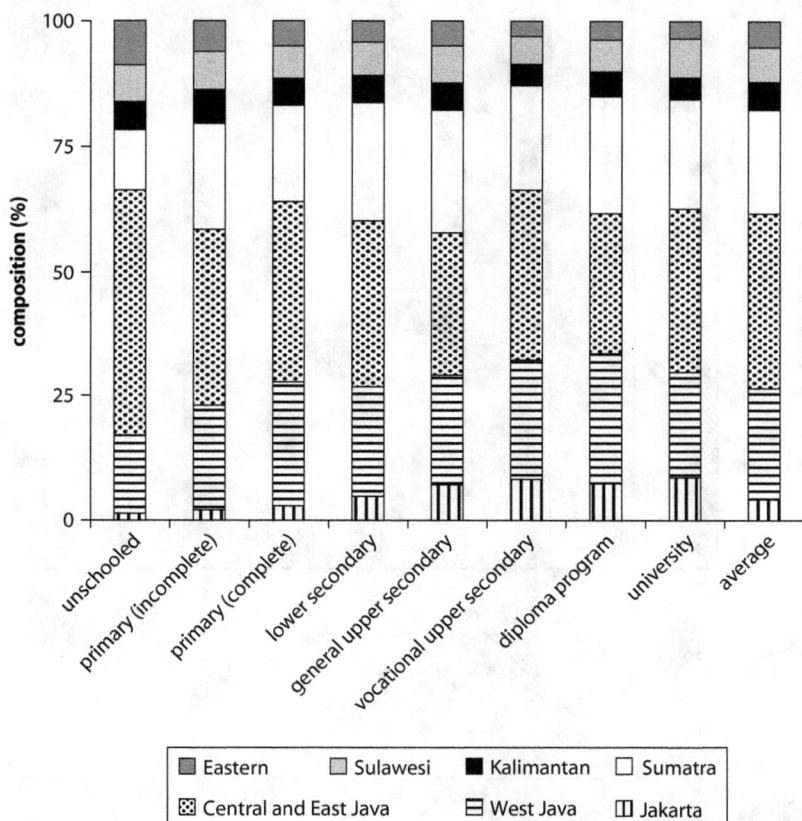

Source: SUSENAS 2007.

economic means to enroll in the first place (see Moeliodihardjo 2010). Given the strong relation between income and attendance in tertiary education, also illustrated by the predicted probability of attending university by selected characteristics (figure 5.9), lack of access to higher education among lower socioeconomic levels is a problem.

Quantifying the coverage of informal education programs and the relief they can provide to disadvantaged groups is difficult, but participation has been increasing. In a context of still limited equitable access to formal education and increased informal programs, more Indonesians—particularly low-income and older workers, as well as out-of-school and unemployed youth—are turning to informal educational providers to

Figure 5.8   Income and Access to Education, by Income Quintile

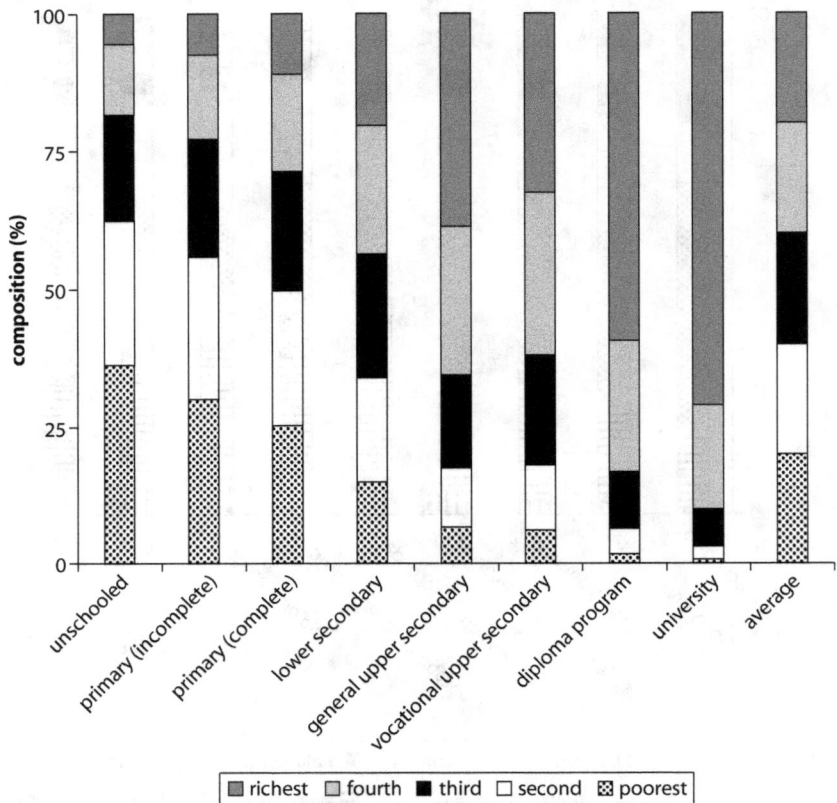

Source: SUSENAS 2007.

develop and upgrade their skills and knowledge. According to SUSENAS (Survei Sosial Ekonomi Nasional, or National Socioeconomic Survey), of the approximately 4.4 million dropouts from formal education in 2003, about 1 million entered the government's equivalency educational system (known as *Paket*).

Policy implications include the following:

- *Sustain expansion of secondary and tertiary enrollment while improving equity of access.* The main findings of this subsection point to the importance of continuing the gradual expansion of secondary and higher education (not losing pace, particularly in higher education, where in comparative terms the GER still has significant room to

Figure 5.9   Predicted Probability of Attending University (Gross Attendance), by Selected Characteristics, 2006

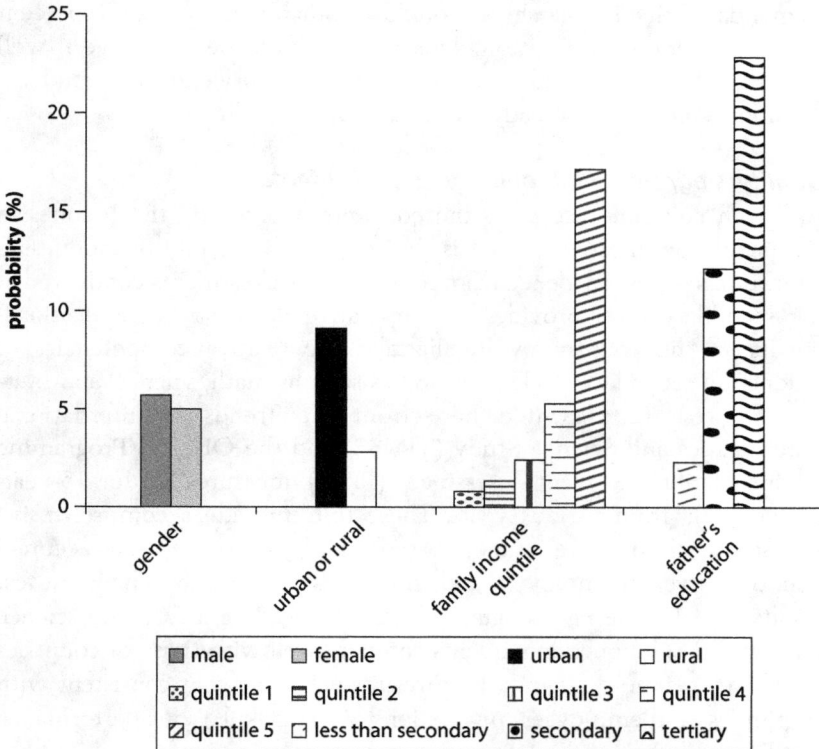

Source: SUSENAS 2006.

grow) while improving the representativeness of all socioeconomic levels in the student population, which is still clearly insufficient. Such efforts should help increase the pool of talented students.

- *Use informal skill provision programs.* Beyond skill upgrading, given the continuing inequalities of access, significant scope seems to exist in Indonesia to prop up informal education. As long as it is of sufficient quality, informal education can usefully complement the country's efforts to make education more inclusive by offering skill development opportunities to groups that continue to be excluded from formal education. Further analysis of informal education is undertaken in chapter 6.

- *Continue with conditional cash transfers, and strengthen the scholarship scheme in tertiary education.* Another line of action, already in place, relates to the increasing use of conditional cash transfers to support the access of disadvantaged groups to formal education. A 2009 law mandated that scholarships should be available for at least 20 percent of the student population. This reform could be attractive if well designed and targeted to include potential tertiary education students and not only those already enrolled.

Quality: Cognitive Skills of Indonesian Students

Although equitable access to the education offered by the Indonesian state could be improved, what is the state of the quality of Indonesia's education system? Evidence from international assessments conducted at the secondary level provides a comparative diagnostic of educational quality in the country by highlighting the relative competencies of Indonesian secondary students in topics such as math, science, and literacy. Figures are presented here from the Trends in International Mathematics and Science Study (TIMSS) and the OECD's Programme for International Student Assessment (PISA); measures are for 15-year-old students from various years. These tests provide a comprehensive assessment of cognitive (subject-based) skills, which are more accurate than the survey of employers' and employees' perceptions. The latest test results reveal some encouraging progress on reading, math, and science skills in PISA; Indonesian students compare well with those of countries of similar income per capita (and results are somewhat consistent with employers' and employees' perceptions of basic skills), but performance is still notably below the international average.

In math on the 2007 TIMSS test, Indonesia performed just better than the Philippines, with a score significantly lower than the TIMSS mean score and even more so the mean score of upper-income East Asia. Although Indonesia placed higher than the Philippines, another middle-income economy, other economies in the region (Hong Kong SAR, China; Japan; the Republic of Korea; and Malaysia) performed significantly better than Indonesia (with differences of about 200 percentage points between, for instance, Hong Kong SAR, China, and Indonesia; figure 5.10). Results have been about stagnant since 1999.

Recent results from Indonesia's participation in PISA indicate that, in absolute terms, the country is performing better than in previous years in reading skills, and the gap with more developed countries has notably decreased; however, the country still has a long way to go to reach the OECD average of 500. Figures 5.11 and 5.12 indicate that Indonesia has performed better consistently from 2000 to 2006 in the

Figure 5.10   TIMSS Math Results, 1999–2007

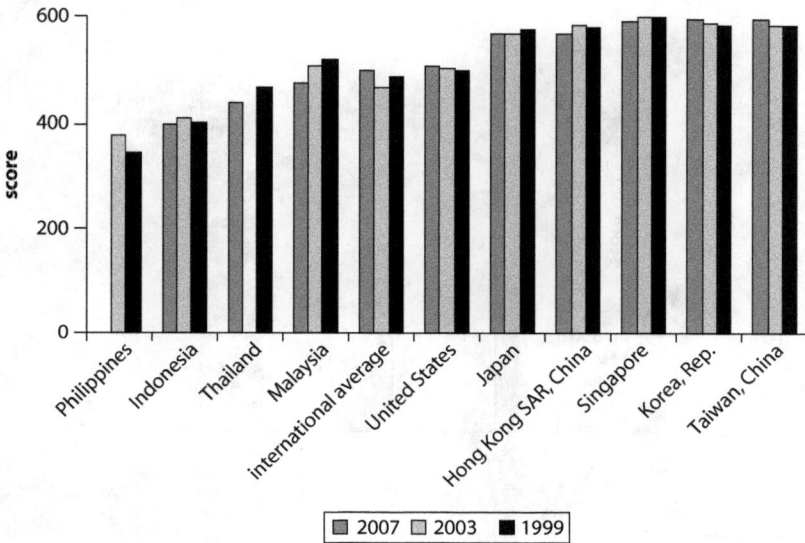

Source: IEA 2008.
Note: TIMSS = Trends in International Mathematics and Science Study.

reading portion of the PISA exam. In all three periods, females performed better than males. In 2000, the average Indonesian female's reading score was 380; in 2003, it was 393; and in 2006, it increased to 402. The respective scores for males during the same periods were 360, 369, and 383. The trend line is encouraging, and the gaps with economies such as Hong Kong SAR, China, and the United States are getting smaller. However, the scores for both females and males and the overall score (393 in 2006) were still well below the PISA reading mean of 500.

The situation is very similar for math skills (figures 5.13), where progress since 2003 is clear and the gap with more developed countries has notably decreased, but the country still has a way to go. In the 2006 PISA, Indonesia's score in math increased by 30 points (or 0.3 of a standard deviation) over the period three years earlier, a remarkable achievement. Males improved their scores by 38 points over this period (from 361 to 399), and females also improved their scores significantly (from 358 to 382). In relative terms, Indonesia's mathematics score still lags that of most of its neighbors, but the gap is getting

Figure 5.11   Trends in Indonesian PISA Reading Scores, Disaggregated by Gender, 2000–06

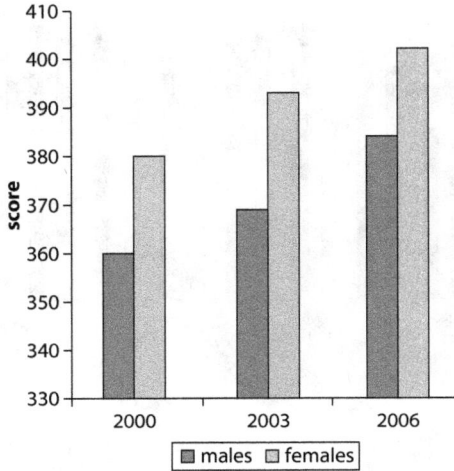

Source: OECD 2007.
Note: PISA = Programme for International Student Assessment.

Figure 5.12   PISA Reading Scores in Selected Countries, 2006

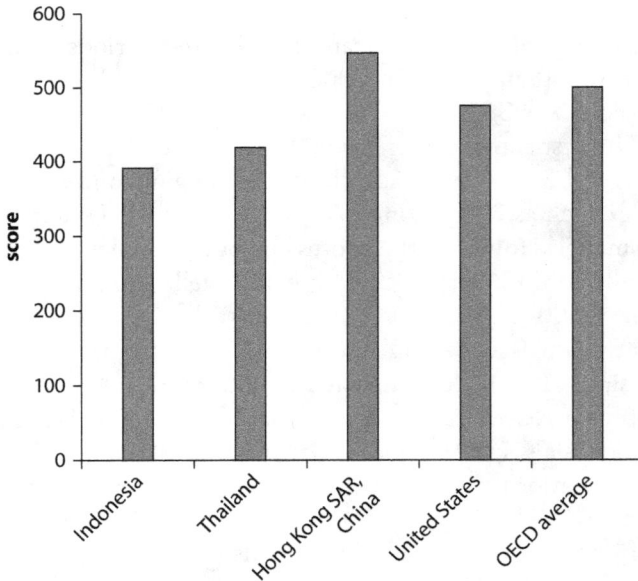

Source: OECD 2007.
Note: OECD = Organisation for Economic Co-operation and Development; PISA = Programme for International Student Assessment.

Figure 5.13   Trends in Indonesian PISA Mathematics Scores, Disaggregated by Gender, 2003 and 2006

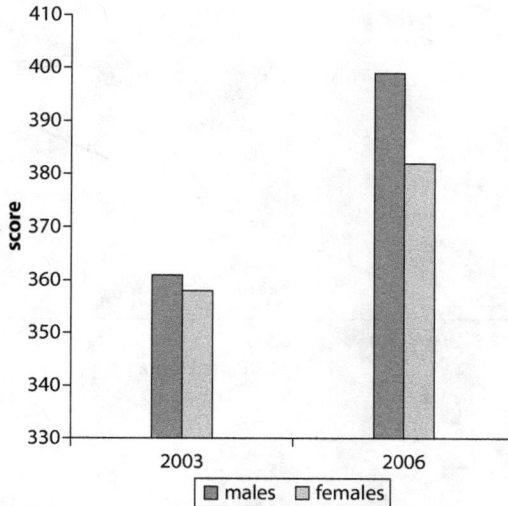

Source: OECD 2007.
Note: PISA = Programme for International Student Assessment.

smaller (and although these tests are not strictly comparable, shrank compared with the score of Hong Kong SAR, China, on the 2003 TIMSS exam). Thailand scored 417 in the 2006 PISA mathematics round, the United States 474, and Hong Kong SAR, China, 547; the OECD average was 498.

Finally, in 2006 Indonesia participated for the first time in the science portion of the PISA exam—with mixed results. As in the case of the reading and math sections of the exam, Indonesia's score of 393 was below the PISA average of 500 and the scores of comparator economies (421 for Thailand, 489 for the United States, and 542 for Hong Kong SAR, China; however, as for math, the gap with Hong Kong SAR, China, decreased relative to the 2003 TIMSS results in science).

Some positives should be noted in these findings, but efforts need to continue to bring Indonesian students' cognitive skills closer to the international standard. Historically, most developing countries have scored near the bottom of the scale in most international achievement tests. Until recently, one could find few examples of significant improvement among developing countries. Indonesia's performance in the 2006 PISA mathematics exam is a case of a developing country showing significant

Figure 5.14   Trend Line of PISA Test Scores against Log GDP Per Capita for Selected Countries, 2003

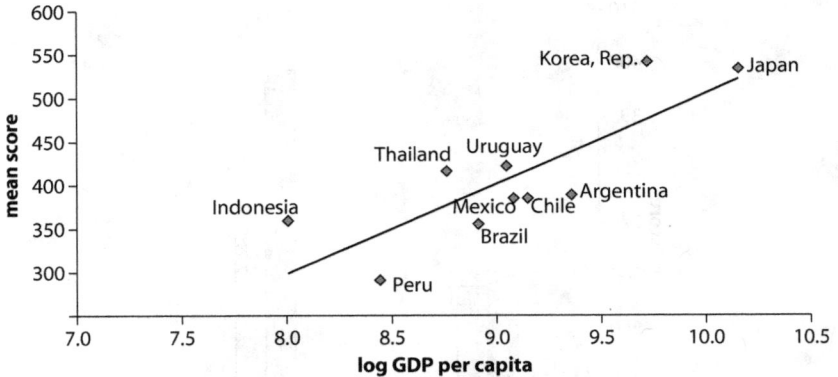

Source: di Gropello 2006.

progress. Moreover, when one looks at PISA scores against countries' income levels, Indonesia performs slightly better than the trend (figure 5.14)—that is, Indonesia is a better performer than other countries at its income level. Nevertheless, these trends do not negate the need for improving the cognitive skills of Indonesian students to bring them closer to the international standard.

As a matter for educational policy, Indonesia needs to continue improving math, reading, and science skills to bring them closer to international standards. This improvement will be critical to help build the basis for the acquisition of higher-order subject-based skills as well as generic and technical skills, which, as has been seen, are still weak. Therefore, the quality of primary and lower-secondary schools can be improved to make sure they can lead to better performance. How to enhance the quality of these schools is something that requires in-depth analysis going beyond the scope of this book.

Strengths and Weaknesses of Secondary and Tertiary Education

This section provides some insights on formal secondary and tertiary education, using further evidence from the employer and employee skill surveys, complemented with results from new country studies, assessments, and background papers. In particular, the employer and employee surveys allow a general picture to be drawn of the education and training sectors in Indonesia not only in terms of their relative merits and weaknesses but also along finer dividing lines, such as between private and public institutions or general and vocational tracks. In the employer survey, employers were asked to characterize the strengths and weaknesses of the institutions from which they have hired fresh graduates. Collectively, the 614 employers surveyed identified 198 general upper-secondary schools (*sekolah menengah umum*, or SMUs); 157 vocational upper-secondary schools (*sekolah menengah kejuruan*, or SMKs); 226 universities; and 137 tertiary vocational institutions.

Secondary Education

Secondary education has both a three-year general track (SMUs) and a three- or four-year vocational track (offered in SMK schools) provided by both public and private institutions. Within SMK institutions are further divisions: generic SMK and SMK plus. Generic SMK institutions are governed exclusively by the Ministry of National Education (MoNE) of Indonesia, which prescribes the curricula at these institutions. On average, generic SMKs require three years of coursework. The curricula at SMK-plus institutions do not have to be designed exclusively by MoNE but may also include the input of other ministries or private institutions. Four years of study are usually required at SMK-plus institutions. MoNE has mandated that SMK students pass five stages of competency before receiving a certificate of graduation,[3] and SMKs, like SMUs, are accredited by the National Accreditation Agency for Higher Education (Badan Akreditasi Nasional Perguruan Tinggi, or BAN-PT) or National Accreditation Agency for Schools and Madrasahs (Badan Akreditasi Nasional Sekolah dan Madrasah, or BAN-S/M) or by the similar provincial accreditation agency. Beyond a minimum common language core, SMUs offer three broad majors (languages, social sciences, and natural sciences), whereas SMKs offer eight specific majors.

Perhaps the most striking development in Indonesia's education sector in the past decade is the plan to significantly expand its formal TVET offerings. Responding to rising unemployment rates and the lack of appropriate skills among workers, MoNE, which oversees and administers formal vocational education, has made TVET expansion a priority and has ramped up investment in the formal TVET subsector. MoNE has set the formal and ambitious goal of shifting the ratio of students enrolled in general upper-secondary education (SMUs) to vocational upper-secondary schools (SMKs) to 30:70 by 2015. This subsection assesses some of the pros and cons of that policy.

The image of formal vocational and general secondary schools from the employer and employee skill surveys is one in which each track has both specific advantages and shortcomings. Employers have an overall positive impression of SMKs, which perform particularly well in areas linked to the labor market while remaining weaker than SMUs in terms of general curriculum coverage. Curriculum coverage is rated higher in the general track, but curriculum specificity and responsiveness to labor-market needs, as well as links to industry, are considered better in the vocational track (table 5.1). SMKs are rated highly on a number of less obvious or predictable criteria, such as quality of teaching, facilities, and curriculum balance. Nonetheless, the less positive perceptions of the SMK general curriculum possibly help explain the similar perceptions in terms of overall graduate quality and are most likely a determinant of the lesser satisfaction of the service sector with SMK graduates.

This employer perception contrasts somewhat with the employees' views. The latter recognize the same strengths of the SMKs but are generally more critical of SMK performance in other dimensions (in line with standardized assessments). In full parallelism with employers, employees recognize significant weaknesses in specific skills and relevance to labor-market needs of the general track, which conversely represent strong points of the vocational track; meanwhile, general skills are stronger in the general track (figures 5.15 and 5.16). Several other quality-related aspects, however, are considered to be weaker in vocational schools, particularly the quality of the teaching-learning process and the facilities, which are

Table 5.1   Major Strengths of Secondary Options

	Share of firms identifying variable as a strength (%)	
Option	General secondary	Formal vocational
Cycle length	75	81
Teaching quality	80	87
Teachers' skills	80	86
Facility quality	77	82
Curriculum balance	53	79
Curriculum general coverage	81	66
Curriculum-specific coverage	33	92
Relevance to labor market	32	86
Links with industry	30	81
Cost	44	43

Source: Indonesia Employer/Employee Survey of Skills/Labor Demand and Job Vacancies 2008, Employer Module.

Figure 5.15   Main Weaknesses of SMUs as Perceived by Employees

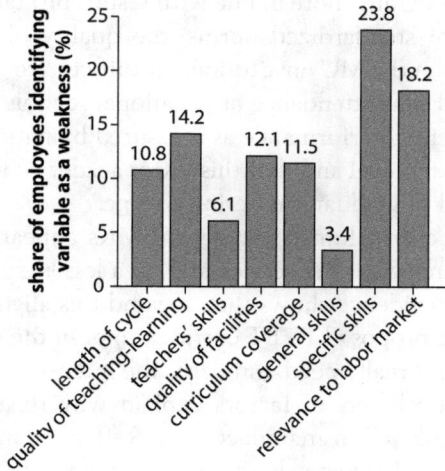

Source: Indonesia Employer/Employee Survey of Skills/Labor Demand and Job Vacancies 2008, Employee Module.
Note: SMU = *sekolah menengah umum*, or general secondary schools.

Figure 5.16   Main Weaknesses of SMKs as Perceived by Employees

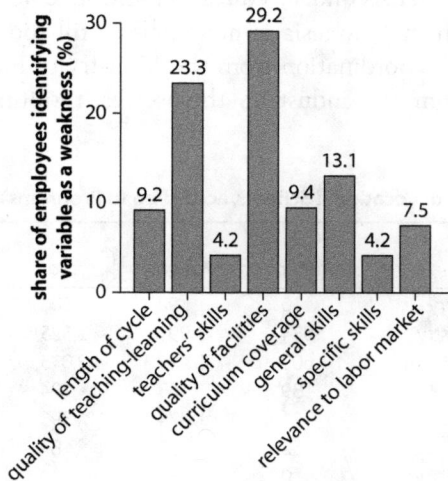

Source: Indonesia Employer/Employee Survey of Skills/Labor Demand and Job Vacancies 2008, Employee Module.
Note: SMK = *sekolah menengah kejuruan*, or vocational secondary schools.

considered significantly weaker than in the general stream. Employees' perceptions are generally more in line with results on standardized exams. In the absence of standardized norms, the quality of education being offered by SMK and SMU institutions is difficult to assess, but Chen (2009) has found that attendance at vocational schools leads to substantially lower academic performance as measured by national test scores at the lower-secondary level and that this lower academic achievement lowers the likelihood of graduates entering college.

Although the curriculum coverage of SMKs appears to be generally aligned with the needs of the service and, to a lesser extent, manufacturing sectors, some evidence shows that, beyond this alignment,[4] gaps may exist between the proposed TVET curriculum or in the way it is designed and what industries really need. Similarly, the intensity of school-industry links is lacking. Both sets of factors explain why relatively few TVET graduates are employed in manufacturing. Reflecting increasing demand from students and relative needs and priorities of the labor market, of the 6,422 vocational secondary schools in the country, more than 5,500 (86 percent) specialize in either technology and industry programs or business and management (table 5.2). Of these schools, 76 percent are private. Overall, more service-related tracks exist, in part reflecting increasing demand in that sector. Nonetheless, a recent TVET assessment (Nazara and Wicaksono 2009) confirms that although considered strong in relation to general secondary education, the specific part of the vocational curriculum in Indonesia is nonetheless still too much driven by MoNE, with little coordination from the Ministry of Industry and insufficient inputs from the industries themselves, resulting in a need for

Table 5.2   Number of Vocational Schools, according to Programs and Providers, 2006

Program	Public	Private	Total	Each program as a % of the total
Agriculture and forestry	110	90	200	3.1
Technology and industry	534	1,991	2,525	39.0
Business and management	600	2,415	3,015	47.0
Community welfare	39	65	104	1.6
Tourism	121	274	395	6.1
Art and handicraft	52	32	84	1.3
Health	0	33	33	0.5
Marine	27	39	66	1.0
Total	1,483	4,939	6,422	100.0

Sources: Data from MoNE; adapted from Martawardaya 2008b.

retraining that can discourage hiring in the first place (particularly, in manufacturing). Furthermore, although compulsory for vocational schools, the quality, length, and relevance of internships vary greatly because of random and unsystematic links between schools and industries, including weak firm participation in internship schemes. Box 5.1 illustrates the main variables explaining firms' decisions whether to participate in the most popular apprenticeship program (the Dual System of Education) and highlighting the role of financial and training capacity constraints. Lack of effective industry links can complicate hiring and job placement even when a firm might have some potential demand. Overall, both sets of issues could contribute to explaining some of the difficulties in finding the right skills for skilled production workers and the unfulfilled TVET vacancies in manufacturing.

Box 5.2 describes a successful example of a demand-driven vocational school in Indonesia that allows some useful lessons to be extracted regarding the need for an industry-based curriculum, strong partnerships between teachers with academic and practitioner backgrounds to ensure both more balanced and more relevant curriculum, and well-working industry-school collaboration in student (and teacher) training. Along that line, the employer survey evidence confirms the effectiveness of the Dual System of Education Program (box 5.1) by indicating that almost one-third of the firms participating in the program ended up hiring their apprentices. In part, this outcome is facilitated by the issuance of a certificate of competency by the partner firm (in parallel with the certificate of graduation issued by the school principal).

TVET graduates do not necessarily perform better in the labor market than general track graduates, despite TVET's greater curriculum specificity and perceived responsiveness to labor-market needs. Possibly this result is due to the high premium on general skills and quality of the teaching-learning process in Indonesia (likely to be more a factor in the service sector) and the likely gap between the design of the TVET specific curriculum and industries' real needs or the intensity of school-industry links (likely to be more important in the manufacturing sector). In fact, as the proportional enrollment share of SMK graduates has continued to decline, the gap in rates of return between SMKs and SMUs also briskly declined, showing evidence of decreased overall demand for SMK students from the labor market. Along the same lines, recent evidence confirms that a significant wage penalty exists for public SMK graduates compared to SMU graduates, which worsens as years elapse. Time-series data from 1994 to 2007 show that although SMK

Box 5.1

Basic Facts on the Dual System of Education Program for Technical and Vocational Education and Training

Of 616 responding firms in the employer skill survey, almost one in three had participated in the Pendidikan Sistem Ganda (Dual System of Education, or PSG) apprenticeship program. Main variables explaining the decision to participate in the PSG included financial and capacity-related factors (see accompanying figure). Interestingly, the variable on vocational schools needing no industry help, which is rather significant overall, loses significance in the manufacturing-only subsample.

Variables Explaining Firms' Decision Whether to Participate in the PSG

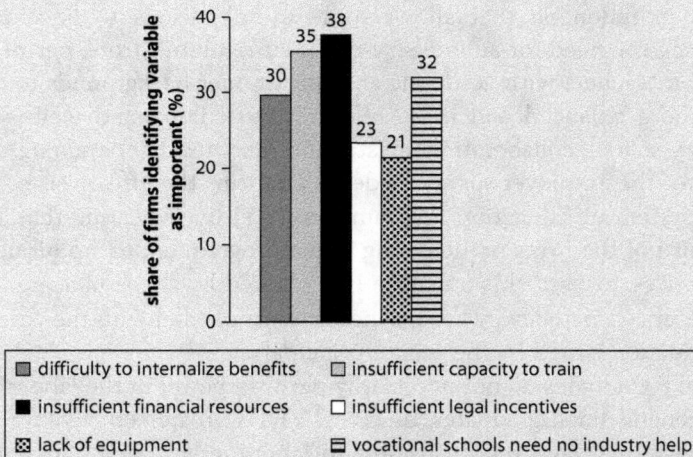

- difficulty to internalize benefits
- insufficient financial resources
- lack of equipment
- insufficient capacity to train
- insufficient legal incentives
- vocational schools need no industry help

Source: Indonesia Employer/Employee Survey of Skills/Labor Demand and Job Vacancies 2008, Employer Module.

Participating firms in the sample took more than 2,500 students in 2007 for an average length of 49 days. Roughly 30 percent of the firms that took in apprentices subsequently hired them. In the case of a PSG graduate, the partner-company plays an important role in verifying the content and result of the graduation exam, resulting in its authority to issue a parallel certificate of competency.

Source: Indonesia Employer/Employee Survey of Skills/Labor Demand and Job Vacancies 2008, Employer Module.

Box 5.2

A Successful Example of Demand-Driven Vocational Schools: The Case of Chemical-Analyst Vocational Secondary Schools

The chemical subsector is one of the most skill intensive and has a fairly high rate of return. At the same time, as seen in the previous analysis, it is also a subsector that does not complain about lack of quantity or quality of staff members and praises their technical skills, knowledge of production cycles and processes in local plants, and organizational and management expertise and creativity. What can be learned from this subsector and, in particular, its relation with vocational secondary education that makes it a successful case?

Chemical-analyst vocational secondary schools (*sekolah menengah analisis kimia*, or SMAK) have a four-year rather than three-year course of study (they are SMK-plus institutions) and adopt a dual curriculum fixed by MoNE and the Ministry of Industry. MoNE sets the curriculum for general and basic subjects such as religion, Bahasa Indonesia, health and sports, English, math, physics, chemistry, biology, and social sciences. The Ministry of Industry determines the curriculum for specific subject matters such as organic chemistry, physical chemistry, environmental chemistry, laboratory procedures, laboratory management, and chemical analysis. Additionally, SMAKs keep their curriculum updated with industry needs through various strategies, such as annual meetings between the school and the companies hosting student internships; periodic meetings with industries, usually represented by the business association; and internships for students and teachers at companies. SMAKs employ both teachers with a practitioner background (coming from the Balai Industri, a Ministry of Industry–owned research institute), who mainly teach with laboratory and technical skills, and teachers with academic backgrounds, who mainly teach basic subjects (with teaching materials often comparable to the ones applied by undergraduate studies).

As a result of these practices, SMAK graduates have excellent labor-market outcomes, and the chemical sector has the skills it needs. Notably, about 80 percent of chemical analysts at the chemical company SUCOFINDO[a] graduated from SMAKs. In comparison, just 15 percent graduated from a tertiary diploma program and only 5 percent had bachelor's degrees. SMAK graduates head most of the SUCOFINDO's laboratories around the country. Because the SMAK educational

(continued next page)

Box 5.2 *(continued)*

system is so oriented toward industrial needs, SUCOFINDO's management could ensure the consistency of laboratorial analysis results with International Organization for Standardization 17025 requirements by employing SMAK graduates rather than holders of diplomas or even bachelor's degrees. Management also perceives that SMAK graduates have the ability to adapt and adjust more quickly to new high-tech laboratory equipment than their counterparts with diplomas or bachelor's degrees. Finally, since the company reorganized its structure in 2002, newly hired employees, whatever their background, have been treated equally, all starting their career as a chemical analyst with only a modest difference in entrance salaries.

This successful program teaches the following lessons:

- Implement an industry-based curriculum, which requires the input of the Ministry of Industry, the companies themselves, and practitioners with an industry background. Strong partnerships between teachers with academic and practitioner backgrounds can ensure both a more balanced and a more relevant curriculum.
- Use varied strategies to keep the curriculum updated to meet industry needs, including regular consultations and internships (for students and teachers), which requires an interested partner industry.
- Increase the government's role (including a mediation role), if necessary, in promoting school-industry links, which are generally left to the initiative of schools and firms.

Source: Nazara and Wicaksono 2009.
a. One of SUCOFINDO'S strategic businesses deals with calibration and testing laboratory services.

graduates consistently experienced higher returns than do SMU graduates, that gap has sharply narrowed (figure 5.17), whereas the gross enrollment rate at SMKs declined between 2000 and 2006. (According to SUSENAS data, the SMK GER was 10.1 percent in 2000 and fell to 7.5 percent in 2006; at the same time, the GER in SMUs increased from 27.5 percent in 2000 to 34.4 percent in 2006.) Furthermore, recent evidence (see World Bank 2010) confirms that public SMK graduates, on average, earn 20 percent lower wages than public SMU graduates (table 5.3), and the wage penalty becomes more severe as more years pass.[5]

Figure 5.17   Wage Premium by Level of Schooling, 1994–2007

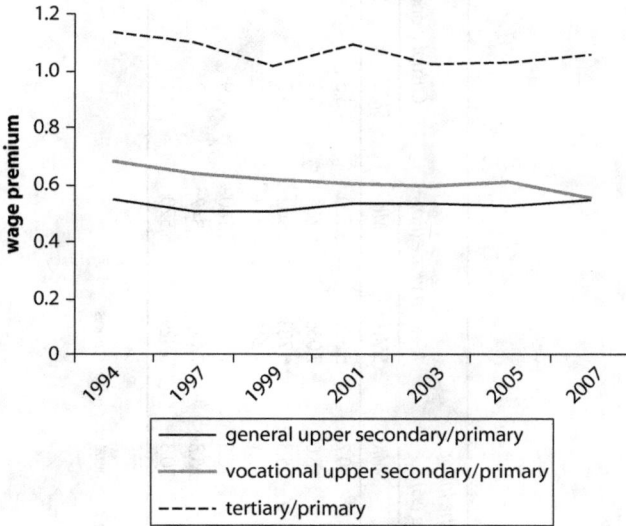

Source: di Gropello 2009, using National Labor Force Survey (Survei Angkatan Kerja Nasional, or SAKERNAS) data.

Further data indicate that SMK graduates are not necessarily more likely to be employed than SMU graduates, with the possible exception of young SMK graduates. In several years, for instance, SMK graduates have experienced higher levels of unemployment than have SMU graduates.[6] Data from the National Labor Force Survey (Survei Angkatan Kerja Nasional, or SAKERNAS) indicate that from 1990 to 1998, SMK graduates did indeed have lower rates of unemployment than SMU graduates. However, from 1999 onward, the unemployment rates for SMK and SMU graduates have been virtually indistinguishable (figure 5.18). Moreover, the recent *Indonesia Jobs Report* (World Bank 2010) estimated that few distinctions occur in employment outcomes between public SMK graduates and public SMU graduates. Public SMK graduates have a 1.1 percent lower probability of being unemployed, but this effect is not statistically significant (table 5.3). An exception needs to be made for young SMK graduates. Those SMK graduates under 24 years of age have a 7 percent lower likelihood of being unemployed than SMU graduates (which is in line with the unemployment data presented in the youth subsection).[7]

With respect to the private-public divide, different conclusions apply for the general and the vocational tracks, with private SMKs

Table 5.3 Labor-Market Outcomes of Public SMU and SMK Institutions

Labor outcome indicator	Unemployment rate (%)		Employment rate (%)		Out of the labor force (%)		Median wage (Rp)		Casual work (%)	
	SMU	SMK	SMU	SMK	SMU	SMK	SMU	SMK	SMU	SMK
Average	4.6	3.7	72.3	76.8	24.4	20.7	6,896	5,520	6.6	7.9
Male	4.8	4.0	82.5	88.2	13.7	8.6	7,065	5,764	5.3	5.7
Female	4.3	3.1	60.7	62.9	36.5	35.3	6,783	4,962	8.7	11.7
Young	18.6	15.0	40.1	53.5	50.7	37.1	3,403	3,213	18.6	18.2
Old	2.0	1.5	82.6	82.8	16.0	16.5	7,403	6,180	4.9	6.2
Advantaged	5.7	3.5	66.2	72.1	30.0	25.3	7,172	5,347	6.2	6.7
Disadvantaged	3.9	3.6	75.8	77.4	21.3	20.3	6,829	5,520	7.1	8.8

Source: World Bank 2010.

Note: SMK = *sekolah menengah kejuruan,* or vocational secondary schools; SMU = *sekolah menengah umum,* or general secondary schools.

Figure 5.18   Unemployment Rates of SMK and SMU Graduates

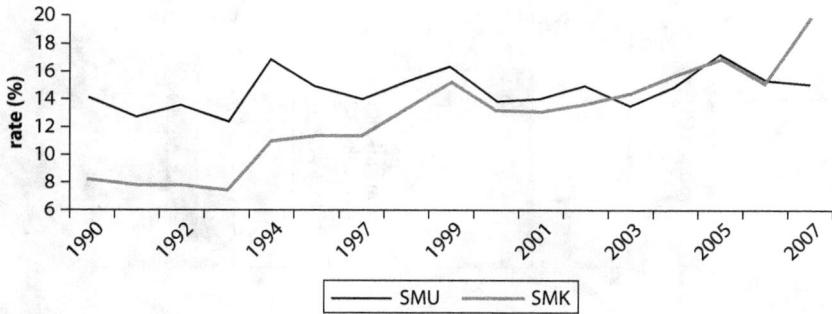

Source: World Bank 2010.
Note: SMK = *sekolah menengah kejuruan*, or vocational secondary schools; SMU = *sekolah menengah umum*, or general secondary schools.

doing particularly poorly. For general secondary education graduates, employers tend to rate equally those who attended public and private institutions (figure 5.19). If anything, variance appears greater in the private sphere (with a higher share of "below average" and "very good" ratings relative to the public sphere). Things are slightly different with regard to vocational schooling. Employers display a clear preference for public school graduates and report high levels of dissatisfaction with students of private secondary institutions (over 27 percent receive "poor" ratings; figure 5.20). This finding is generally in line with the findings of the *Indonesia Jobs Report* (World Bank 2010) that public SMK school graduates perform far better than private SMK graduates, perhaps in part because private vocational schools, which are generally much smaller than the public ones, do not have the scale to provide appropriate vocational training. Moreover, private SMK graduates face a 7 percent higher probability of being unemployed than public SMK graduates while also earning significantly less, further illustrating the employability issues of a mostly private SMK sector. In contrast, no difference in likelihood of unemployment existed between public and private SMU graduates, which tends to confirm the earlier finding of similar quality levels between public and private SMUs; however, there is evidence that for SMUs, too, graduates of private schools earned significantly less than those of public ones (about 19 percent less), pointing to a possible inconsistency between employers' perceptions of private SMU graduates and their real career prospects (table 5.4).

In sum, this mixed bag suggests that no track is clearly superior to the other, but each has advantages and disadvantages. Whereas SMKs have

Figure 5.19   Quality of Recruits from the Formal Secondary Education Track

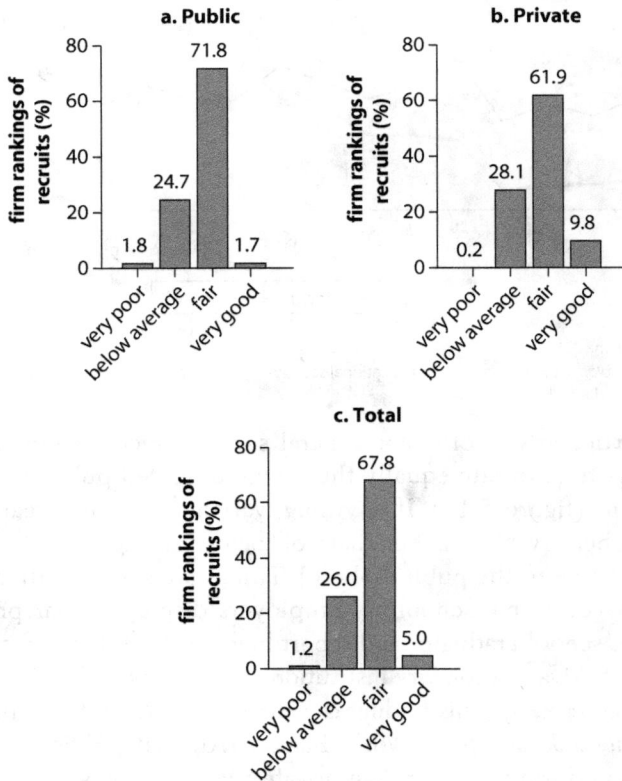

Source: Indonesia Employer/Employee Survey of Skills/Labor Demand and Job Vacancies 2008, Employer Module.

an advantage in terms of curriculum relevance to specific labor-market needs and links with the productive world that may somewhat increase employability (in particular, of current youth), they have disadvantages in terms of general curriculum and related skills and quality of the teaching-learning process that hamper earnings (in particular, in the medium or longer term and possibly in the service sector) and employment in jobs for which graduates are qualified. At the same time, the curriculum of SMKs may not be specific enough for the manufacturing sector, and the schools' links with the sector may not be strong enough to allow SMKs to fully meet the sectors' needs. Conversely, the SMUs produce more well-rounded and flexible graduates who clearly satisfy an important fraction of the labor market (and have more options of

Figure 5.20   Quality of Recruits from the Formal Vocational Secondary Institutions

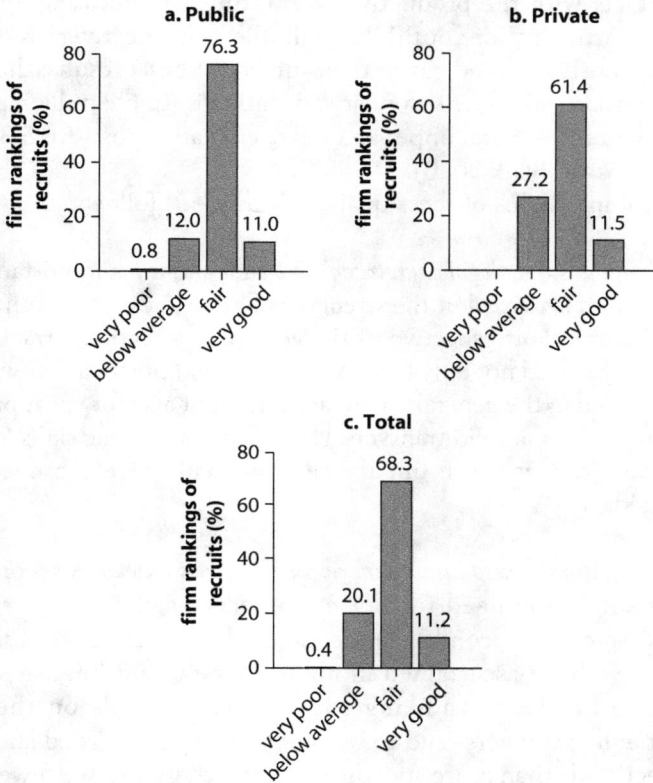

a. Public

b. Private

c. Total

Source: Indonesia Employer/Employee Survey of Skills/Labor Demand and Job Vacancies 2008, Employer Module.

Table 5.4   Labor-Market Indicators, SMUs and SMKs, Public versus Private

	SMU		SMK	
Labor-market indicator	Public	Private	Public	Private
Unemployment rate (%)	4.6	4.6	3.7	6.8
Employment rate (%)	72.3	72.2	76.8	68.9
Out of the labor force (%)	24.4	24.6	20.7	26.3
Median wage (Rp)	6,896	4,857	5,520	4,067
Casual work (%)	6.6	9.2	7.9	11.0

Source: World Bank 2010.
Note: SMK = *sekolah menengah kejuruan*, or vocational secondary schools; SMU = *sekolah menengah umum*, or general secondary schools.

mobility across jobs), but these graduates lack significantly in specificity and contacts with the productive world, thus complicating job placement (in particular, for youth). Overall, the cost-effectiveness of SMKs can be seriously doubted, given their mixed (at best) results; the cost of a public vocational upper-secondary education is Rp 6.8 million per year, whereas a public general upper-secondary education costs Rp 5.3 million per year (World Bank 2010).

Policy implications of these quality issues are as follows:

- *Build on the strengths of each track.* The first and most important policy implication is to exploit the strengths of both tracks and maintain balanced curricula irrespective of the general or vocational track, which implies the need not only for more specific and practical knowledge to be included in the general secondary track, but also for vocational education to retain a solid transversal set of core academic skills. The current situation is quite imbalanced and will therefore need to be changed.

- *Improve subject-based and generic skills across tracks.* A second overall lesson is the need for better subject-based and generic skills across tracks in secondary education, which derives from the gaps that have been ascertained in math, literacy, and English skills on the one hand and thinking and behavioral skills on the other. Although employers tend to be generally less concerned about core subject skills than more specific skills and therefore see fewer weaknesses from this perspective, the general coverage of the curriculum is clearly an issue in vocational schools, and the quality of teaching and learning could be further improved in both tracks (at least according to employees' perceptions). Vocational schools in particular need to ensure a good balance between teachers with academic and practitioner backgrounds.

- *Better design and implement the specific components of the curriculum in secondary vocational schools.* Schools should learn from the SMAK and German experience with vocational education to design a more demand-driven curriculum, which in turn requires more systematic industry input, more practitioners on staff, and stronger consultation mechanisms with industry and other relevant ministries and bodies. Indonesia should also continue to support the dual education system methodology through extensive internships in firms. This approach, which is now being more widely applied, seems particularly relevant to improving the demand-driven focus of the technology and industry curriculum, which, by its nature, is more difficult to design and implement well than the business and management curriculum (probably explaining the lesser relative number of TVET graduates in manufacturing). Some caveats do exist to this approach: (a) it requires the active participation of subsectors and firms not only in designing the curriculum and accepting and training intern students, but also in sharing training and even facility costs to make expenses manageable for the school; (b) along the same lines, it should rely as much as possible on the industry's facilities to decrease costs for the school; (c) as a consequence of the first two caveats, this approach clearly works better in subsectors with large firms, which have more means and expertise;[8] and (d) finally, it requires the government to play an intermediary, regulatory, and even possibly financial role to ensure that schools and industries connect the way they should.[9] In Indonesia, where firms and SMKs tend to be small (the chemical sector is probably one of the few exceptions with larger firms),[10] the government may need to step up its role to make the model work, which necessarily implies selective rather than broad-based support with consequences on school and enrollment targets, unless a policy of consolidating private SMKs is also implemented, which could help ease the financial burden.

- *Emphasize specific skills more and improve links with industry for the general stream.* This change would not imply adding very specific technical subjects, but rather more applied subjects, such as business, economics, and strengthened computing and English. It would also mean making the pedagogy itself more varied by supporting ways to communicate more effectively and planning short internships in relevant economic sectors.[11] Strengthening the emphasis in general curricula on science, math, and information and communication technology, together with further emphasizing developing analytical and creative thinking, could better serve the needs of the manufacturing sector. Overall, effective general secondary curricula can be designed in many different ways, and the country could learn from some successful examples around the world. As things stand, general upper-secondary graduates have too few tools for insertion in the labor market (which is particularly critical for youth with no job experience). This situation is an issue, given that only a minority of graduates, at least for a while, will continue to tertiary education.

- *Keep current the SMK:SMU enrollment ratio.* The evidence presented in this book does not support MoNE's target of shifting the ratio of students enrolled in SMUs and SMKs to 30:70 by 2015. Although vocational secondary graduates are quite intensively used in the service sector and generally appreciated in both sectors, their returns and employment prospects have, in fact, been declining and there is no sign of an overall increasing demand or shortage of such graduates. In contrast, general secondary graduates continue to be in higher demand, as returns, enrollment trends, and employment prospects seem to confirm. More than the existence of an overall shortage, the situation seems to suggest that TVET graduates could be used more intensively in the manufacturing sector and therefore should be better prepared for that role. In addition, the presence of general secondary graduates could be further increased in the service sector by improving, among other things, their practical skills. A reallocation in priorities within the TVET sector would therefore be a more helpful strategy. Other reasons that justify this strategy rather than an overall increase are related to the significant cost that would be entailed in the increase and the enrollment shift. The World Bank (2010) has estimated that achieving the 2015 target will require increased public investments of Rp 5.8 trillion per year, as well as the shift of 4.1 million students from SMUs to SMKs. This huge cost is not justified by the benefits; moreover, the cost may rise to accommodate the needed changes in the vocational model. Additionally, enrollment in SMUs has been declining, and given the recent enrollment trends, achieving the shifted ratio appears unlikely. Overall, keeping a similar ratio but improving both tracks to bring them to their full potential would be the most advisable option at this stage.

- *Review the efficiency and effectiveness of private SMKs.* The particularly poor performance of private SMKs needs special scrutiny. There may be grounds for closing or consolidating institutions to improve the quality of facilities and instruction as well as reduce costs.

- *Undertake a thorough set of tracer studies to follow secondary education graduates to learn lessons about the relevance of their education.* Such studies could interview both graduates and employers on a regular basis, ascertain what the most desirable skills for particular industries are, determine fields of education in increased or decreased demand, identify where secondary institutions can benefit from this information, and incorporate this information into their curricula.

Tertiary Education

Over the past five years, Indonesia has paid increasing attention to the higher-education subsector. Since 1999, a shift has occurred toward more public sector and fiscal decentralization, particularly in the higher-education subsector. The government's Higher Education Long-Term Strategy (HELTS), 2003–10, constituted an important part of that reform package. Seeking to remedy the relative delay of higher education in relation to the other education levels, the government designed HELTS to improve the quality of higher education, thereby helping to alleviate the shortages of higher-level skills that are slowing investment in the economy and absorption of new technologies. Box 5.3 provides a brief description of the structure of the higher-education sector.

The employer survey shows strengths and weaknesses of general (university) and technical tertiary institutions that, to a large extent, mirror the differences between general and vocational secondary education. Universities are stronger in quality of facilities, variety of fields of study, and research capacity, whereas technical institutes have closer links with industry and appear more relevant and adaptable to labor-market needs (table 5.5). They also have the benefit of a shorter cycle length. The constraints that universities seem to be facing to be more responsive to labor-market needs provide grounds for continuing support of the innovations introduced by HELTS in the ways that higher education is managed and financed. HELTS focuses on decentralizing public HEIs and making them more autonomous, thereby allowing public funding to become more demand driven. These reforms will be instrumental to creating stronger university-industry links.

Accreditation data confirm that the majority of higher-education institutions do rather well, and quality is slowly improving, but a significant proportion of institutions are still just borderline or below, suggesting room for improvement. By the standards of Indonesia's own BAN-PT,[12] the quality of education is slowly improving. The BAN-PT certified about 13 percent of undergraduate study programs as "excellent" in 2006, up from 9.1 percent in 2000 (table 5.6); 49 percent were categorized as "good," up from 38.9 percent in 2000; and only 3 percent were considered

Box 5.3

Structure of the Higher-Education Sector in Indonesia

Indonesia has five types of higher-education institutions (HEIs): single-faculty academies (*akademi*), advanced schools (*sekola tinggi*), polytechnic schools (*polteknik*), institutes (*instituti*), and universities (*universitas*). Academies are legally defined as higher-education institutions that provide instruction in only one field; most offer diplomas and certificates for technician-level courses in applied science, engineering, or art at both public and private institutions. Advanced schools provide academic and professional university-level education in one particular discipline. Polytechnic schools are attached to universities and provide subdegree junior technician training. Institutes are those HEIs that offer several fields of study by qualified faculty and are ranked as universities with full degree-granting status. Universities are larger than institutes and offer training and higher education in various disciplines.

MoNE, through the Directorate-General of Higher Education, exercises overall authority over both state and private institutions. Public universities and institutes are certified by the Directorate-General of Higher Education. Private universities are governed by the Directorate of Private Universities within the Directorate-General of Higher Education. Islamic institutes, which have the same rank as universities, are administered by the Ministry of Religious Affairs.

Structurally, Indonesia's higher-education subsector is notable for its high private sector participation: 81 public and more than 2,000 private HEIs operate in the country. According to the Directorate-General for Higher Education, 2,235 private HEIs now operate in Indonesia (see the accompanying table).

Indonesian Higher-Education Institutions, 2006

Type	Public	Private
Academies	0	715
Polytechnics	25	89
Advanced schools	0	1,043
Institutes	10	43
Universities	46	345
Total	81	2,235

Source: Data from Directorate-General of Higher Education.

Box 5.3 *(continued)*

Within this system, several stages of education are offered. Higher technical and vocational education is offered by academies, which confer diploma-level qualifications (up to three years' study) and also by polytechnic schools, which also confer diplomas. Diploma programs are considered to be professional rather than academic.

At the university level, the first stage of study is classified as Sarjana (S1). The Sarjana (or *Strata Satu*) is awarded after four years of full-time study at a recognized university, institute, or school. To obtain the S1 certification, students must obtain 144 credits, and for the fields of medicine, dentistry, veterinary science, pharmacy, and engineering, an additional two to six semesters must be added.

The Magister (S2, or *Strata Dua*) is awarded after a further two years' study in addition to research. Between 36 and 50 credits beyond S1 are required. Doktor (S3, or *Strata Tiga*) degrees require an additional two to four years beyond the Magister level. In some cases, students can pursue Doktor degree programs immediately after the first degree. They have a residential requirement of two years, and students must pass the examinations that are organized every year to check their research progress. The Doktor degree is the highest award conferred by Indonesian universities or institutes.

At the tertiary level, polytechnic schools and academies are accredited by the BAN-PT, which also accredits institutes and universities.

Source: Moeliodihardjo 2008.

"failing," down from 7.2 percent in 2000. However, about one-third of higher-education institutions are still just borderline or below. No obvious differences are seen between general or technical modalities.

Employment data confirm quality and relevance issues for higher education, which are more serious for diploma graduates, confirming a premium on curriculum coverage and general skills at that level of education. Although, as shown in previous chapters, demand for higher-education graduates remains sustained and unemployment has been decreasing, generally significant search times for new tertiary graduates (figure 5.21) combined with still significant unemployment rates confirm issues with the quality and relevance of educational results. Practical knowledge of the job remains weak across the board for university graduates, and urgent action is needed to make these graduates more appealing across all sectors.

Table 5.5   Major Strengths of Tertiary Options

Option	Share of firms identifying variable as a strength (%)	
	University	Tertiary vocational
Cycle length	54	85
Teaching quality	85	84
Teachers' skills	87	86
Facility quality	86	82
Curriculum balance	80	51
Curriculum general coverage	80	72
Curriculum-specific coverage	53	88
Relevance to labor market	50	75
Links with industry	55	78
Cost	30	41

Source: Indonesia Employer/Employee Survey of Skills/Labor Demand and Job Vacancies 2008, Employer Module.

Table 5.6   Indonesian Study Program Accreditation Levels, 2006

Type of program	A (excellent)	B (good)	C (fair)	D (failing)	Total
Diploma I	1	5	3	0	9
Diploma II	2	19	22	0	43
Diploma III	90	533	333	15	971
Diploma IV	3	9	10	1	23
S1 (bachelor's degree)	785	2,766	1,921	202	5,674
S2 (master's degree)	309	185	66	2	562
S3 (doctoral degree)	15	18	4	0	37
Total	1,205	3,535	2,359	220	7,319

Source: Data from National Accreditation Agency for Higher Education.

Additionally, shortages of higher-education graduates in manufacturing[13] (where they are quite appreciated) are likely indicative of skill mismatches that may derive from a lack of manufacturing-relevant university fields of study, in turn caused by weak links between universities and manufacturing firms. In this context, ensuring that universities become flexible and connected enough to lead to curriculum choices that satisfy the needs of manufacturing subsectors experiencing shortages (now and in the future) will be important. At the same time, the system should continue to ensure a sufficient supply of service-relevant professions (responding to the sustained demand and immediate shortages, such as those in financial services). Despite being more connected to labor markets, diploma graduates

Figure 5.21   Number of Months to Find a Job, New Graduates, 2006

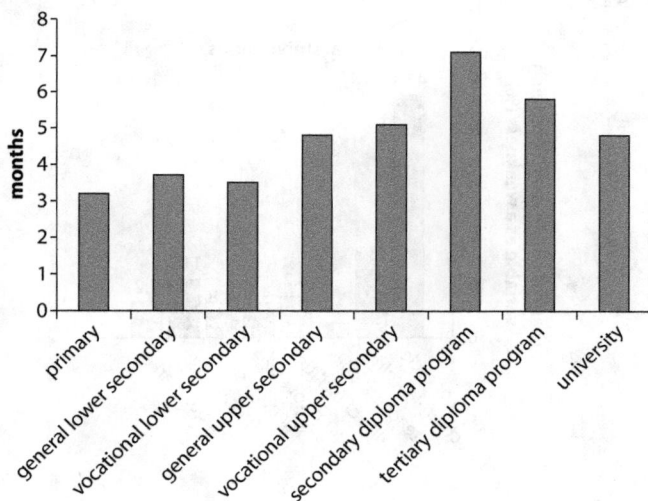

Source: Moeliodihardjo 2008.

are performing even more poorly than university graduates, judging from longer search times and lower quality of jobs eventually occupied by diploma graduates, according to the employer survey.[14] This result, which is somewhat inconsistent with employers' more rosy view of technical higher education, suggests that curriculum balance, variety, and flexibility remain at a premium in higher education in Indonesia. Laid-off university graduates in several fields and occupations—notably, architects, pharmacists, teachers, lecturers, managers, wholesale owners, insurance salespeople, and some professional technicians—are known to spend less than one month on their job search, indicating more sustained demand than for many diploma fields (Moeliodihardjo 2008).

Along these lines, although employees' perspectives somewhat mirror employers' about the relative strengths and weaknesses of both tertiary modalities, employees have a generally less positive outlook on diplomas. Universities are considered to have the same relative strengths in terms of quality of facilities, curriculum coverage, and general skills, but differences regarding the diplomas are more marked (figure 5.22). The cycle length is confirmed to be a key weakness of universities.

At the tertiary level, graduates of public institutions fare better across the board. Clearly, more private universities are performing below average

Figure 5.22   Main Weaknesses of Universities and Diploma Programs as Perceived by Employees

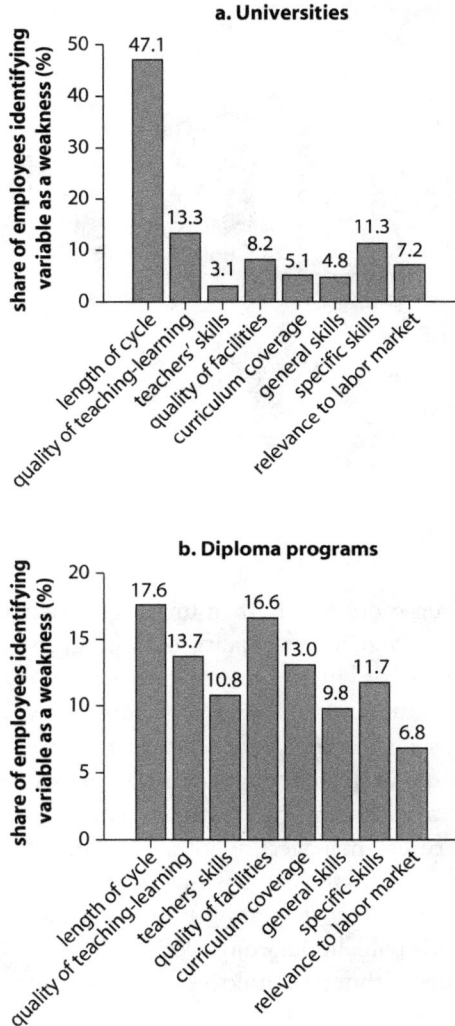

a. Universities

b. Diploma programs

Source: Indonesia Employer/Employee Survey of Skills/Labor Demand and Job Vacancies 2008, Employee Module.

than public ones, and public technical institutes perform better than private ones (figures 5.23 and 5.24). Other sources confirm these findings. In addition to the BAN-PT's assessments, which generally show lower quality for private institutions, some anecdotal evidence suggests poor quality in many private HEIs in Indonesia. The World Bank (2010), for instance,

Figure 5.23   Quality of Recruits from Universities

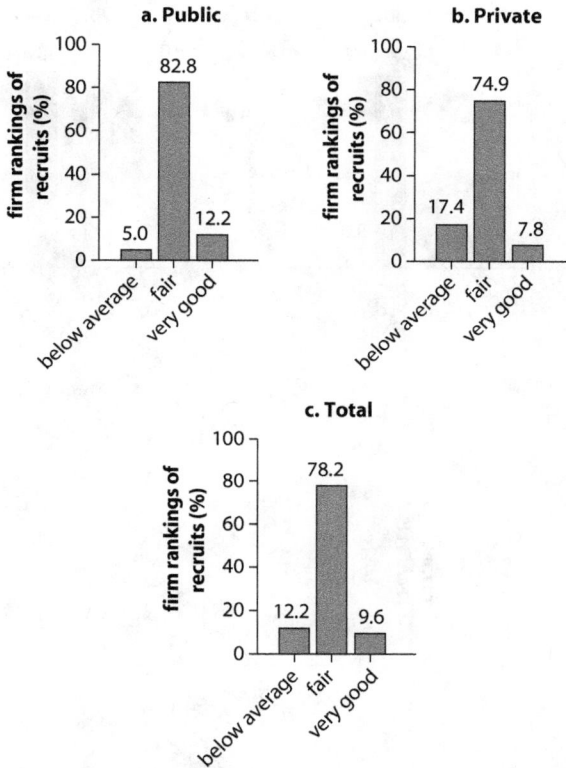

a. Public

b. Private

c. Total

Source: Indonesia Employer/Employee Survey of Skills/Labor Demand and Job Vacancies 2008, Employer Module.

noted that despite the high prevalence of private HEIs operating in the country, most are of poor quality. They acknowledge that private schools in Indonesia are often a prospective student's second choice after public schools, and they also claim that shortages of qualified staff and underdeveloped systems for supporting and financing high-quality study programs and research continue.

Finally, beyond the need to satisfy employers and the current labor market in general, strong grounds exist for strengthening the role of the higher-education sector as a driver of innovation or at least increased economic productivity and competitiveness (by creating more science and technology graduates, more PhDs, higher-level skills, and greater research capacity in general). In this area, Indonesia has an even longer

Figure 5.24   Quality of Recruits from Formal Tertiary Vocational Institutions

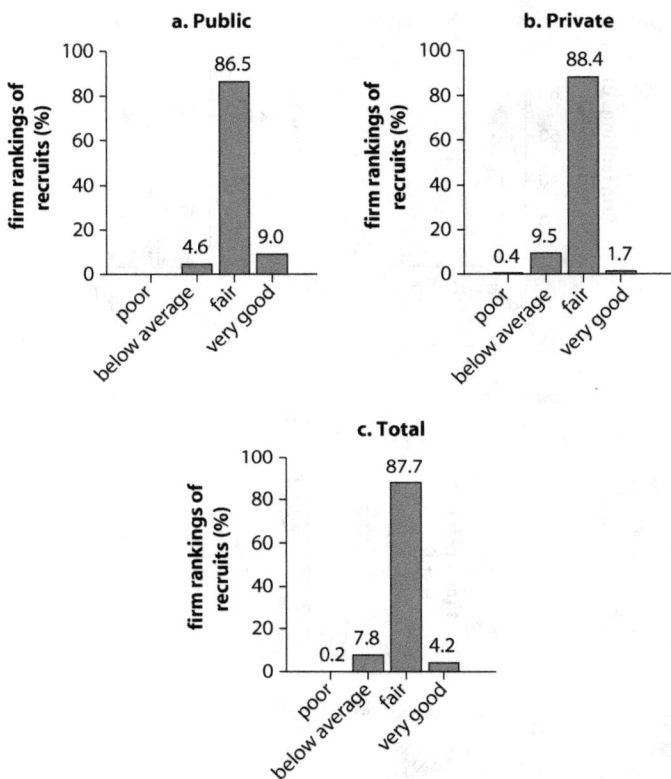

a. Public

b. Private

c. Total

Source: Indonesia Employer/Employee Survey of Skills/Labor Demand and Job Vacancies 2008, Employer Module.

way to go. Available evidence indicates that Indonesia's higher-education system is being outpaced by many of its neighbors'. Figure 5.25 provides information on patents granted, journal publications, and the number of researchers working in research and development (R&D) in Indonesia. It shows that Indonesia is significantly behind the top innovating countries, such as the Republic of Korea, as well as its more immediate neighbor, Malaysia, particularly in terms of patents granted and number of researchers.

Indonesia invests much less in R&D than many Asian countries do when measured as a percentage of GDP. It invests less than 0.5 percent of its GDP in R&D. In contrast, high innovators, such as Korea, invest over 2.5 percent. Singapore invests over 2 percent. Indonesia invests less

Figure 5.25   Innovation Indicators, Selected Asian Countries

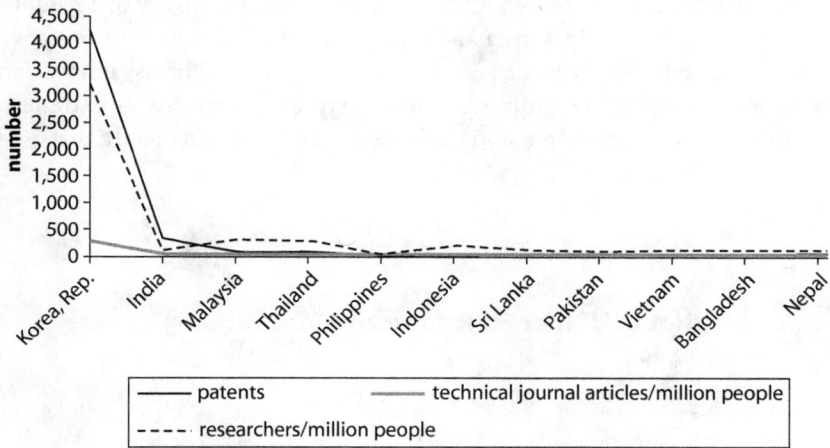

Source: Moeliodihardjo 2008.
Note: Countries are ordered by amount of GDP. Patents are the average number granted by the U.S. Patent and Trademark Office from 2001 to 2005. Technical journal articles are those published in 2003. Researchers are those working in R&D in 2004.

Figure 5.26   R&D as a Percentage of GDP, Selected Asian Countries, 1999 to Latest Available Date

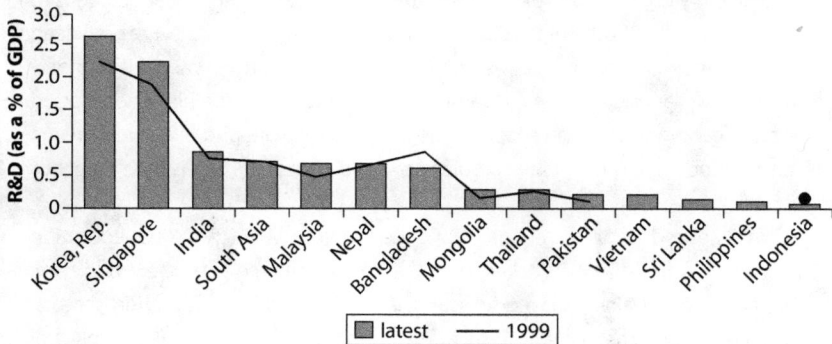

Source: Moeliodihardjo 2008.
Note: There are no data for 1999 for Vietnam, Sri Lanka, and the Philippines.

in R&D as a proportion of its GDP than Mongolia, Thailand, Pakistan, Vietnam, and the Philippines (figure 5.26). These data indicate that Indonesia has not prioritized R&D as much as some other countries, and the recent higher-education assessment has called for more investment in this area.

Microeconomic information also indicates that the innovation capacity of universities appears to be limited. A recent in-depth survey of 12 "innovative" firms in manufacturing and services suggests that universities have a very limited effect through applied research on the firms' innovation performance (box 5.4). Employers may see research capacity as a strength of university education in comparison to the diploma, but clearly this type

Box 5.4

A Snapshot of Higher Education and Innovation in Indonesia

Higher education has the potential to play two major roles in improving productivity and growth. First, it needs to provide high-quality skills that are relevant to current and developing labor-market needs. This human capital formation allows professionals and managers to perform well and efficiently in the workplace and thus support productivity and competitiveness. Second, a well-performing higher-education system should contribute to research and innovation. It should help develop a country's technological capability, which in turn supports productivity and competitiveness improvements in the longer run by reorienting, upgrading, and diversifying the country's economic base. To do so, higher education needs to be a provider of R&D by producing graduates in the hard sciences with advanced degrees and outstanding skills, as well as by developing its own capacity to undertake world-class research. In Indonesia, the extent to which the higher-education system can undertake this second function—to innovate and effectively create, supply, and spread new technologies now and in the future—is the subject of much debate.

In October 2009, to better understand the extent to which the higher-education system in Indonesia contributes to innovation at the firm level, the World Bank interviewed 12 Jakarta-based firms in the service and manufacturing sectors. Service sector firms included providers of mining services, education, financial services, research, and logistics. Manufacturing sector firms included providers of pharmaceuticals, wireless technology, and palm oil processing. Respondents were asked questions related to (a) the education levels of the top manager and employees, (b) R&D expenditure and staff training, (c) relationships with universities, and (d) innovation activities. The last topic included details of the innovation, the person who introduced it, the requisite education and skill levels, and the constraints encountered. Respondents were also asked to provide any general

Box 5.4 *(continued)*

recommendations on innovation policy as it relates to Indonesia's higher-education system.

Education Levels

These firms had a well-educated workforce by Indonesian standards. In four of the firms, 100 percent of employees were university graduates, and the figure was 60 percent to 80 percent in four more. As expected, the four firms with a highly educated workforce were in the education and research sectors. In only one firm was the percentage of employees with at least a bachelor's degree quite low—20 percent, similar to the national average. Thus, these firms are atypical in this sense and therefore might be expected to be among the more innovative. Similarly, the education of the top managers was generally high. Four had PhDs, and another five had master's degrees.

R&D and Training

Most firms were active in R&D at levels well above the national average. As would be expected, the pharmaceutical firms spent a significant proportion of their operating budget on R&D, in the range of 15 percent to 20 percent. Also not surprisingly, the wireless technology firm was the most active in R&D, spending 25 percent. Staff training varied considerably among the firms. Half of the firms had formal technical training programs of at least two weeks per year and more if needed for new projects. As expected, these firms were typically in R&D-intensive activities, where such investments are essential to retain competitive advantages. Most of the other firms arranged training on an informal and ad hoc basis.

Recent Innovation Activity

All but one firm reported some sort of innovation activity. As expected, these activities were typically "process" in nature and involved modifying and improving existing activities rather than conducting more fundamental research. Some of the innovations were embodied in recently established plants incorporating modern technology, as in the case of the mining services provider, one of the pharmaceuticals firms, and the palm oil refiner. The sectors these firms represent have been growing strongly in Indonesia over the past decade, and this growth provides the opportunity to invest in modern technology. Several firms reported information technology–based innovations, including for product grading,

(continued next page)

Box 5.4 *(continued)*

accounting systems, output monitoring, company financial reports, and inventory management. Here, also, the active innovators appeared to be those with higher levels of R&D expenditures, those with more highly qualified staff, and those in more R&D-intensive industries.

These innovations were typically top-down in nature. The chief executive officer or deputy was directly involved in four of them. Staff members with the relevant expertise (engineering or accounting) were the decision makers in another four cases. Three of the firms engaged international consultants. International sources of technology—acquired at arm's length or from the company's parent—were directly present in five cases, and probably indirectly present in most of the others. This finding highlights the importance of connections to international technology sources (which did not come up strongly in the employer skill survey, probably because of the sample's composition).

Links with Universities

Most firms had some sort of relationship with universities, although few of these relationships were richly developed. Several offered internships, apparently as a means of informal recruitment and talent spotting. Some firms engaged university staff members as consultants and guest lecturers. The wireless technology manufacturer had a formal, ongoing training relationship with a foreign university. This firm also spent the most on R&D and was clearly the most innovative in the sample, a factor no doubt dictated by its location in an R&D-intensive industry.

Innovation, Education, and Skills

Respondents varied as to the importance of education levels in the innovation process. Two regarded PhDs as necessary—not surprisingly, the wireless technology manufacturer and one of the pharmaceutical firms. The majority of the remaining respondents thought that a master's degree was sufficient. Two firms reported that the requisite skills were obtained through outsourcing. On-the-job experience was also mentioned and was presumably relevant in most cases.

As to the skill levels required, all firms (except one nonrespondent) emphasized the importance of relevant industry-specific technical knowledge and a broad understanding of the company's general operations. Several referred to the importance of understanding international best practice. Some respondents emphasized the importance of generic skills such as being curious, proactive, and creative; significantly, these remarks originated from firms with a general commitment to R&D and education.

Box 5.4 *(continued)*

Constraints to Innovation

The constraints to innovation were diverse. The more innovative firms drew attention to the difficulty of recruiting overseas workers and the country's weak protection of intellectual property rights. Several firms mentioned a general lack of international exposure and knowledge on the part of staff members; language barriers are presumably also relevant here. Firms also pointed to the lack of original, commercially relevant research originating in Indonesian universities and the lack of a central or regional research hub. The poor technical quality of Indonesian university graduates was also highlighted, with the notable exception of the country's premier institute, the Bandung Institute of Technology. A lack of clustering opportunities was also seen as an obstacle. This common observation from Indonesian field research reflects the absence of scale in some cases. Financial constraints were reported in only one case. These issues are discussed in more detail in the World Bank's upcoming regional flagship study *Higher Education, Skills, and Innovation in East Asia* (di Gropello forthcoming).

Source: Hill and Tandon 2010.

of research does not really support innovation. Higher potential through higher-level skills seems possible, as long as universities produce sufficient postgraduate students and the combination of job-specific and generic skills that enhances the propensity to innovate. Unfortunately, employers complain about gaps in theoretical job knowledge, creative thinking, and knowledge of English, which require action at a more basic level.

A need exists for stronger links between universities and industries. The capacity to innovate and to leverage this investment depends, too, on the capacity of faculty and researchers in the higher-education system who perform this work. Several universities in Indonesia have high concentrations of PhD holders, which indicates that these universities likely have strong capacities to innovate that could be better exploited by offering better and more incentives for research—including stronger links between universities and firms, which would support more applied research. These links are obviously weak now, as shown by the field-work evidence. Box 5.5 illustrates the recent Chinese experience with commercialization of university research, which could provide a useful example for some Indonesian universities.

Box 5.5

University-Industry Links in Beijing

In China, several universities and research institutes have put significant emphasis on the commercialization of their research. In Beijing in particular, universities have developed close relationships with industry through joint projects, professional consulting, and training. According to a 2000 survey, among 8,278 research projects under way in Beijing universities, 1,540 were conducted in cooperation with firms, and another 795 were technology service contracts. To promote the commercialization of university research results and patent licensing, Beijing universities signed 1,159 technology transfer contracts with industry worth more than 800 million yuan. Moreover, Beijing universities have worked with industry to establish numerous spin-offs and for-profit enterprises. Beijing has the most university-affiliated enterprises, and they are the largest in terms of sales and profit; the two leading universities in terms of commercialization are Tsinghua University and Peking University. Each has established an internal technology licensing organization to promote collaboration with industry and industrial technology transfer.

Source: Wu 2010.

In summary, although universities are generally considered to be of better quality than secondary education institutions, they still have a way to go to produce higher-quality graduates who are sufficiently relevant to the needs of both the manufacturing and service sectors. Practical knowledge is still weak across the board, and universities remain quite unconnected from the needs of the labor market, judging from rather negative opinions on their capacity to link with industries and adapt to changing labor-market needs. Lack of links is likely to be particularly serious in manufacturing, given the difficulty that the sector encounters in filling its professional positions. To be able to support innovation through applied research, universities have an even longer way to go, and the provision of skills for innovation also needs to be improved. Although more connected to labor markets, diploma graduates are, in fact, performing even more poorly than university graduates, suggesting that curriculum balance, variety, and flexibility remain at a premium in higher education in Indonesia. Finally, weaknesses are stronger for private tertiary institutions across the board.

Policy implications for tertiary institutions are as follows:

- *Build on the strengths of each track.* Building on the strengths of each tertiary education track and maintaining more balanced curricula are important and require universities to become stronger in providing practical knowledge and in adapting to labor-market needs generally. Institutions granting diplomas need to make sure that they provide a solid transversal set of core academic skills. The role and focus of diplomas in Indonesia need to be reassessed given their poor labor-market outcomes.

- *Provide incentives to improve university-industry links.* Universities need to be further encouraged to link with industries for purposes of curriculum (particularly critical for the manufacturing sector), training, and research. More management flexibility will help, but the government may also need to play a role in improving the legal framework and other incentives for collaboration. More incentives for technology transfer are needed, including setting up internal technology licensing organizations within universities to help promote collaboration with industry and industrial technology transfer. The country's weak protection of intellectual property rights should also be strengthened.

- *Provide skills for innovation.* Additional emphasis needs to be put on providing skills for innovation. In that respect, universities would be particularly well positioned to address the general lack of international exposure and knowledge on the part of staff members, which is presumably linked to language barriers. They should also enhance creative thinking through exposure to different learning and teaching methodologies.

- *Review quality of private institutions and publish accreditation results.* Although private tertiary education institutions are part of the BAN-PT accreditation process, the quality of such institutions remains an issue and should be more closely monitored. Remedial actions should be taken to decrease the number of underperforming institutions, including, if needed, closing failing or nonperforming HEIs. Together with regular publication and dissemination of outcomes of accreditation results, this action would signal a commitment to quality, guide and influence the behavior of tertiary education institutions, and inform students more clearly about which institutions provide better education.

- *Undertake a thorough set of tracer studies to follow tertiary education graduates to learn lessons about the relevance of their education.* Such studies could interview both graduates and employers on a regular basis, ascertain what are the most desirable skills for particular industries, determine fields of education with increased or decreased demand, and identify where HEIs can benefit from this information and incorporate this information into their curricula.

Notes

1. The Islamic levels of education are Islamic kindergarten, *ibtidaiyah* (primary), *tsanawiyah* (lower secondary), *aliyah* (upper-secondary general and vocational), and the Islamic institute or university.
2. Data are from the World Bank's EdStats database.
3. These stages are as follows: Level Examination (Uji level); Dual System of Education Exam (Pendidkan Sistem Ganda); Competency Examination (Uji Kompetensi); National Examination (Ujian Nasional); and School Final Exam (Ujian Akhir Sekolah).
4. This alignment between vocational schools and labor-market needs is clearly closer than in general secondary education.
5. This finding is in line with a lot of the international evidence, which shows that difficulties in retraining vocational graduates may explain their decreased probability of employment and earning potential over time.
6. It is important to note here that SMK and SMU graduates have similar socioeconomic backgrounds in Indonesia.
7. With regard to gender, female SMK graduates have a 2 percent lower likelihood of being unemployed. However, the same data suggest that although female SMK graduates are slightly more likely to be employed, they are also more likely to have an inferior job. For instance, they are 3.5 percent more likely to be engaged in casual work than are SMU graduates.
8. This conclusion is corroborated by the constraints that lack of capacity and means represent for participation in the PSG.
9. This role will be inversely proportional to the size and means of schools and firms.
10. The chemical sector, which has larger firms, is probably one of the few exceptions.
11. Incidentally, these are all changes that would make general secondary graduates more appealing to the service sector, which is currently overusing vocational graduates in relative terms.

12. The BAN-PT was established to introduce a quality-awareness and self-assessment tradition among public and private sector providers. It has recently begun to reference international benchmarks in its accreditation processes (though this process is still incipient). Ratings are based on assessors' views of an institution's (a) quality of institutional governance, (b) faculty quality, (c) training program quality and content, (d) facility quality, and (e) student quality. Ratings are valid for four years, after which each vocational provider must seek reaccreditation.

13. Fairly high rates of return on these graduates in that sector (higher than in the service sector) combined with particular difficulties in filling professional positions and the role of quantity constraints in manufacturing illustrate these shortages.

14. As mentioned in chapter 2, there is strong evidence that the diploma stream may be operating mainly as an extension of secondary education. Graduates of diploma schools perhaps command higher positions than students who achieved only a secondary-level education, but a diploma does not really open the door to occupations dominated by university graduates.

References

Chen, Dandan. 2009. "Vocational Schooling, Labor Market Outcomes, and College Entry." Policy Research Working Paper 4814, World Bank, Washington, DC.

di Gropello, Emanuela, ed. 2006. *Meeting the Challenges of Secondary Education in Latin America and East Asia: Improving Efficiency and Resource Mobilization.* Washington, DC: World Bank.

———. 2009. "Demand for Skills and Skill Gaps in Indonesia." Background report for *Indonesia Jobs Report: Towards Better Jobs and Security for All,* World Bank, Jakarta.

———. Forthcoming. *Higher Education, Skills, and Innovation in East Asia.* Washington, DC: World Bank.

Embassy of the Republic of Indonesia in London. 2000. "Education System in Indonesia." http://www.indonesianembassy.org.uk/education_system.html.

Hill, Hal, and Prateek Tandon. 2010. "Higher Education and Technological Capability in Indonesia." Background paper for *Higher Education, Skills, and Innovation in East Asia,* World Bank, Washington, DC. http://siteresources .worldbank.org/EASTASIAPACIFICEXT/Resources/226300- 1279680449418/HigherEd_InnovationandTechnologicalCapabilityinIndonesia .pdf.

IEA (International Association for the Evaluation of Educational Achievement). 2008. *TIMSS 2007 International Mathematics Report*. Boston: TIMSS & PIRLS International Study Center, Lynch School of Education, Boston College.

Martawardaya, Berly. 2008a. "Characteristics and Outcomes of the Education System in Indonesia." Background paper prepared for this book, World Bank, Washington, DC.

———. 2008b. "Policy Note on TVET/Secondary Education in Indonesia." Background paper prepared for this book, World Bank, Washington, DC.

Moeliodihardjo, Bagyo. 2008. "Higher Education Sector Assessment." World Bank, BAPENAS (National Development Planning Agency, and Ministry of National Education, Jakarta.

———. 2010. "Equity and Access in Higher Education: The Case of Indonesia." Background paper for *Higher Education, Skills, and Innovation in East Asia*, World Bank, Washington, DC. http://siteresources.worldbank .org/INTEAST ASIAPACIFIC/Resources/Indonesia-EquityandAccessinHigherEducation .pdf.

Nazara, Suahasil, and Padang Wicaksono. 2009. "Skills Development Strategy: The Indonesian Case Study on the Pre-employment Vocational Education and Training (VET)." Background study in collaboration with the World Bank, Demographic Institute, Faculty of Economics, University of Indonesia, Jakarta.

OECD (Organisation for Economic Co-operation and Development). 2007. *PISA 2006: Science Competencies for Tomorrow's World*. 2 vols. Paris: OECD.

———. 2009. *PISA 2009 Assessment Framework: Key Competencies in Reading, Mathematics and Science*. Paris: OECD.

World Bank. 2010. *Indonesia Jobs Report: Towards Better Jobs and Security for All*. 2 vols. Jakarta: World Bank.

Wu, Weiping. 2010. "Higher Education Innovation in China." Background paper for *Higher Education, Skills, and Innovation in East Asia*, World Bank, Washington, DC. http://siteresources.worldbank.org/INTEASTASIAPA CIFIC/Resources/China-HigherEducationInnovation.pdf.

CHAPTER 6

Training the Unskilled and Updating the Skills of the Labor Force

A Brief Overview of the Informal Education and Training System and On-the-Job Training

This chapter provides some insights on informal education and training as well as on-the-job training, using further evidence from the employer and employee skill surveys, complemented with results from new country studies, assessments, and background papers. In particular, the employer survey includes a fairly comprehensive section on firm training, assessing coverage, content, structure, and incentives. The analysis of this chapter is nevertheless more limited than the chapter on formal education because of the lack of comprehensive data and evaluations and because of the difficulties of categorizing and covering all the programs that are directed to the unskilled (young or old) or address skill obsolescence. For instance, beyond analyzing the survey results of on-the-job training and documenting the new qualification framework, the chapter deals little with issues related to the implementation of a lifelong learning system. Still, some of the constraints for lifelong learning are identified. The first section of the chapter briefly summarizes the state of the country's informal education offerings, and the second section reviews the main characteristics of on-the-job training and its effectiveness in allowing workers to update and improve their skills.

Despite little available data and lack of comprehensive impact evaluations, this chapter finds that informal programs are flourishing and producing some initially positive results. Quality is still very much at stake, but the development of a skill-based competency and qualification framework that creates bridges between the informal and formal sectors has the potential to improve quality. This framework will help set the stage for a still largely absent lifelong learning approach in Indonesia, the need for which is illustrated by the remedial or short-term nature of upgrading and updating of the country's on-the-job training. Consistent with the lack of preparation of young workers and the importance of practical on-the-job skills and in a context of budget constraints, formal on-the-job training is very much focused on young and relatively skilled workers, with an overall emphasis on job-specific skills and more emphasis on generic skills in the service sector.

Informal Education

Increasing numbers of Indonesians—particularly low-income and older workers as well as unemployed youth—are turning to informal educational providers to upgrade their skills and knowledge. Although improving, educational attainment remains quite low overall; many youth are not in school, and significant inequities exist in access to formal education. In this context, informal education becomes a critical tool to provide a bridge to skill acquisition. Almost all of those who entered informal education programs dropped out of the formal education system before completing secondary school. Indeed, according to the National Socioeconomic Survey (Survei Sosial Ekonomi Nasional, or SUSENAS), of the approximately 4.4 million dropouts from formal education in 2003, about 1 million entered the government's equivalency educational system as a means of finding second-chance opportunities and alternative pathways to employment.

The goals of Indonesia's informal education programs are to substitute and in some cases supplement formal education within the context of lifelong learning (provision of skills for life, or life skills). Articulating a strategic direction, Law 20/2003 stated that national informal education offerings should consist of life skills, early childhood education, youth education, women's empowerment education, literacy, vocational skills and training, equivalency, and other education. The government has categorized informal education along the following lines:

- Equivalency program (an alternative to formal education)
- Community education (functional literacy and life skills)
- Commercial courses (vocational skills)

The government's informal education offerings encompass all age levels, from early childhood education and development to youth education to vocational training to equivalency certification. Of these, the most popular programs are the equivalency initiatives—*Pakets* A, B, and C—and informal vocational training, that is, the public vocational training centers (*balai latihan kerja*, or BLKs) and private training centers (see box 6.1 for a description and some characteristics of these programs). In recent years, the government has stepped up efforts to tackle youth unemployment by

Box 6.1

Structure of the Informal Education Sector in Indonesia

Equivalency Program

The Directorate for Equivalency Education, under the Ministry of National Education (MoNE), administers the equivalency program in Indonesia (although it receives funds from different sources). The program allows participants who have not had access to the formal educational system to achieve formal qualifications. The country's equivalency program is known as *Paket*. *Paket* A is equivalent to primary school, *Paket* B to lower-secondary school, and *Paket* C to upper-secondary school. Together, *Pakets* A and B fulfill the requirement of basic education. These programs are especially vital to those living in remote and isolated areas. In 2006, more than 8 million children were enrolled in *Paket* programs (World Bank 2010a, chapter 9). Most of these children were overage. In the absence of systematic data (for example, the age and number of participants, enrollment rates, and dropout rates), evaluating the quality and effectiveness of the country's equivalency programs is difficult. More and better information is obviously needed. The equivalency program relies on a very active dissemination and socialization strategy to reach out to the most remote areas.

Informal Vocational Training

In addition to equivalency programs, both public and private institutions offer short-term informal vocational training opportunities. These programs are alternatives to formal vocational education offerings and focus on preparing workers and trainees to enter the job market with specific, upgraded skills. They are largely under the auspices of the Ministry of Manpower and Transmigration (MoMT).

(continued next page)

Box 6.1 *(continued)*

BLKs

Public informal vocational training centers (known as BLKs) are administered by district governments in a decentralized system. Originally administered under a centralized system, they were created to target poor individuals who had dropped out of the primary or secondary education cycle. Currently, 162 BLKs are operating in Indonesia. They are financed mainly through government budget allocations. Some BLKs also perform modest revenue-generating activities.

BLKs provide four types of training: institutional training, noninstitutional training, apprenticeship programs, and demand-based training. Institutional training is defined as those job-training programs that aim to increase the skills of job seekers. Noninstitutional training is provided for people in remote areas through mobile training units. Apprenticeship programs work directly in industries. Demand-based training caters to industries' demand.

Three types of BLKs exist, defined by their geography. Type A (20 percent of all BLKs) are the largest training providers and are located in urban areas; type B (10 percent) are located in smaller urban centers; and type C (70 percent) are the smallest providers and are located in rural areas. Larger centers provide industrial and service skills training, whereas smaller ones offer training in appropriate technologies and skills for self-employment. In 2003–04, about 34,759 trainees went through regional or local BLKs, and 7,873 trainees went through MoMT BLKs. By 2007, only 11 BLKs remained under the auspices of the MoMT; the rest had shifted to the administration of regional and local governments.

Most BLK participants receive certificates of completion. They then have the option of taking a company trainee exam as well as a professional association exam to receive certificates from the company and association in addition to the completion certificate. The basis for most association examination systems is Indonesia's National Qualification Framework (Kerangka Kualifikasi Nasional Indonesia, or KKNI) and National Competency Standard (Standar Kompetensi Kerja Nasional Indonesia, or SKKNI).

Private Informal Training Centers

Private informal training centers are administered under the auspices of MoMT or MoNE. To be registered with the government, these providers must provide MoNE with a training curriculum, a list of staff qualifications, a description of their training facilities, a financial statement, a proposed evaluation and certification system,

Box 6.1 *(continued)*

and evidence of an education governance and management scheme. Each training center has to be accredited by the National Accreditation Agency for Informal Educational Units (Badan Akreditasi Nasional Pendidikan Nonformal, or BAN-PNF).

MoNE has classified three types of private informal training:

- Training to increase proficiency in specific subjects, such as math, English, or science
- Training to enhance various technical skills, such as computer literacy and electronics
- Professional development training, such as secretarial and public relations training.

The majority of training centers fall under the second category and teach practical skills, such as sewing, hairdressing, and computer literacy. Training in computer literacy, accounting, and English has been the most in demand. These private training centers receive funding through tuition fees and contracts with employers.

Private training centers are much more numerous than their public counterparts (in 2005, there were about 25,000 training centers registered at MoNE or MoMT that offered more than 100 types of skills divided into 10 categories). They also reach many more students: 4.5 million, compared with 50,000 students reached by public institutions.

Sources: Martawardaya 2008; Nazara and Wicaksono 2009.

leveraging the informal sector more aggressively. In consultation with the World Bank, it has developed the Education for Youth Employment (EYE) program, which supplements *Paket* B with life skills training, improved education management, and teacher training modules, while placing youth in jobs through networking in the industrial or business world. The program focuses on uneducated or undereducated youth, between 16 and 24 years of age, who are poor and jobless. Programs to support a more effective school-to-work transition also include the Professional Course (Kursus Para Profesi, or KPP) program to create alternative paths to employment. The KPP program provides training and education to disadvantaged youth, concentrating on job skills that are directly in demand by employers. It is a government-initiated program designed to address current market constraints and failures by giving incentives to private training providers so that they provide demand-driven training to disadvantaged youth and link them to domestic and overseas jobs.

The results from the employer survey indicate that informal secondary and postsecondary options are still below par with formal programs, although doing relatively well in terms of relevance and adaptability to labor-market needs. Employees generally share similar perceptions but place more emphasis on quality weaknesses. Quality of facilities, curriculum balance, and generic curriculum coverage are clear weaknesses for secondary equivalency or training programs, whereas quality of facilities, variety of fields of study, and research capacity are, not surprisingly, weaknesses for postsecondary programs (see figure 6.1). Informal programs do not have the same overall quality as formal education and training, at least according to employers. Interestingly, however, the secondary-level informal programs (judged of overall better quality than the postsecondary ones according to the previous evidence on quality of graduates) perform quite well in terms of links with the productive world and relevance to labor-market needs, according to employers. Employees' perceptions of informal skill training programs (figure 6.2) confirm weaknesses in terms of quality of facilities and strengths in terms of specific skills and relevance to labor-market needs. Interestingly, however, they find stronger relative weaknesses in the quality of the teaching-learning process in these programs than do employers, but at the same time, employees find curriculum design and general skills to be more of a strength than a weakness. This finding may suggest that employers are overall more attentive to relevance than quality issues, while the converse is true of employees, who are the ones who actually attend the programs.

Although quality issues are real, it is encouraging to see that a rather comprehensive National Qualification Framework (KKNI) and National Competency Standard (SKKNI) has been put in place in Indonesia (under the auspices of MoMT[1]) to build a bridge between competencies acquired in the formal and informal systems. One hopes the KKNI and SKKNI will encourage better quality of the informal system while also laying the groundwork for lifelong learning. In particular, after they obtain their certificate of completion, BLK graduates have the option of getting a professional association–issued certificate so that their skills are more broadly recognized. To be acknowledged at the national level, BLK graduates have to be awarded national-level professional certification (*lembaga sertifikasi profesi*), which needs to refer to the KKNI and SKKNI.

Figure 6.1   Main Strengths of Informal Education as Perceived by Employers

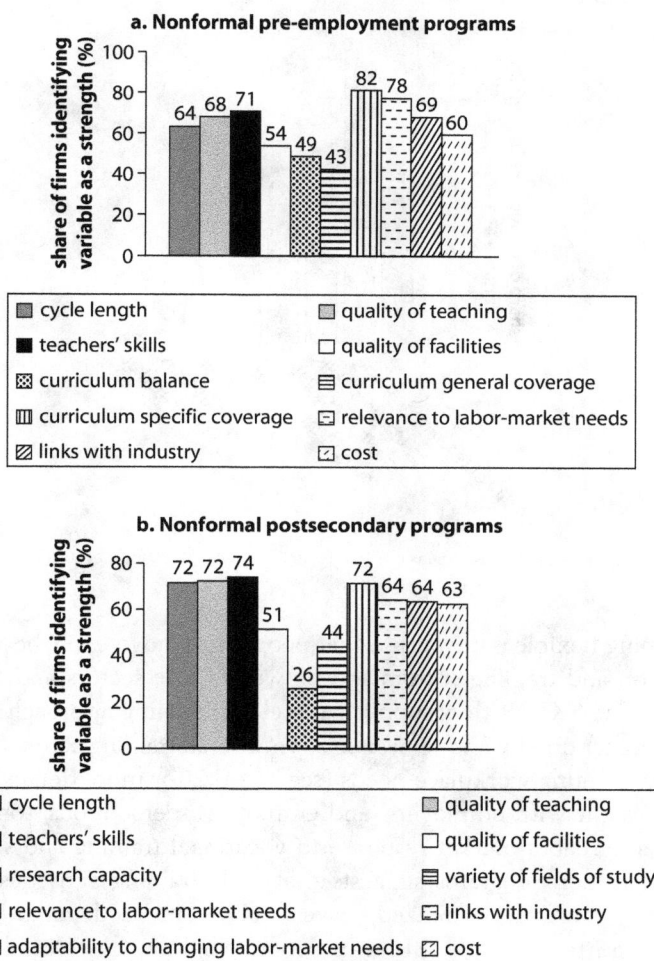

a. Nonformal pre-employment programs

share of firms identifying variable as a strength (%)

Values shown: 64, 68, 71, 54, 49, 43, 82, 78, 69, 60

Legend:
- cycle length
- teachers' skills
- curriculum balance
- curriculum specific coverage
- links with industry
- quality of teaching
- quality of facilities
- curriculum general coverage
- relevance to labor-market needs
- cost

b. Nonformal postsecondary programs

share of firms identifying variable as a strength (%)

Values shown: 72, 72, 74, 51, 26, 44, 72, 64, 64, 63

Legend:
- cycle length
- teachers' skills
- research capacity
- relevance to labor-market needs
- adaptability to changing labor-market needs
- quality of teaching
- quality of facilities
- variety of fields of study
- links with industry
- cost

Source: Indonesia Employer/Employee Survey of Skills/Labor Demand and Job Vacancies 2008, Employer Module.

Furthermore, they can get their skills acknowledged internationally by seeking a certification from the International Professional Association, which will provide opportunity to work overseas as an expert. Overall, the SKKNI not only will provide nationally consistent recognition of outcomes achieved in postcompulsory education or promote national and international recognition of qualifications, but also will help with

Figure 6.2   Main Weaknesses of Informal Skills Training Programs as Perceived by Employees

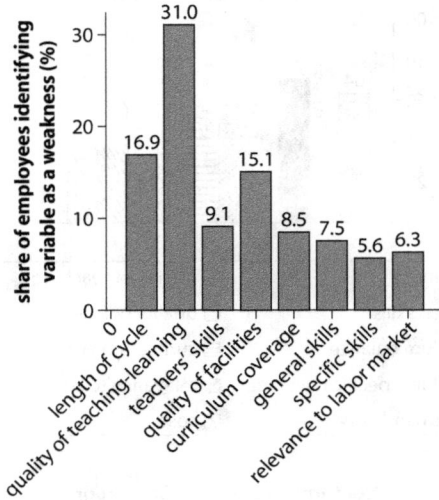

Source: Indonesia Employer/Employee Survey of Skills/Labor Demand and Job Vacancies 2008, Employee Module.

developing flexible pathways so that people can move easily between the education and training sectors and between those sectors and the labor market. The SKKNI thus supports a lifelong learning approach and promotes higher quality and relevance of vocational training across the board through meeting workplace needs (see box 6.2 for more details).

Consistent with employers' and employees' perceptions, some initial evidence on labor-market response to vocational training and school-to-work transition programs suggests that BLK training activities, beyond becoming more decentralized, have become more demand oriented. During the past decade, BLKs' program portfolio has steadily shifted from institutional and noninstitutional government-sponsored training to demand-based training. Demand-based training is tailored to company needs. In 1993–94, only 20 percent of BLK graduates participated in demand-based training; this figure increased to 45 percent in 2003. The fact that BLK graduates still need to take an additional company exam to have their skills recognized by the company may, however, imply either that this vocational training is still not demand driven enough (more company input into curriculum design or more internships may be needed) or that the completion exam is not taken as an accurate skill predictor.[2] Poor quality of BLKs may also be an issue, according to MoMT

Box 6.2

Introducing Skill-Based Competencies in Indonesia

In partnership with the Australian government, MoMT is drawing on the Australian Qualification Framework to develop its own system of defining skill competencies, known as SKKNI.

The objectives of the SKKNI initiative are as follows:

- Provide nationally consistent recognition of outcomes achieved in postcompulsory education.
- Help in developing flexible pathways that allow people to move easily between the education and training sectors and between those sectors and the labor market by providing the basis for recognition of prior learning, including credit transfer, work experience, and life experience.
- Integrate and streamline the requirements of participating providers, employers and employees, individuals, and interested organizations.
- Offer flexibility to suit the diversity of purposes of education and training.
- Encourage individuals to progress through the levels of education and training by improving access to qualifications, clearly defining avenues for achievement, and generally contributing to lifelong learning.
- Encourage the provision of more and higher-quality vocational education and training through qualifications that normally meet workplace requirements and vocational needs, thus contributing to national economic performance.
- Promote national and international recognition of qualifications offered.

Although the system is still under development and recently began a pilot rollout, its intention is to help ensure a well-designed curriculum that is demand led and competency based and an examination, assessment, and qualification system that involves industries' participation and ensures the consistent quality of the technical and vocational training outputs.

Source: MoMT Web site (http://www.nakertrans.go.id/).

evaluations in 2004 and 2006, which found that approximately 60 percent of all BLKs are in poor condition in terms of facilities, equipment, and human resources, and very few instructors have a tertiary education.

One step beyond, over two years, the KPP program has trained and linked approximately 40,000 out-of-school youth to domestic and overseas jobs. Developed by MoNE's Directorate-General for Nonformal and

Informal Education in 2006 and 2007, the KPP program is reported to have reached 39,315 youth (through 214 private training providers teaching 45 unique courses or skills) across 24 Indonesian provinces and at a total cost of approximately US$12 million, or at an average cost of US$305 per individual recruited for domestic or overseas work.

Two steps beyond, the EYE program has also had some initial success in terms of labor-market responsiveness, this time going all the way to absorption and even permanence. This outcome is encouraging, given the critical gaps identified in youth skills and the high level of youth unemployment. The EYE program was evaluated by two independent teams and the World Bank in 2006. Although these evaluations were not as rigorous as desired, they found some evidence of success. The evaluations found that the EYE's training program, certification, and domestic placement certified and placed 5,128 youth in formal jobs across six Indonesian districts.[3] Of these participants, 82 percent (more than 5,100 beneficiaries) were employed after three to four months of training, at a unit cost of US$300 per individual (figure 6.3). These results need to be taken with care because they do not control for the possibility of selection biases, but they are still encouraging. Employee retention rates remained above 80 percent after three years, and average wages were mostly on par with the minimum wage for the location—if not higher. Part of the success of the program lies in the way it is delivered: it provides skill training through

Figure 6.3   Number of EYE Program Trainees Hired: Domestic Placement over Six Indonesian Districts, 2004–06

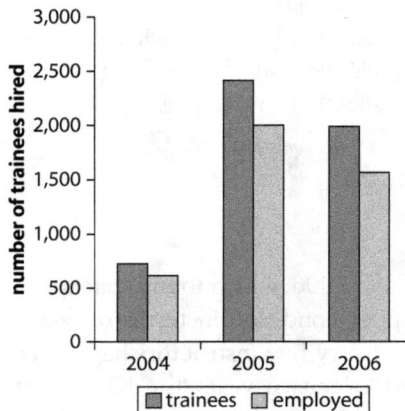

Source: Data from EYE evaluation conducted in 2006.

community centers and dual skill training and apprenticeship programs with local industry (public-private partnerships) while improving the curriculum and managerial skills of the community learning centers.

In sum, the evidence on school-to-work transition programs in Indonesia is still scarce, which makes looking at what happens beyond the country's borders particularly important to help with the critical issue of youth skills and unemployment.

Few hard facts allow an overall judgment to be made on the coverage, quality, and relevance of informal education programs in Indonesia. The employer and employee skill surveys suggest that such programs are of lower quality than formal programs but that they tend to be reasonably responsive to labor-market needs (along the same lines as formal vocational options). The initial results of programs such as KPP and EYE are similar; however, they need to be more thoroughly evaluated. An achievement is the recent development of a skill-based competency and qualification framework that creates bridges between the informal and formal sectors and lays the groundwork for a lifelong learning approach.

Policy implications of these findings include the following:

- *Obtain better data and institute monitoring and evaluation.* The informal programs described here have a huge potential in Indonesia, given the needs of youth and the unskilled population. These programs need to be more fully assessed by gathering more data and undertaking regular monitoring and evaluation. Monitoring and evaluation should be used in particular for interventions that change the incentives of providers and users of training services. Information systems should be set up, including systems to collect data on individual programs and participants, and tracer studies should be carried out.
- *Learn from international experience in setting up successful school-to-work transition programs.* Indonesia has started putting in place programs with good potential, but it needs to look at successful examples elsewhere. Examples from Latin America could be drawn on.
- *Improve input quality in school-based vocational training.* More emphasis needs to be put not only on ensuring that all programs are more demand driven but also on improving their core weaknesses in teaching-learning processes, quality of facilities, instructors' qualifications, and curriculum coverage—all aspects that are stronger in the formal system. Revitalization of BLKs should clearly continue to be a priority. Reexamining the role of the BLKs in light of an increasing focus on lifelong learning may also be useful.

- *Pursue efforts to develop the skill competency and qualification framework*. Efforts to develop a well-functioning competency and qualification framework should be pursued to help support better quality of the informal system (also through improved skill certification) and build a lifelong learning approach to education and training.

Postemployment Firm Training

This section reviews practices of on-the-job training in Indonesia using the results of the employer skill survey. Workers are generally given the opportunity to upgrade, complement, or update their skills to enhance and maintain productivity while on the job. As such, on-the-job training can be considered a form of lifelong learning. In the Indonesian case, however, more focus seems to be put on upgrading and complementing the generally insufficient skills of the educated youth than on updating the skills of older workers. Such training therefore fulfills more of a remedial function for the deficiencies of the preemployment education and training system than a lifelong learning role. A short-term upgrading role of training makes sense given the emphasis on job-specific skills and experience that can best be provided on the job, but the lack of youth preparedness hampers training from also playing a longer-term role in skill acquisition and updating.

Formal training programs that firms offer to their employees constitute an important source of practical on-the-job skills. Given the importance employers place on such skills in Indonesia, firms not surprisingly are actively training their staff in house or through outside training providers. Consistent with the employers' perception of needs (or usefulness), training appears to be targeted at relatively skilled and young workers (table 6.1). Beyond the well-known complementarity between education and training, this finding appears to confirm the importance of practical on-the-job skills in Indonesia and the insufficient preparation provided by some education levels—in particular, secondary education, which largely trains skilled production and sales workers.

Despite firms quite actively offering training (particularly in the service sector), the share of firms offering formal training appears to be on the low side at the regional level (although not for skilled production and some other specific categories of workers). Although comparisons are difficult because of different surveys and ways of asking the questions, the share of firms offering training appears to be lower than in China, the Republic of Korea, Malaysia, Mongolia, and Thailand (tables 6.1 and 6.2).

Table 6.1   Share of Firms Offering In-House or Outside Training to Staff

Position	Share of firms (%)	
	Manufacturing	Noneducation services
Directors	18	25
Professionals	19	23
Administrative workers	28	32
Sales workers	21	34
Skilled production workers	40	38
Unskilled workers	15	10
Temporary workers	17	16
Workers under age 30	33	38

Source: Indonesia Employer/Employee Survey of Skills/Labor Demand and Job Vacancies 2008, Employer Module.

Table 6.2   Share of Firms Offering Formal Training for Permanent Employees

Country	All employees (%)	Skilled employees (%)	Unskilled employees (%)	Nonproduction employees (%)
Cambodia	22	—	—	—
China	85	—	—	—
Korea, Rep.	57	63.16	55.79	53.61
Malaysia	42	—	—	—
Mongolia	47	19.13	—	—
Thailand	76	—	—	—
Vietnam	34	45.19	28.37	27.88

Sources: Investment Climate Surveys: Vietnam 2005; Thailand and Republic of Korea 2004; Cambodia and China, 2003; Malaysia 2002.
Note: — = not available.

This finding is, however, less true for skilled production workers, who are quite intensively trained in Indonesia, as well as for administrative and sales workers in the service sector. Young workers also receive higher priority in training.

The reasons advanced by firms that provide no formal training give more preeminence to the existence of informal in-house training, sufficient skills, and good existing skill-technology match than lack of access to finance or lack of information on training needs. Interestingly, access to finance or lack of information on training needs, which elsewhere are often put forward by employers, do not seem to play a dominant role in Indonesia in explaining lack of training; the driving factor is much more workers' skills and informal on-the-job training (figure 6.4). In combination with relatively low shares of firms training managers and professionals, this finding suggests relatively higher preparation of employed

Figure 6.4   Main Reasons Firms Do Not Provide Training

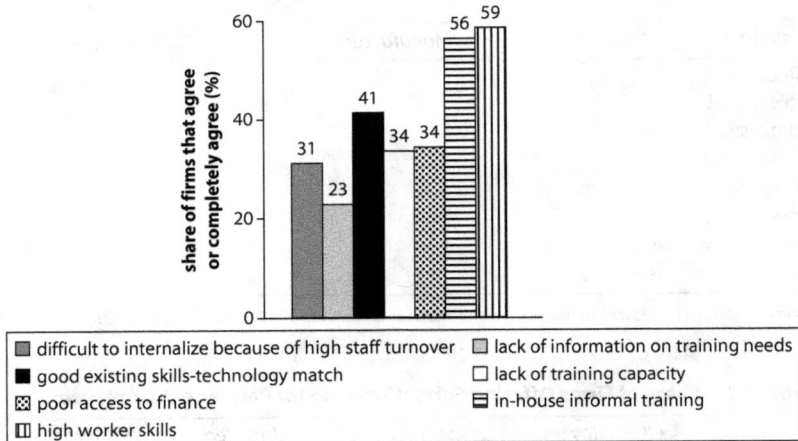

Source: Indonesia Employer/Employee Survey of Skills/Labor Demand and Job Vacancies 2008, Employer Module.

tertiary-level workers (at least for mature workers) or substantial informal on-the-job training offered to them. In-house informal training is widely used in both the service and the manufacturing sectors (and in the exporting and nonexporting sectors). Although less preeminent overall than other reasons for offering no formal training, lack of access to finance and training capacity are nonetheless a more significant constraint in the manufacturing sector (figure 6.5).

The survey provides a wealth of specific information behind the firms' training decisions. For instance, although budgets may not be a strong determinant of the decision to train, they largely drive decisions on numbers of participants and duration of training, and firm needs are key in determining the training subject matter.

Along these lines, the paucity of financial incentives in place is a concern. And confirming more serious financial constraints for the manufacturing sector, manufacturing firms tend to receive even fewer financial incentives for training than those in the service sector. In addition, exporting sectors receive less financial support than nonexporting ones. Firms' decisions to train (and the extent to which firms train) are—at least in part—determined by government support and incentives to encourage training programs. The results of the employer survey give the general impression that relatively few incentives are in place and that they mostly benefit firms in the service sector and firms producing for the domestic

Figure 6.5   Main Reasons Manufacturing and Noneducation Service Firms Do Not Provide Training

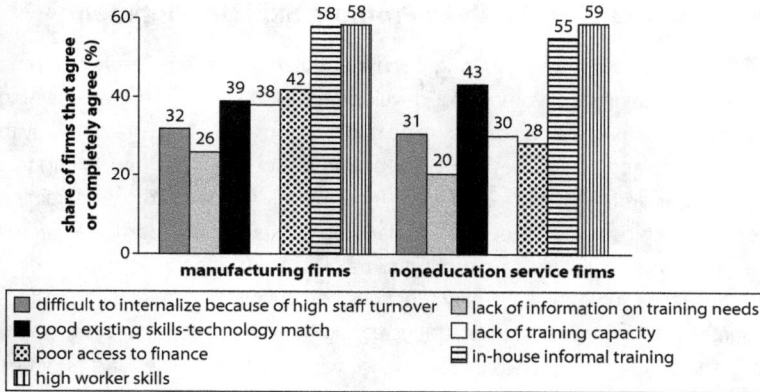

Legend:
- difficult to internalize because of high staff turnover
- good existing skills-technology match
- poor access to finance
- high worker skills
- lack of information on training needs
- lack of training capacity
- in-house informal training

Source: Indonesia Employer/Employee Survey of Skills/Labor Demand and Job Vacancies 2008, Employer Module.

market (9 percent of service firms receive financial incentives versus 5 percent of manufacturing firms, and 7 percent of nonexporting firms receive financial incentives versus 2 percent of exporting firms). Examples in other countries of efficient and effective ways of financing training—particularly firm-based training—are available that would be worthwhile to look at in this context (see box 6.3 for a review of training funds).

Similarly, for employees wishing to obtain training by their own means, direct financial incentives tend to be relatively scarce. Professional growth seems to be a main source of motivation (figure 6.6).

Formal training in the manufacturing sector is clearly focused on job-specific skills; general thinking and behavioral skills are also prioritized in services (figures 6.7 and 6.8). Industrial firms appear to put stronger relative emphasis on job-specific skills (in particular for skilled production workers). Beyond job-specific skills, which also generally maintain the first position (except for directors), general thinking and behavioral skills are given strong importance in the service sector (which underscores their importance for the sector and the existing gaps). Interestingly, training in computer skills is also quite significant in the service sector, underscoring the relatively higher importance and ascertained gaps.

Service firms as well as exporting firms appear more prone to send their staff members to outside training programs and to invest more in

Box 6.3

National Training Funds to Promote Skill Development

National training funds have long been a popular instrument for encouraging firm-based training to promote skill development of the workforce. These training funds buy training services for firms and target groups and offer a practical way to consolidate and administer government and donor spending on training in a cohesive and strategic manner. Training funds usually support short-term training for firm employees to meet rapidly changing skill needs of a particular sector. More and more countries are turning to training funds as a financial instrument because they serve three primary functions particularly well: (a) unifying various sources of financing for training, (b) increasing the volume of resources for training, and (c) allocating funds in accordance with national policies and priorities.

Administering these funds and coordinating what are often diverse and fragmented communities of training providers, however, can be a substantial challenge for governments. Ministries of education, ministries of labor, other technical ministries, national and regional training authorities, nongovernmental organizations, and private training providers all must work together with employers under the administrative umbrella of training funds to deliver the training that firms demand. So that these various actors can be accommodated, training funds are usually administered under the aegis of federal governments and managed by a governing board that includes employer representatives. This method helps ensure that feedback from the labor market is incorporated into the training content. Governing boards meet on a regular basis, are tasked with setting the strategic direction for skill development, and monitor and guide the activities supported by the training fund.

Training funds are usually financed by general taxation or by donor agencies. In many countries, training funds use competitive procedures or levy-grant arrangements to disburse funds to firms to carry out board-sanctioned training programs and courses. In recent years, several Latin American countries have begun to introduce innovative financing mechanisms, such as performance-based budgeting or competitive funding schemes.

Among the most well-known training funds in Latin America is National Industrial Apprenticeship Service (Serviço Nacional de Aprendizagem Industrial, or SENAI). SENAI is financed through a 1 percent payroll levy assessed on industrial enterprises as well as fisheries and transportation and communications firms. It is managed through the National Confederation of Industry and is structured with a national department and 27 regional departments. The national office provides

Box 6.3 *(continued)*

overall guidance, technical assistance, and coordination, while the regional councils function as executive arms of SENAI and operate vocational training centers as well as provide training services to enterprises. SENAI's training structure includes more than 500 vocational training centers, more than 200 mobile training units, and several personnel development centers, many of which are joint ventures with industry. SENAI trains more than 2.8 million people per year, administers a network of 726 operational units, and has enrolled 30 million trainees since its creation in 1942.

Another well-known and effective training fund is Malaysia's Human Resource Development Fund (HRDF). Established in 1993 with a matching grant from the government, HRDF is financed by a payroll levy of 1 percent for employers with more than 50 employees (or 0.5 percent for small enterprises that wish to participate) and offers firms several training options for these firms' employees: (a) approved training courses provided by registered external institutions, (b) ad hoc in-plant or external training courses provided on an as-needed basis, and (c) annual training programs. Between 1992 and 2006, HRDF reimbursed firms over 70 percent of the costs of training conducted for 5.3 million workers. Critics have pointed to three main drivers of HRDF's success: (a) active employer involvement in the governance and operating committees, (b) a lean bureaucracy that reduces administrative burden, and (c) its continuous efforts to disseminate information to firms about the importance of human resource development for raising productivity and competitiveness.

Sources: Dar, Canagarajah, and Murphy 2003; Johanson 2009; World Bank 2010b.

such training. Service firms use external training more intensively than manufacturing ones (30 percent of their staff members benefit from outside training versus 20 percent for manufacturing firms), and the average duration of their external training is also a bit longer than for manufacturing firms (whereas the contrary happens for internal training, with the exception of professionals and skilled production workers). In line with higher use and duration, service firms also spend much more per year on external training than manufacturing firms, whereas the opposite is true for internal training. Exporting sectors also appear more prone to send their employees to outside training program (33 percent of their staff members benefit from outside training versus 24 percent for nonexporting sectors), although for lesser duration, thereby saving on costs.

Figure 6.6   Incentives for Workers to Pursue Outside Training on Their Own

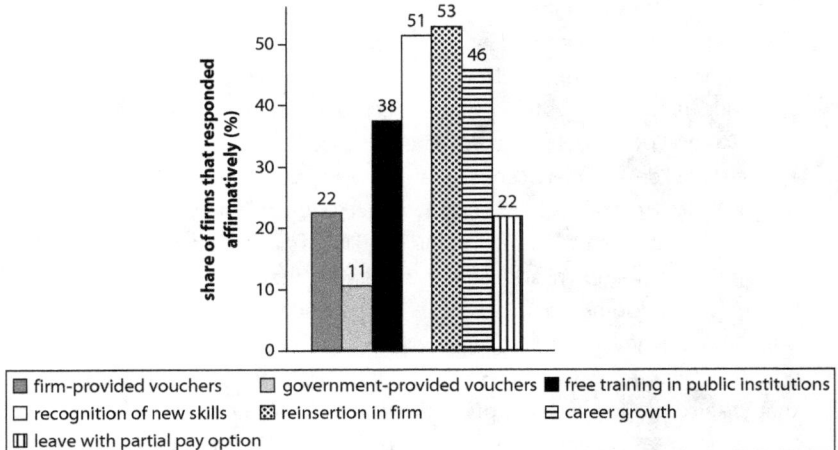

Source: Indonesia Employer/Employee Survey of Skills/Labor Demand and Job Vacancies 2008, Employer Module.

Interestingly, although sources of internal training are similar across sectors, some differences exist in the sources of external training. No major differences exist across sectors for sources of in-house training, but service firms appear to rely much more heavily on private institutes and "partners" for outside training, whereas manufacturing firms appear more eager to train employees through government institutes and industry associations (figure 6.9). This finding probably also contributes to explaining the cost differential. The differences between exporting and nonexporting firms in this case reflect, to a rather large extent, the differences between manufacturing and services.

Finally, with respect to quality of outside training institutions, the level of satisfaction is generally quite high and, unlike in the case of education, private institutions seem to have a small but significant edge. A large majority of institutions are considered to be of "good" quality, and private institutions elicit fewer "poor" or "average" ratings and more "very good" assessments (figure 6.10). This finding suggests that postemployment training may be of better quality than preemployment training.

In sum, the picture coming from this brief review is one of a relatively financially constrained firm sector, which—in the absence of significant financial incentives to train—focuses most of its efforts on young and skilled production workers while relying, to a large extent, on informal

Figure 6.7   In-House and Outside Training Provided by Manufacturing Firms

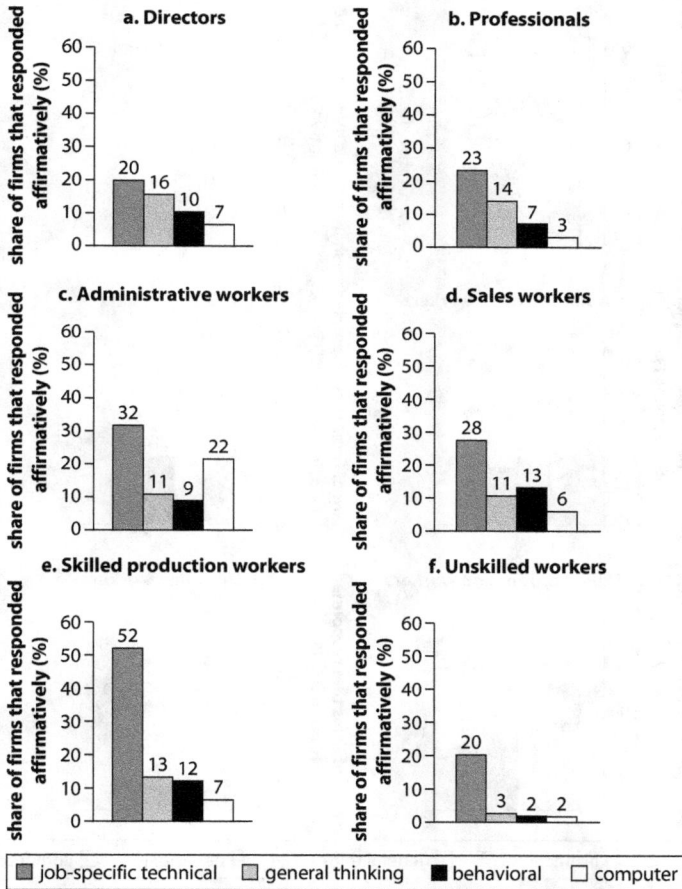

Source: Indonesia Employer/Employee Survey of Skills/Labor Demand and Job Vacancies 2008, Employer Module.

training and learning by doing for professionals and managers. Training subject areas tend to reflect the ascertained skill gaps and firms' relative strengths by focusing on job-specific skills across the board and more thinking, behavioral, and computing skills in the service sector. Less financially constrained service firms make more use of external training and the private sector. These findings confirm rationality in firms' decisions while supporting the previous diagnostics. At the same time, they confirm that firm training seems to be used more as a minimum remedial and upgrading mechanism to address the deficiencies of the preemployment

Figure 6.8   In-House and Outside Training Provided by Service Firms

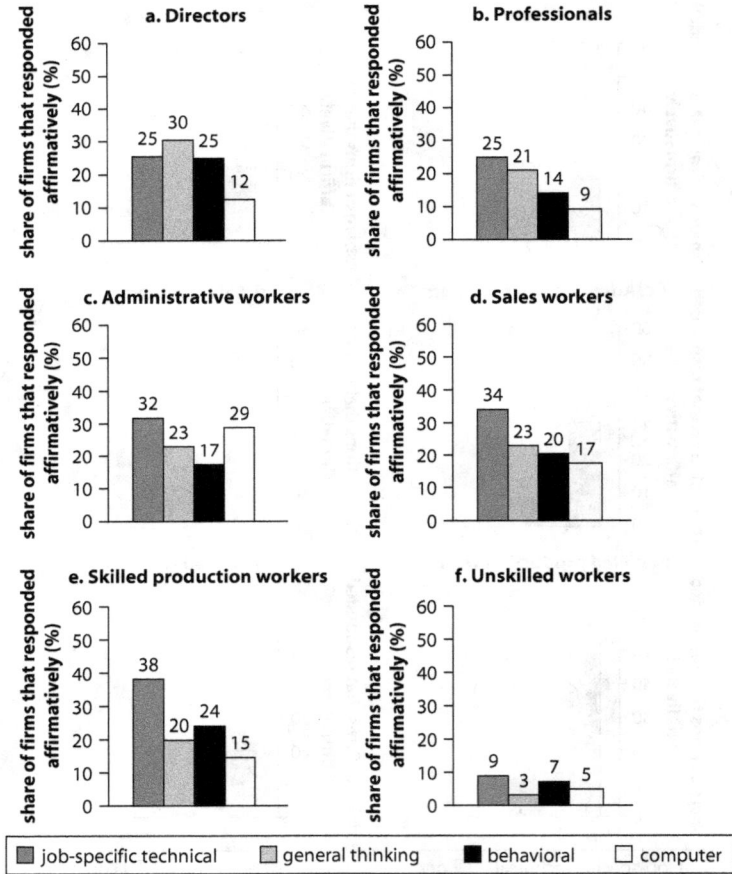

Source: Indonesia Employer/Employee Survey of Skills/Labor Demand and Job Vacancies 2008, Employer Module.

education and training system, while exploiting some of the firms' skill provision strengths, than as a mechanism with a real lifelong learning perspective. Along these lines, one also gets a sense that manufacturing and exporting firms, in particular, may not train enough, and certainly not to the level that would allow their professional and managerial staff members to become generally more competitive and innovative (which would require more investment in generic skills and a higher level of industry knowledge).

Figure 6.9   Sources of Outside Training Provided

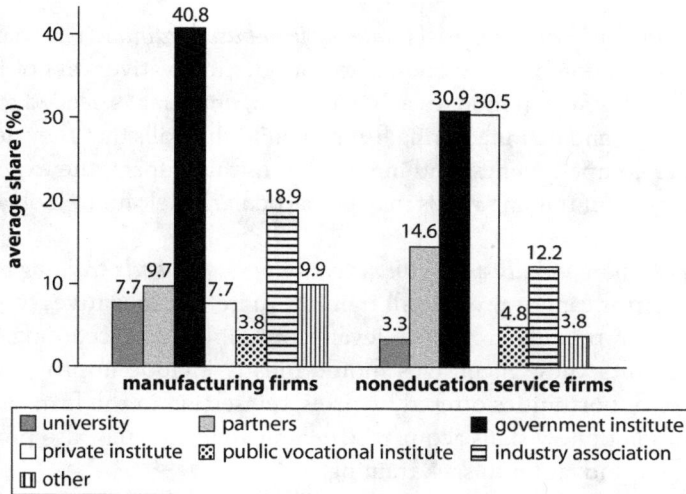

Source: Indonesia Employer/Employee Survey of Skills/Labor Demand and Job Vacancies 2008, Employer Module.

Figure 6.10   Quality of Outside Training Institutes as Evaluated by Respondents

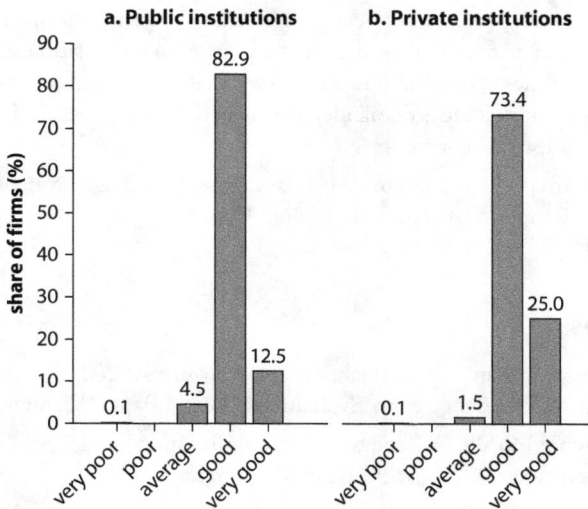

Source: Indonesia Employer/Employee Survey of Skills/Labor Demand and Job Vacancies 2008, Employer Module.

Policy implications in relation to these findings are as follows:

- *Consider innovative ways of financing firm-based training.* The main policy implication of this section is to consider innovative ways of financing firm training in Indonesia. In particular, financing is needed to allow exporting and manufacturing firms to build the skills that they need for higher competitiveness and innovation. In this respect, the experience of successful training funds may be particularly helpful to look at.

- *Provide more incentives for employees to pursue outside training on their own.* Firms cannot provide all training; therefore, incentives to pursue their own training are very relevant for employees. According to survey results, these incentives should mostly include improvement of career opportunities offered by firms, reinsertion in the firm, and certification of new skills acquired. Training vouchers may also provide a further motivation to seek training.

Notes

1. MoMT is responsible for the regulation, quality assurance, and implementation of vocational training.

2. MoMT has recently begun a further effort to revitalize the nation's 162 vocational education and technical training facilities. Following a market-oriented "three-in-one" approach of vocational education, certification, and job placement, MoMT is overhauling the existing vocational education and technical training facilities across Indonesia to ensure that skill training centers are training students in skill areas demanded by the private sector. SKKNI provides the framework for this approach.

3. These districts were Cianjur, West Java; Pasuruan, East Java; Badung, Bali; Lombok Barat, West Nusa Tenggara; Kupang, East Nusa Tenggara; and Donggala, Central Sulawesi.

References

Dar, Amit, Sudharshan Canagarajah, and Paud Murphy. 2003. "Training Levies: Rationale and Evidence from Evaluations." World Bank, Washington, DC.

Johanson, Richard. 2009. "A Review of National Training Funds." Social Protection Discussion Paper 0922, World Bank, Washington, DC.

Martawardaya, Berly. 2008. "Policy Note on TVET/Secondary Education in Indonesia." Background paper prepared for this book, World Bank, Washington, DC.

Nazara, Suahasil, and Padang Wicaksono. 2009. "Skills Development Strategy: The Indonesian Case Study on the Pre-employment Vocational Education and Training (VET)." Background study in collaboration with the World Bank, Demographic Institute, Faculty of Economics, University of Indonesia, Jakarta.

World Bank. 2010a. *Indonesia Jobs Report: Towards Better Jobs and Security for All.* 2 vols. Jakarta: World Bank.

———. 2010b. *Reducing Inequality for Shared Growth in China: Strategy and Policy Options for Guangdong Province.* Washington, DC: World Bank.

APPENDIX A

Main Tables

Table A.1 Global Competitiveness Index and Rankings

Country or economy	Global Competitive Index 2008–09		Basic requirements		Institutions		Infrastructure		Macroeconomic stability		Health and primary education		Efficiency enhancers		Higher education and training		Technological readiness	
	Rank	Score	Rank	Score	Rank	Score	Rank	Score	Rank	Score	Rank	Score	Rank	Score	Rank	Score	Rank	Score
Singapore	5	5.53	3	6.14	1	6.19	4	6.39	21	5.74	16	6.24	2	5.52	8	5.56	7	5.65
Japan	9	5.38	26	5.36	26	4.99	11	5.80	98	4.53	22	6.11	12	5.22	23	5.08	21	5.11
Hong Kong SAR, China	11	5.33	5	6.05	9	5.78	5	6.32	3	6.26	43	5.82	6	5.43	28	4.78	10	5.60
Korea, Rep.	13	5.28	16	5.71	28	4.95	15	5.63	4	6.15	26	6.10	15	5.15	12	5.51	13	5.51
Taiwan, China	17	5.22	20	5.53	40	4.67	19	5.46	18	5.82	20	6.16	18	5.06	13	5.46	15	5.34
Malaysia	21	5.04	25	5.42	30	4.91	23	5.25	38	5.43	23	6.11	24	4.82	35	4.63	34	4.41
China	30	4.70	42	5.01	56	4.18	47	4.22	11	5.95	50	5.71	40	4.41	64	4.05	77	3.19
India	50	4.33	80	4.23	53	4.23	72	3.38	109	4.32	100	4.99	33	4.49	63	4.06	69	3.27
Thailand	34	4.60	43	4.97	57	4.17	29	4.67	41	5.41	58	5.61	36	4.45	51	4.31	66	3.37
Indonesia	55	4.25	76	4.25	68	3.89	86	2.95	72	4.91	87	5.26	49	4.29	71	3.88	88	3.02
Philippines	71	4.09	85	4.17	105	3.44	92	2.86	53	5.21	90	5.17	68	4.02	60	4.10	70	3.26
United States	1	5.74	22	5.50	29	4.93	7	6.10	66	4.99	34	5.97	1	5.81	5	5.67	11	5.57
Switzerland	2	5.61	2	6.14	5	5.97	3	6.40	10	5.97	17	6.22	8	5.35	7	5.60	5	5.76
Finland	6	5.50	1	6.18	2	6.18	9	5.94	8	6.01	1	6.57	13	5.21	1	6.07	14	5.46

Source: Schwab 2009.

Table A.2 Skill Composition of Labor Force in Indonesia, 1994–2007

Indicator	1994[a]	1997	1999	2001	2003	2005 (November)	2007 (August)
Schooling							
Years of schooling	7.99	8.52	8.75	9.64	10.17	10.33	10.33
Primary incomplete (% of labor force)	19.9	16.8	14.9	8.3	5.3	4.6	6.0
Primary complete (% of labor force)	31.5	28.5	28.0	24.5	20.1	20.2	21.2
Lower-secondary school (% of labor force)	13.8	15.1	15.5	17.7	20.0	19.4	17.2
Upper-secondary school, general (% of labor force)	14.0	16.8	17.8	19.9	25.9	24.7	22.3
Upper-secondary school, vocational (% of labor force)	13.6	13.4	12.8	15.8	14.0	14.2	12.3
Diploma program (% of labor force)	4.0	4.3	5.2	6.4	6.2	7.3	8.8
University (% of labor force)	3.2	5.0	5.8	7.3	8.4	9.6	12.1
Occupation							
Professional (% of labor force)	11.3	11.1	11.9	12.7	12.4	14.1	14.4
Manager (% of labor force)	0.6	0.4	0.7	0.7	0.6	0.8	1.1
Official or administrative (% of labor force)	13.4	14.4	14.4	15.5	17.5	15.3	14.4
Sales (% of labor force)	5.9	7.4	6.9	7.6	8.8	9.0	9.6
Labor (% of labor force)	10.1	9.7	10.3	11.2	10.8	11.6	14.1
Agriculture (% of labor force)	18.2	15.5	17.8	10.2	8.3	7.5	7.5
Production (% of labor force)	13.5	14.1	13.5	16.5	17.5	16.1	14.6
Transportation (% of labor force)	7.5	7.8	7.9	8.2	8.8	9.5	8.5
Laborers (% of labor force)	19.4	19.6	16.5	17.3	15.4	16.1	15.8
Skill classification							
Skilled, secondary and above (% of labor force)	34.8	39.6	41.6	49.4	54.5	55.7	53.4
Skilled, tertiary and above (% of labor force)	7.2	9.3	11.0	13.7	14.6	16.9	16.7
Sample size	43,450	40,965	27,267	21,037	37,756	27,441	125,654

Source: SAKERNAS (Survei Angkatan Kerja Nasional, or National Labor Force Survey) 1994–2007 (employed for wages).
a. Industry controls included at the one-digit (Standard Industrial Classification) level.

Table A.3   Evolution of Skill Premiums, by Education, Year, Sector, and Country

Indicator	Indonesia	Philippines	Thailand	Vietnam	Cambodia	China	Mongolia
Upper-secondary or higher							
1988							
Agriculture or mining	—	0.192	—	—	—	—	—
Manufacturing	—	0.343	—	—	—	—	—
Trade or services	—	0.539	—	—	—	—	—
1990							
Agriculture or mining	—	—	1.812	—	—	—	—
Manufacturing	—	—	0.642	—	—	—	—
Trade or services	—	—	0.969	—	—	—	—
1991							
Agriculture or mining	—	0.186	—	—	—	—	—
Manufacturing	—	0.322	—	—	—	—	—
Trade/services	—	0.560	—	—	—	—	—
1992							
Agriculture or mining	—	—	—	−0.586	—	—	—
Manufacturing	—	—	—	−0.102	—	—	—
Trade or services	—	—	—	−0.237	—	—	—
1994							
Agriculture or mining	0.809	0.161	1.148	—	—	—	—
Manufacturing	0.419	0.301	0.665	—	—	—	—
Trade or services	0.722	0.469	1.065	—	—	—	—
1997							
Agriculture or mining	—	0.204	—	—	−0.263	—	—
Manufacturing	—	0.255	—	—	0.115	—	—
Trade or services	—	0.511	—	—	0.190	—	—

	C1	C2	C3	C4	C5	C6	C7
1998							
Agriculture or mining	—	—	—	−0.243	—	—	0.381
Manufacturing	—	—	—	0.00	—	—	0.266
Trade or services	—	—	—	0.00	—	—	0.280
1999							
Agriculture or mining	0.634	—	—	—	—	0.454	—
Manufacturing	0.375	—	—	—	—	0.165	—
Trade or services	0.689	—	—	—	—	0.348	—
2000							
Agriculture or mining	—	—	0.898	—	—	—	—
Manufacturing	—	—	0.644	—	—	—	—
Trade or services	—	—	0.990	—	—	—	—
2001							
Agriculture or mining	—	0.140	—	—	—	—	—
Manufacturing	—	0.197	—	—	—	—	—
Trade or services	—	0.621	—	—	—	—	—
2002							
Agriculture or mining	—	—	—	—	—	—	0.388
Manufacturing	—	—	—	—	—	—	0.371
Trade or services	—	—	—	—	—	—	0.296
2003							
Agriculture or mining	0.551	—	0.571	—	0.262	—	—
Manufacturing	0.394	—	0.642	—	0.225	—	—
Trade or services	0.689	—	0.811	—	0.516	—	—
2004							
Agriculture or mining	—	0.145	—	0.208	—	—	—
Manufacturing	—	0.189	—	0.328	—	—	—
Trade or services	—	0.609	—	0.463	—	—	—

(continued next page)

Table A.3 (continued)

Indicator	Indonesia	Philippines	Thailand	Vietnam	Cambodia	China	Mongolia
2005							
Agriculture or mining	—	—	—	—	—	0.301	—
Manufacturing	—	—	—	—	—	0.380	—
Trade or services	—	—	—	—	—	0.541	—
2006							
Agriculture or mining	—	0.122	—	0.410	—	—	—
Manufacturing	—	0.201	—	0.232	—	—	—
Trade or services	—	0.698	—	0.249	—	—	—
2007							
Agriculture or mining	0.605	—	—	—	0.157	—	1.025
Manufacturing	0.463	—	—	—	0.156	—	0.631
Trade or services	0.734	—	—	—	0.541	—	0.833
Tertiary or higher							
1988							
Agriculture or mining	—	0.364	—	—	—	—	—
Manufacturing	—	0.497	—	—	—	—	—
Trade or services	—	0.726	—	—	—	—	—
1990							
Agriculture or mining	—	—	2.010	—	—	—	—
Manufacturing	—	—	1.182	—	—	—	—
Trade or services	—	—	1.048	—	—	—	—
1991							
Agriculture or mining	—	0.355	—	—	—	—	—
Manufacturing	—	0.387	—	—	—	—	—
Trade or services	—	0.742	—	—	—	—	—

	1	2	3	4	5	6	7
1992							
Agriculture or mining	1.432	—	—	-0.233	—	—	—
Manufacturing	1.075	—	—	0.084	—	—	—
Trade or services	0.770	—	—	-0.050	—	—	—
1994							
Agriculture or mining	—	0.336	2.436	—	—	—	—
Manufacturing	—	0.405	1.190	—	—	—	—
Trade or services	—	0.644	1.067	—	—	—	—
1997							
Agriculture or mining	—	0.405	—	—	—	—	—
Manufacturing	—	0.389	—	—	-0.677	—	—
Trade or services	—	0.715	—	—	0.325	—	—
1998							
Agriculture or mining	—	—	—	0.304	—	—	0.382
Manufacturing	—	—	—	0.382	—	—	0.259
Trade or services	—	—	—	0.191	—	—	0.289
1999							
Agriculture or mining	1.128	—	—	—	—	0.356	—
Manufacturing	0.797	—	—	—	—	0.318	—
Trade or services	0.691	—	—	—	—	0.475	—
2000							
Agriculture or mining	—	—	2.051	—	—	—	—
Manufacturing	—	—	1.070	—	—	—	—
Trade or services	—	—	1.003	—	—	—	—
2001							
Agriculture or mining	—	0.350	—	—	—	—	—
Manufacturing	—	0.339	—	—	—	—	—
Trade or services	—	0.769	—	—	—	—	—

(continued next page)

Table A.3 *(continued)*

Indicator	Indonesia	Philippines	Thailand	Vietnam	Cambodia	China	Mongolia
2002							
Agriculture or mining	—	—	—	—	—	—	0.519
Manufacturing	—	—	—	—	—	—	0.400
Trade or services	—	—	—	—	—	—	0.287
2003							
Agriculture or mining	0.976	—	1.487	—	—	—	—
Manufacturing	0.752	—	1.077	—	0.423	—	—
Trade or services	0.678	—	0.97	—	0.601	—	—
2004							
Agriculture or mining	—	0.354	—	0.503	—	—	—
Manufacturing	—	0.301	—	0.517	—	—	—
Trade or services	—	0.752	—	0.594	—	—	—
2005							
Agriculture or mining	—	—	—	—	—	0.497	—
Manufacturing	—	—	—	—	—	0.477	—
Trade or services	—	—	—	—	—	0.655	—
2006							
Agriculture or mining	—	0.303	—	0.384	—	—	—
Manufacturing	—	0.328	—	0.377	—	—	—
Trade or services	—	0.809	—	0.547	—	—	—
2007							
Agriculture or mining	1.213	—	—	—	—	—	0.868
Manufacturing	0.903	—	—	—	1.045*	—	0.560
Trade or services	0.787	—	—	—	0.843	—	0.742

Source: Labor force and household surveys (various years).

Note: — = not available. Survey results were not available for every year in every country.

* = not statistically significant.

Table A.4 Employment, Wage Skill Premium, and Wage Bill Share of Skilled Labor, by Manufacturing Subsector, 1975–2005

Item/subsector	1975	1986	1996	2000	2005
A. Employment share of nonproduction workers (%)					
Food products, beverages, and tobacco	16.0	21.2	24.1	19.0	18.9
Textiles, garments, and leather	11.1	12.4	10.8	10.9	10.7
Wood and wood furniture	18.4	15.1	13.6	13.1	13.2
Paper products and printing	22.9	24.4	23.9	23.8	22.9
Chemicals, rubber, plastics, and petroleum	22.9	26.1	24.0	20.7	24.1
Nonmetallic minerals	17.5	14.5	18.8	16.3	19.1
Basic metals	22.9	29.9	22.5	19.5	21.6
Fabricated metal products, machinery, and equipment	19.4	24.9	18.9	18.5	18.2
Other manufactured products	8.6	14.5	10.2	13.3	9.9
B. Wage skill premium (%)					
Food products, beverages, and tobacco	1.9	2.2	1.5	2.0	1.8
Textiles, garments, and leather	2.3	2.4	2.6	2.2	2.1
Wood and wood furniture	1.4	1.8	1.9	1.9	1.7
Paper products and printing	2.1	1.7	2.1	1.9	1.6
Chemicals, rubber, plastics, and petroleum	2.4	2.4	2.3	2.7	2.1
Nonmetallic minerals	2.1	2.7	2.2	2.3	2.5
Basic metals	1.7	1.1	1.6	2.7	1.5
Fabricated metal products, machinery, and equipment	2.5	2.0	2.3	2.5	1.9
Other manufactured products	3.4	2.6	2.5	3.2	2.2

(continued next page)

Table A.4 *(continued)*

Item/subsector	1975	1986	1996	2000	2005
C. Wage bill share of nonproduction workers (%)					
Food products, beverages, and tobacco	27.0	37.9	32.9	37.1	30.5
Textiles, garments, and leather	22.1	25.1	24.3	19.1	20.2
Wood and wood furniture	24.0	24.0	22.8	19.7	20.4
Paper products and printing	38.2	35.2	39.6	32.7	34.8
Chemicals, rubber, plastics, and petroleum	41.2	46.7	42.5	37.4	39.8
Nonmetallic minerals	31.2	31.3	33.6	29.3	37.5
Basic metals	33.6	31.9	32.2	27.7	29.7
Fabricated metal products, machinery, and equipment	37.3	39.9	35.5	36.8	29.7
Other manufactured products	24.3	31.2	22.4	22.2	19.7

Source: Fernandes and Sundaram 2008. Calculations are based on Indonesia's Manufacturing Survey of Large and Medium-Size Firms (Survei Industri).

Note: The years shown in the table delimit the four periods used in the book's analysis: (a) 1975–86 (import substitution), (b) 1987–96 (export orientation), (c) 1997–99 (financial crisis), and (d) 2000–05 (postcrisis).

Table A.5   Correlation between Openness and Skilled Labor Share

Indicator	Average employment share of skilled workers (%)		Average wage bill share of skilled workers (%)	
	For plants that	For plants that do not	For plants that	For plants that do not
Receive foreign direct investment	0.214***	0.146	0.351***	0.212
Export	0.159***	0.147	0.261***	0.209
Import inputs	0.190***	0.141	0.305***	0.201

Source: Fernandes and Sundaram 2008. Calculations are based on Indonesia's Manufacturing Survey of Large and Medium-Size Firms (Survei Industri).

Note: The results are based on data for the 1990–2005 period.

*** indicates that the difference between the average share for plants engaged in an international activity and the average share for plants not engaged in that international activity is significant at the 1 percent confidence level.

Table A.6   Share of Plants That Receive Foreign Direct Investment, Export, or Import Their Intermediates across Industries, 1988–2005

Item/subsector	1988–96	1997–99	2000–05
A. Average share of plants with foreign direct investment (%)			
Food products, beverages, and tobacco	2.5	3.3	3.7
Textiles, garments, and leather	5.0	6.2	7.2
Wood and wood furniture	3.8	3.8	5.0
Paper products and printing	3.2	3.9	3.8
Chemicals, coal, rubber, and plastics	9.4	12.1	13.2
Nonmetallic minerals	2.1	2.6	3.5
Basic metals	19.3	25.4	22.3
Fabricated metal products, machinery, and equipment	11.3	19.4	20.9
Other manufactured products	10.3	11.6	12.3
B. Average share of plants that import their inputs (%)			
Food products, beverages, and tobacco	9.4	8.4	10.5
Textiles, garments, and leather	24.5	22.6	24.9
Wood and wood furniture	7.6	7.8	10.9
Paper products and printing	28.1	21.4	22.1
Chemicals, coal, rubber, and plastics	45.5	38.6	37.7
Nonmetallic minerals	13.5	10.1	12.6
Basic metals	50.4	48.5	49.0
Fabricated metal products, machinery, and equipment	38.3	37.9	40.7
Other manufactured products	37.4	30.2	30.0

(continued next page)

Table A.6   *(continued)*

Item/subsector	1988–96	1997–99	2000–05
C. Average share of plants that export (%)			
Food products, beverages, and tobacco	9.2	6.2	10.3
Textiles, garments, and leather	18.6	10.3	19.5
Wood and wood furniture	37.8	20.7	45.9
Paper products and printing	6.1	4.3	7.6
Chemicals, coal, rubber, and plastics	17.8	10.2	18.9
Nonmetallic minerals	5.3	3.6	8.4
Basic metals	26.1	15.0	20.7
Fabricated metal products, machinery, and equipment	13.1	9.4	16.2
Other manufactured products	31.1	14.1	34.3

Source: Fernandes and Sundaram 2008. Calculations based on Indonesia's Manufacturing Survey of Large and Medium-Size Firms (Survei Industri).

Table A.7 Openness, Technological Innovation, and the Demand for Skills (Sample of Eight East Asian Countries)

Indicator	(1)	(2)	(3)	(4)	(5)	(6)	(7)
Exporter	-0.177***	0.043	0.041	-0.017	-0.019	-0.029	-0.058
	[0.0350]	[0.0350]	[0.0359]	[0.0389]	[0.0388]	[0.0387]	[0.0388]
Foreign ownership	0.429***	0.358***	0.354***	0.283***	0.278***	0.262***	0.211***
	[0.0386]	[0.0374]	[0.0381]	[0.0395]	[0.0394]	[0.0393]	[0.0394]
Technological innovation	—	—	—	—	0.246***	0.230***	0.226***
					[0.0316]	[0.0316]	[0.0318]
Age of firm	-0.00907***	-0.00320***	-0.00377***	-0.00719***	-0.00706***	-0.00713***	-0.00672***
	[0.00130]	[0.00121]	[0.00121]	[0.00127]	[0.00127]	[0.00125]	[0.00124]
Public ownership	0.261***	0.268***	0.291***	0.274***	0.267***	0.260***	0.256***
	[0.0486]	[0.0449]	[0.0454]	[0.0486]	[0.0484]	[0.0482]	[0.0483]
Managerial postsecondary education	—	—	—	—	—	0.745***	0.696***
						[0.0877]	[0.0911]
Sales per employee (log)	—	—	—	—	—	—	0.0447***
							[0.00814]
Industry fixed effects?	No	Yes	No	No	No	No	No
Country fixed effects?	Yes	Yes	No	No	No	No	No
Country-industry fixed effects?	No	No	Yes	No	No	No	No
Country-industry-size fixed effects	No	No	No	Yes	Yes	Yes	Yes
Observations	8,087	8,087	8,087	8,087	8,047	8,047	7,746
R^2	0.09	0.23	0.25	0.32	0.33	0.34	0.34

Source: Almeida 2009; Investment Climate Surveys.

Note: — = not available. Dependent variable is share of workers in the firm with more than secondary education (12 years of schooling).
*** indicates significance at the 1 percent level.

Table A.8 Openness, Technological Innovation, and the Demand for Skills: Robustness to Alternative Samples

Item	Cambodia (1)	China (2)	Indonesia (3)	Malaysia (4)	Philippines (5)	Korea, Rep. (6)	Thailand (7)	Vietnam (8)
A. Excluding one country at a time								
Exporter	-0.0683*	0.118***	-0.0888**	-0.0725*	-0.056	-0.061	-0.130***	-0.0776*
	[0.0386]	[0.0426]	[0.0397]	[0.0393]	[0.0395]	[0.0393]	[0.0475]	[0.0455]
Foreign ownership	0.201***	0.186***	0.234***	0.216***	0.229***	0.208***	0.255***	0.0969**
	[0.0393]	[0.0448]	[0.0405]	[0.0411]	[0.0402]	[0.0401]	[0.0474]	[0.0441]
Technological innovation	0.240***	0.123***	0.227***	0.234***	0.205***	0.232***	0.251***	0.250***
	[0.0322]	[0.0379]	[0.0326]	[0.0326]	[0.0324]	[0.0322]	[0.0363]	[0.0364]
Baseline firm characteristics?	Yes	Yes	Yes	Yes	Yes	Yes	Yes	Yes
Country-sector size effects?	Yes	Yes	Yes	Yes	Yes	Yes	Yes	Yes
Observations	7,443	4,931	7,270	7,427	7,255	7,261	6,451	6,184
R^2	0.313	0.36	0.333	0.343	0.351	0.332	0.344	0.355
B. Including one country at a time								
Exporter	1.531***	-0.406***	0.388**	0.336	-0.028	0.015	0.142**	-0.050
	[0.542]	[0.0755]	[0.159]	[0.228]	[0.166]	[0.210]	[0.0562]	[0.0665]
Foreign ownership	0.628	0.191***	-0.118	0.131	-0.231	0.419***	0.012	0.400***
	[0.422]	[0.0705]	[0.178]	[0.138]	[0.198]	[0.156]	[0.0618]	[0.0797]
Technological innovation	-0.161	0.342***	0.247*	0.007	0.497***	0.051	0.134**	0.055
	[0.179]	[0.0555]	[0.139]	[0.135]	[0.142]	[0.168]	[0.0564]	[0.0592]
Baseline firm characteristics?	Yes	Yes	Yes	Yes	Yes	Yes	Yes	Yes
Country-sector size effects?	Yes	Yes	Yes	Yes	Yes	Yes	Yes	Yes
Observations	303	2815	476	319	491	485	1,295	1,562
R^2	0.366	0.344	0.303	0.172	0.246	0.383	0.22	0.259

Sources: Almeida 2009; Investment Climate Surveys.

Note: Dependent variable is share of workers in the firm with more than secondary education (12 years of schooling). Item A excludes from the sample one country at a time. Item B restricts the sample to one country at the time.

* indicates significance at the 10 percent confidence level; ** indicates significance at the 5 percent confidence level; *** indicates significance at the 1 percent confidence level.

Table A.9   Openness, Technological Innovation, and the Demand for Skills: Robustness Technological Variables (Regional Sample)

Indicator	(1)	(2)	(3)	(4)	(5)
Exporter	−0.0634	−0.135***	−0.137***	−0.228***	0.00842
	[0.0415]	[0.0467]	[0.0469]	[0.0647]	[0.0429]
Foreign ownership	0.208***	0.247***	0.232***	0.0691	0.142***
	[0.0411]	[0.0473]	[0.0474]	[0.0606]	[0.0442]
Technological innovation	0.199***	0.204***	0.244***	0.264***	0.0616
	[0.0341]	[0.0410]	[0.0405]	[0.0469]	[0.0376]
International Organization for Standardization certificate	0.267***	—	—	—	—
	[0.0381]				
Research and development	—	0.295***	—	—	—
		[0.0424]			
Research and development or sales	—	—	0.00603***	—	—
			[0.00214]		
Use of computers	—	—	—	0.642***	—
				[0.0543]	
Use of e-mail and Internet	—	—	—	—	0.558***
					[0.0434]
Baseline firm characteristics?	Yes	Yes	Yes	Yes	Yes
Country-sector size effects?	Yes	Yes	Yes	Yes	Yes
Observations	7,208	5,069	5,069	4,059	4,928
R^2	0.346	0.302	0.297	0.394	0.385

Sources: Almeida 2009; Investment Climate Surveys.

Note: — = not available. Dependent variable is the share of workers in the firm with more than secondary education (12 years of schooling).

*** indicates significance at the 1 percent confidence level.

References

Almeida, Rita. 2009. "Openness and Technological Innovation in East Asia: Have They Increased the Demand for Skills?" Social Protection Discussion Paper 0919, World Bank, Washington, DC.

Fernandes, Ana, and Ramya Sundaram. 2008. "Skill Demand and Openness in Indonesia." Background paper prepared for this book, World Bank, Washington, DC.

Schwab, Klaus, ed. 2009. *The Global Competitiveness Report 2009–2010*. Geneva: World Economic Forum.

APPENDIX B

Empirical Framework for Estimating the Effects of Openness on the Demand for Skills

This appendix provides the empirical framework for the plant-level regressions undertaken by Fernandes and Sundaram (2008). As Goldberg and Pavcnik (2005) argue, the literature has so far provided little evidence on how plant heterogeneity within industries influences the demand for skilled labor. Within a given industry, different products are produced using very different factor proportions, and plants vary substantially in terms of efficiency, quality, and types of workers employed. Openness to trade and investment is shown—theoretically and empirically—to result in important compositional changes within industries, namely, a reallocation of labor and capital toward plants with higher efficiency or quality (for example, Melitz 2003). Moreover, openness to trade is also likely to lead to an upgrading in the quality of plants, as plants in import-competing sectors try to avoid competition by improving their own efficiency and quality (for example, Fernandes 2007).

The crucial issue then is whether the compositional changes within industries as a result of trade openness (which serves as a driving force toward more efficient plants) lead to a higher demand for skilled labor. If openness is measured by foreign ownership, and foreign ownership is associated with direct technological transfer to subsidiaries, then one could expect openness to lead to a higher demand for skilled labor. Similarly, if openness is measured by imports of intermediate inputs that can bring about learning from embodied technologies, once again openness could lead to a higher demand for skilled labor. If openness is measured by exports, then an increase in the demand for skilled labor would result if production for export markets was more skill intensive than production for domestic markets. However, Schott (2004) shows that countries abundant in unskilled labor, such as Indonesia, specialize completely in the export of low-unit-value products (that is, those of lower quality and thus likely to be produced by less skill-intensive plants).

A discussion of the econometric framework used to investigate the effect of various openness channels as well as of capital deepening on the demand for skilled labor at the plant level follows. Plants are assumed to choose their levels of skilled and unskilled labor by minimizing a restricted cost function subject to a value-added constraint and to capital stock being a quasi-fixed input. The logarithmic variable cost function is assumed to be of the translog form. In this framework, the estimating equation for the wage bill share of skilled labor $\dfrac{w^s_{ijrt} L^s_{ijrt}}{VC_{ijrt}}$ is given by:[1]

$$\frac{w^s_{ijrt} L^s_{ijrt}}{VC_{ijrt}} = \alpha + \beta_2 \ln\left(\frac{K_{ijrt}}{VA_{ijrt}}\right) + \beta_3 \ln VA_{ijrt} + \gamma O_{ijrt} + I^t + I^r + I^j + \varepsilon_{ijrt}, \quad \text{(B.1)}$$

where K_{ijrt} is the capital stock of plant I in industry j, region r, at time t; VA_{ijrt} is value added; O_{ijrt} is a vector of international integration measures (including dummies for foreign direct investment, exports, and imported inputs); I^t is a vector of year indicators; I^r is a vector of province indicators; I^j is a vector of industry indicators (at two- or three-digit International Standard Industrial Classification level); and ε_{ijrt} is a plant-specific time-varying error term. This discussion also estimates a modified version of equation B.1, where the dependent variable is the employment share of skilled workers. A positive β_2 provides evidence of capital-skill complementarity, whereas a positive β_3 indicates the presence of increasing returns to scale. The main coefficients of interest are those included in the vector γ, which indicate if and how the relative demand for skilled labor changes with international integration.

The error term ε_{ijrt} is assumed to be decomposed into a plant-specific fixed component f_i and an independent identically distributed residual u_{ijrt}. The presence of a plant fixed-effect component in the residual will make ordinary least squares estimates of equation (B.1) inconsistent.

Nevertheless, such estimates will be obtained to see what type of relationship they identify between openness and the relative demand for skilled labor. Then equation (B.1) is estimated using plant fixed effects to find out whether, after unobserved plant-level characteristics are controlled for, a significant relationship still exists between openness and the relative demand for skilled labor. A complete description of the variables used in the analysis is provided in the appendix of Fernandes and Sundaram (2008).

Note

1. The use of this framework follows the seminal study by Berman, Bound, and Griliches (1994), as well as other studies such as those by Doms, Dunne, and Troske (1997), Pavcnik (2003), and Fernandes and Fajnzylber (2009). Those studies provide details on the derivation of the estimating equation for the wage-bill share of skilled labor. In very summarized terms, that equation is derived by (a) differentiating the cost function with respect to the wage of skilled labor, (b) using Shephard's lemma, (c) assuming symmetry in the effect of relative input prices on input demands, and (d) assuming homogeneity of degree one in input prices. Moreover, this discussion follows Berman, Bound, and Griliches (1994) and most other studies in dropping from the right-hand side of the equation a term derived from theory: the ratio of the wage of skilled labor to the wage of unskilled labor. The identification of its effect is difficult, given that most of the observed variation in relative wages is due to the variation in the unobserved quality of labor and is therefore endogenous to skilled labor demand. The inclusion of industry and region dummy variables in the equation partly accounts for differences in the excluded term.

References

Berman, Eli, John Bound, and Zvi Griliches. 1994. "Changes in the Demand for Skilled Labor within U.S. Manufacturing: Evidence from the Annual Survey of Manufactures." *Quarterly Journal of Economics* 109 (2): 367–97.

Doms, Mark, Timothy Dunne, and Kenneth Troske. 1997. "Workers, Wages, and Technology." *Quarterly Journal of Economics* 112 (1): 253–90.

Fernandes, Ana. 2007. "Trade Policy, Trade Volumes, and Plant-Level Productivity in Colombian Manufacturing Industries." *Journal of International Economics* 71 (1): 52–71.

Fernandes, Ana, and Pablo Fajnzylber. 2009. "International Economic Activities and Skilled Labour Demand: Evidence from Brazil and China. *Applied Economics* 41 (5): 563–77.

Fernandes, Ana, and Ramya Sundaram. 2008. "Skill Demand and Openness in Indonesia." Background paper prepared for this book, World Bank, Washington, DC.

Goldberg, Pinelopi K., and Nina Pavcnik. 2005. "Trade, Wages, and the Political Economy of Trade Protection: Evidence from the Colombian Trade Reforms." *Journal of International Economics* 66 (1): 75–105.

Melitz, Marc. 2003. "The Impact of Trade on Intra-industry Reallocations and Aggregate Industry Productivity." *Econometrica* 71 (6): 1695–725.

Pavcnik, Nina. 2003. "What Explains Skill Upgrading in Less Developed Countries?" *Journal of Development Economics* 71 (2): 311–28.

Schott, Peter. 2004. "Across-Product versus Within-Product Specialization in International Trade." *Quarterly Journal of Economics* 119 (2): 646–77.

Index

Boxes, figures, notes, and tables are indicated by *b*, *f*, *n*, and *t*, respectively.